ROT & RUIN

"Rot & Ruin won me over with its dark imagery and constantly moving storyline..."
— *Rhymes With Geek*

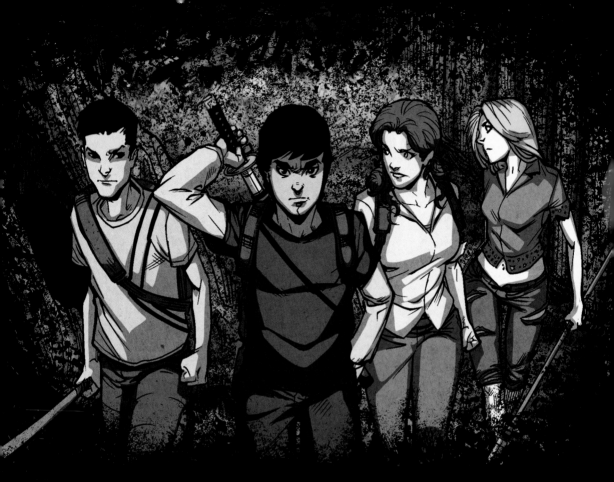

Written by Jonathan Maberry

Illustrated by Tony Vargas

Colored by Oliver Lee Arce

Lettered by Robbie Robbins, Chris Mowry, and Shawn Lee

Series Edited by David Hedgecock

Cover by Alex Ronald

Collection Edited by Justin Eisinger and Alonzo Simon

Collection Designed by Clyde Grapa

ISBN: 978-1-63140-186-2

18 17 16 15 1 2 3 4

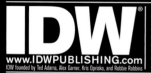

IDW®
www.IDWPUBLISHING.com
IDW founded by Ted Adams, Alex Garner, Kris Oprisko, and Robbie Robbins

Ted Adams, CEO & Publisher
Greg Goldstein, President & COO
Robbie Robbins, EVP/Sr. Graphic Artist
Chris Ryall, Chief Creative Officer/Editor-in-Chief
Matthew Ruzicka, CPA, Chief Financial Officer
Alan Payne, VP of Sales
Dirk Wood, VP of Marketing
Lorelei Bunjes, VP of Digital Services
Jeff Webber, VP of Digital Publishing & Business Development

Facebook: facebook.com/idwpublishing
Twitter: @idwpublishing
YouTube: youtube.com/idwpublishing
Instagram: instagram.com/idwpublishing
deviantART: idwpublishing.deviantart.com
Pinterest: pinterest.com/idwpublishing/idw-staff-faves

Originally published as ROT & RUIN issues #1–5.

Story so Far

The zombie apocalypse was nearly 15 years ago. The dead rose, we fell. No one knows why. Everyone who dies, for any reason, rises as a mindless, shambling, flesh-eating ghoul. There are seven billion zombies and thirty thousand humans. The survivors of this apocalypse live in nine small fenced-in towns along the Sierra Nevadas in Central California.

Benny Imura is a fifteen-year-old who was a toddler during "First Night," the beginning of the end. His older half-brother, Tom, was a twenty-year-old police cadet. Tom rescued Benny after their parents were infected and, after many hardships, found other survivors and helped build Mountainside, the first of the nine towns. Everything beyond the fence line is the great Rot and Ruin.

At least, that's what Benny and his friends thought until they saw the jumbo jet fly across the sky. Now Benny, his girlfriend, Nix, his best friend, Chong, and the feral girl, Lilah, have set out to find that jet...

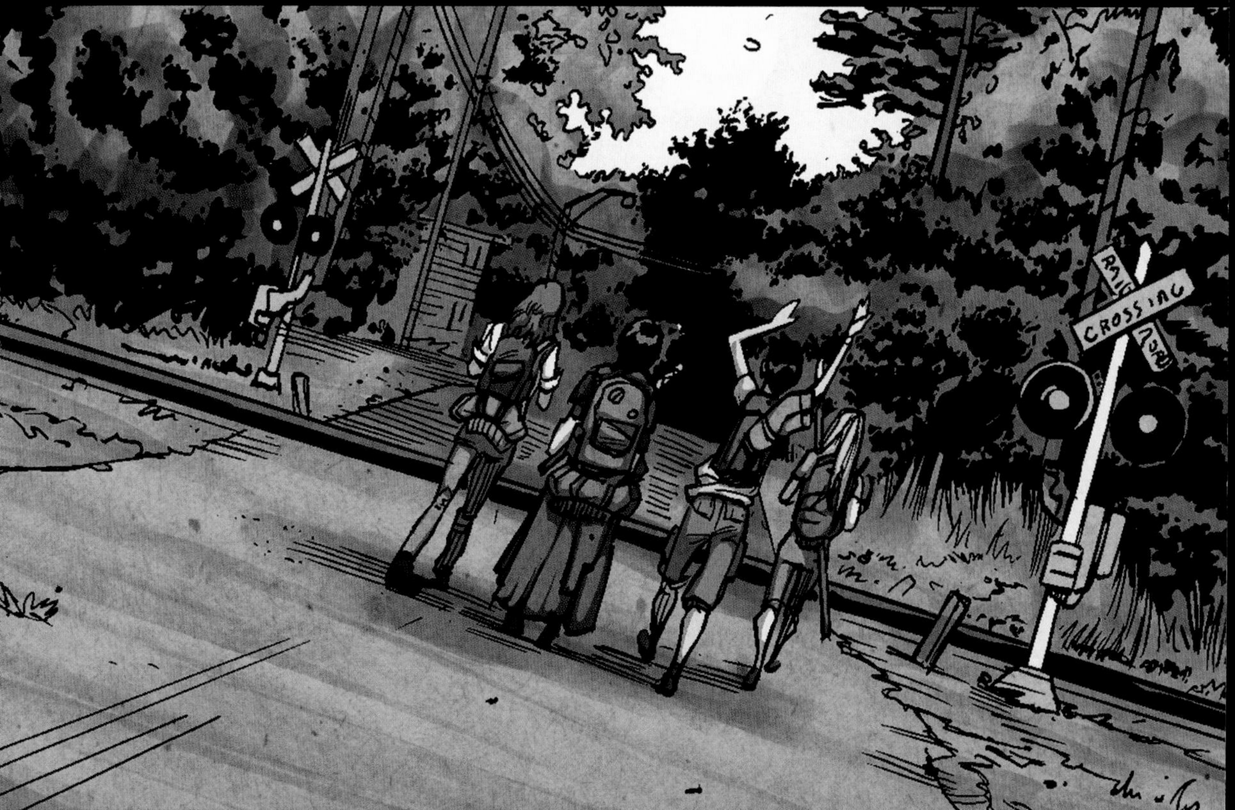
CROSSING

Art by Alex Ronald

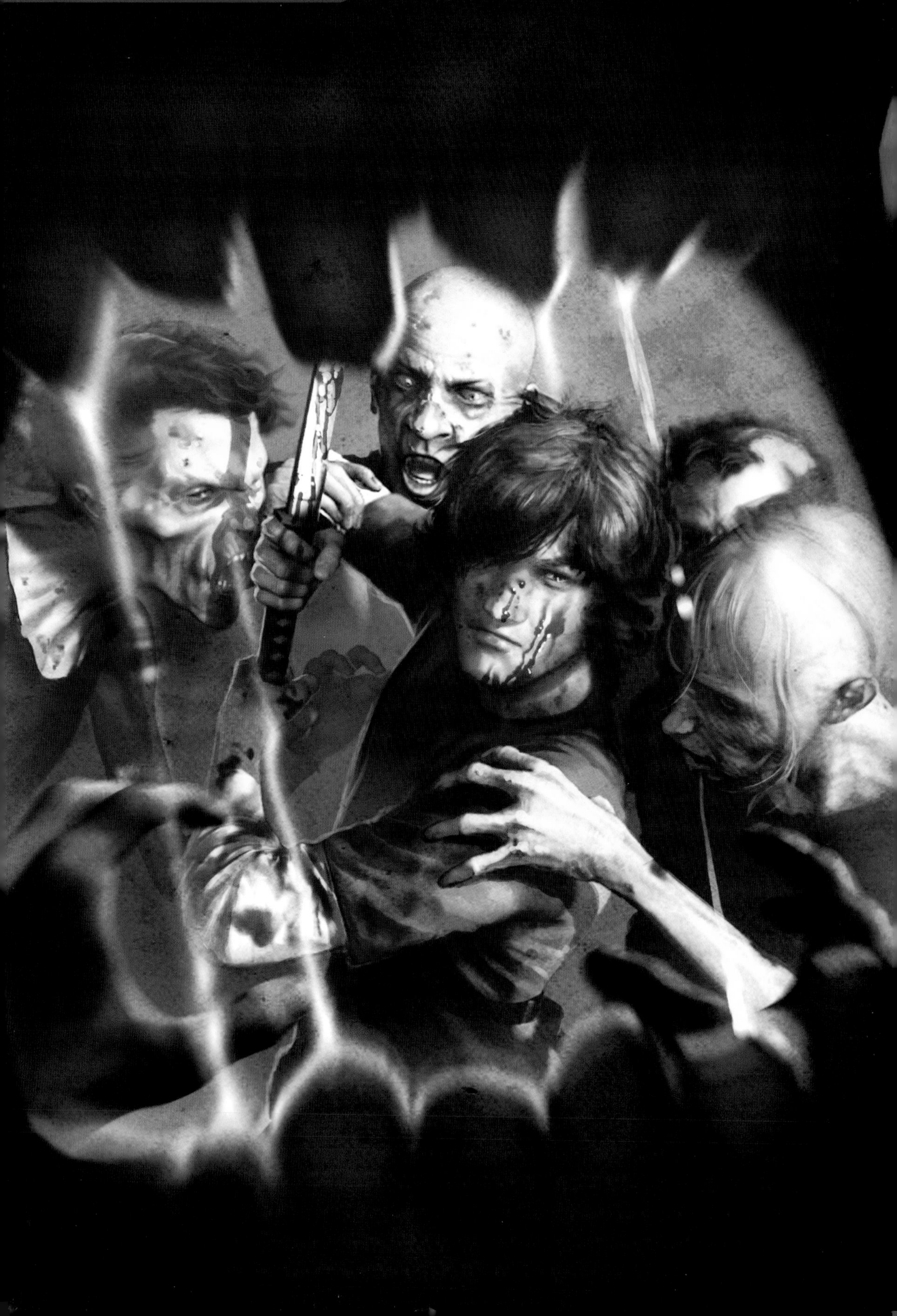

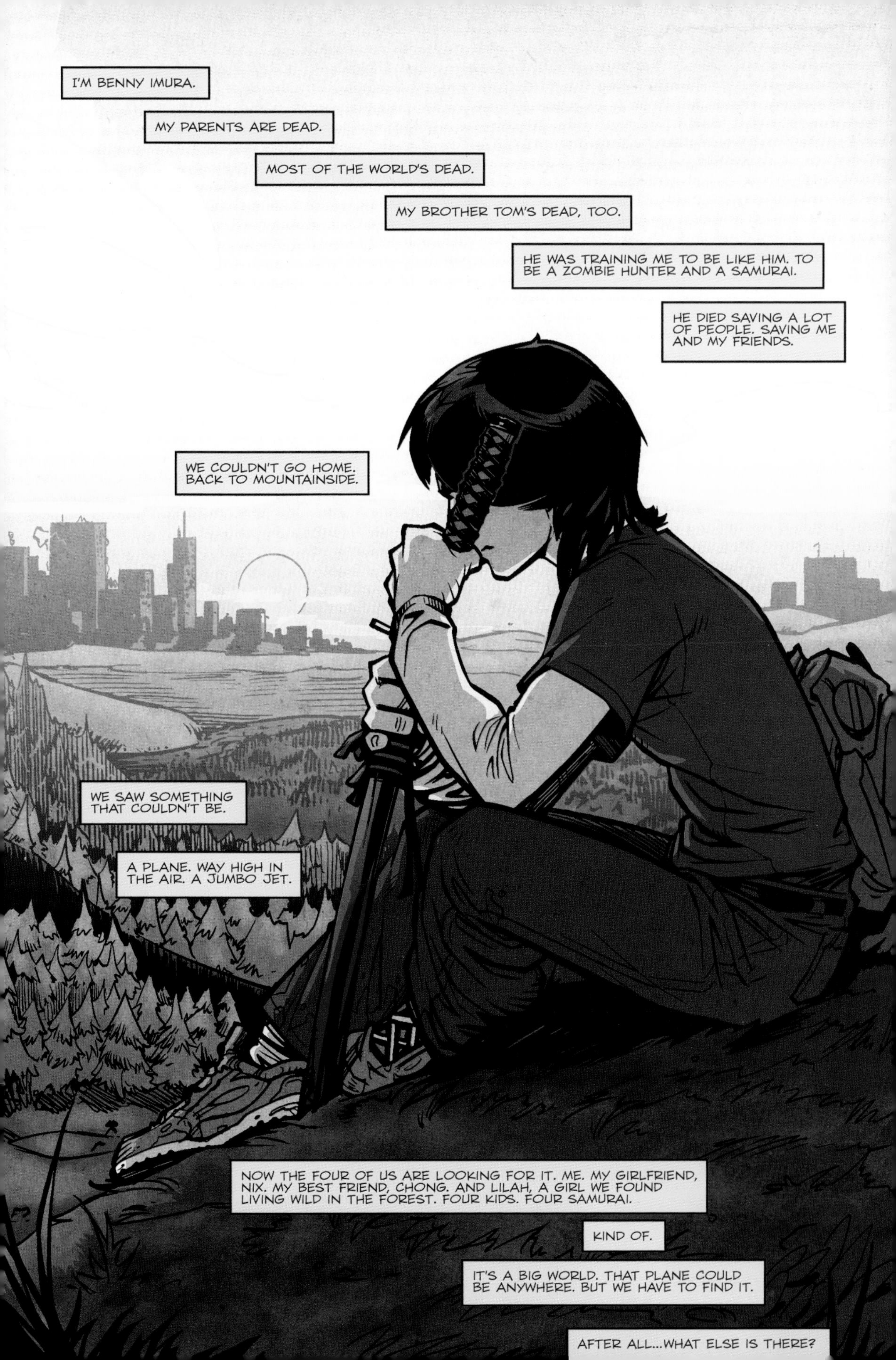
I'M BENNY IMURA.
MY PARENTS ARE DEAD.
MOST OF THE WORLD'S DEAD.
MY BROTHER TOM'S DEAD, TOO.
HE WAS TRAINING ME TO BE LIKE HIM. TO BE A ZOMBIE HUNTER AND A SAMURAI.
HE DIED SAVING A LOT OF PEOPLE. SAVING ME AND MY FRIENDS.
WE COULDN'T GO HOME. BACK TO MOUNTAINSIDE.
WE SAW SOMETHING THAT COULDN'T BE.
A PLANE. WAY HIGH IN THE AIR. A JUMBO JET.
NOW THE FOUR OF US ARE LOOKING FOR IT. ME. MY GIRLFRIEND, NIX. MY BEST FRIEND, CHONG. AND LILAH, A GIRL WE FOUND LIVING WILD IN THE FOREST. FOUR KIDS. FOUR SAMURAI.
KIND OF.
IT'S A BIG WORLD. THAT PLANE COULD BE ANYWHERE. BUT WE HAVE TO FIND IT.
AFTER ALL...WHAT ELSE IS THERE?

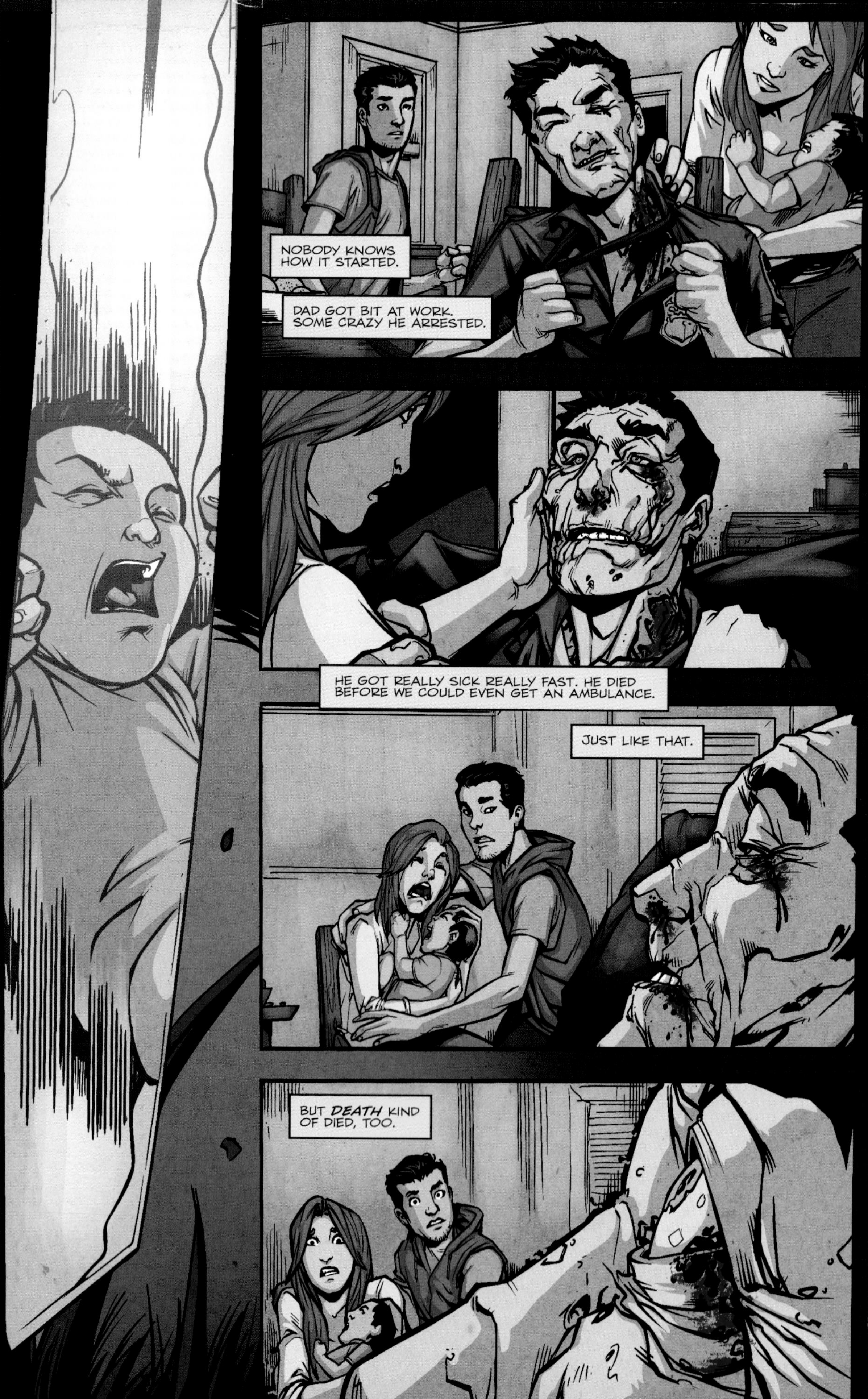
NOBODY KNOWS HOW IT STARTED.
DAD GOT BIT AT WORK. SOME CRAZY HE ARRESTED.
HE GOT REALLY SICK REALLY FAST. HE DIED BEFORE WE COULD EVEN GET AN AMBULANCE.
JUST LIKE THAT.
BUT *DEATH* KIND OF DIED, TOO.

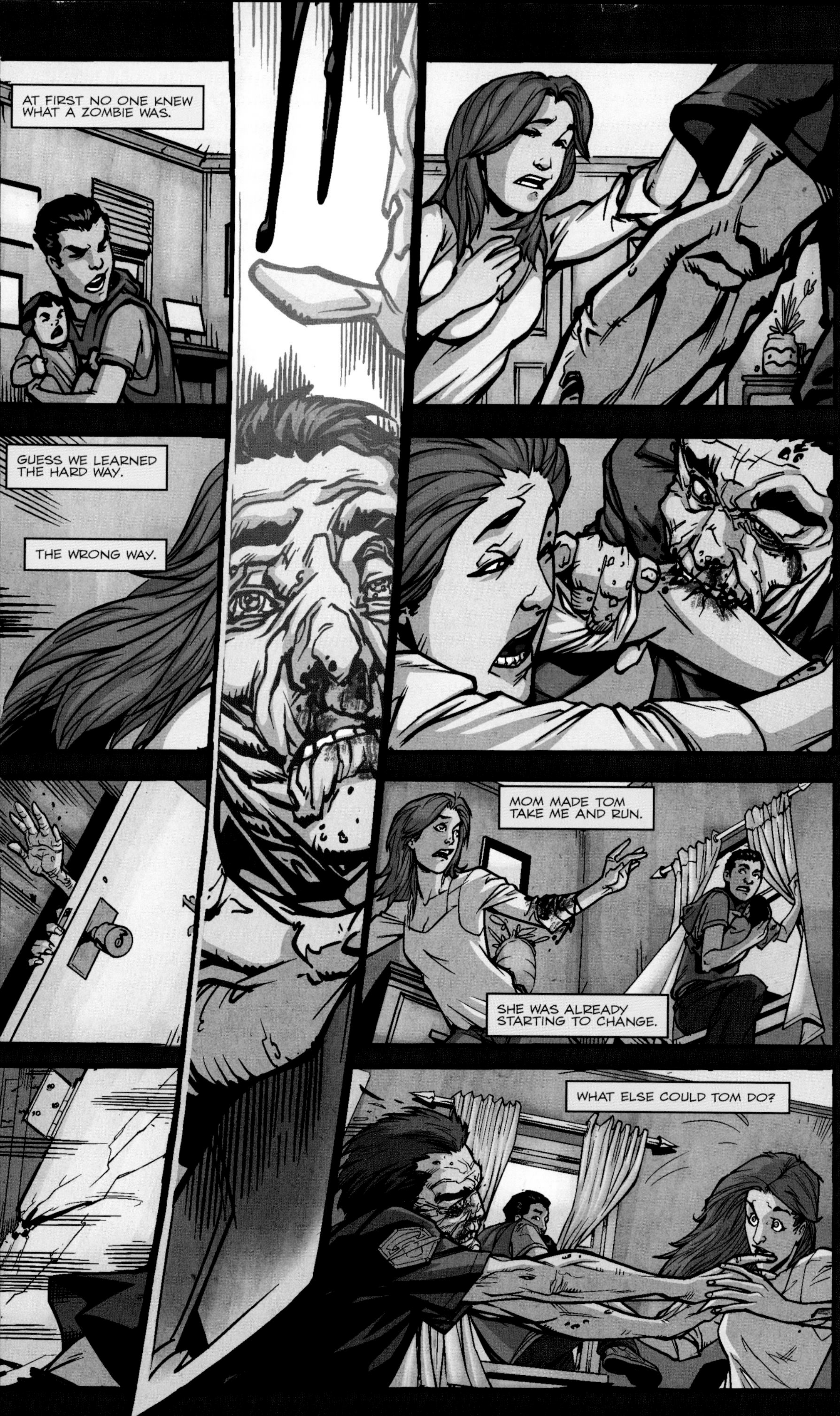
AT FIRST NO ONE KNEW WHAT A ZOMBIE WAS.
GUESS WE LEARNED THE HARD WAY.
THE WRONG WAY.
MOM MADE TOM TAKE ME AND RUN.
SHE WAS ALREADY STARTING TO CHANGE.
WHAT ELSE COULD TOM DO?

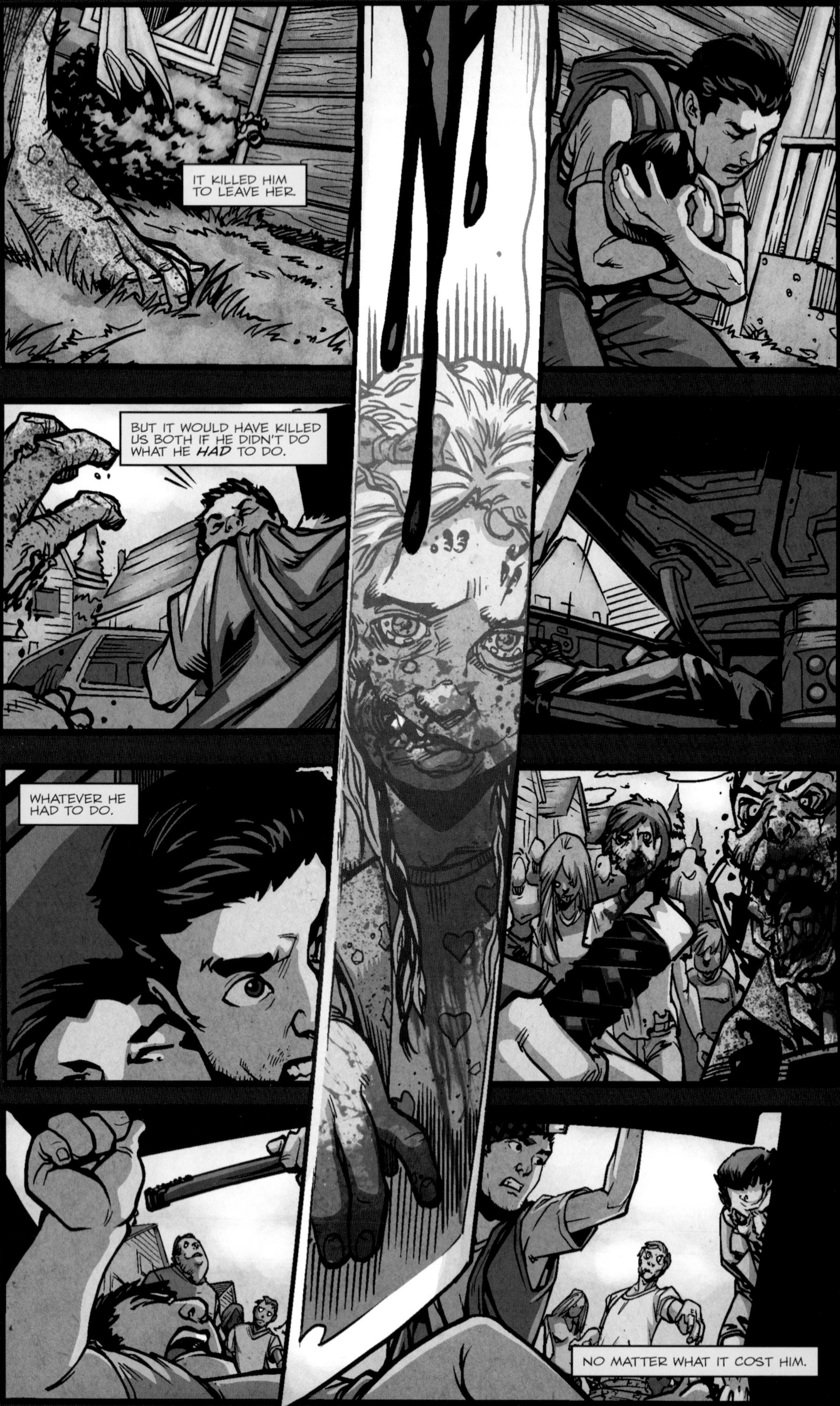
IT KILLED HIM TO LEAVE HER.
BUT IT WOULD HAVE KILLED US BOTH IF HE DIDN'T DO WHAT HE *HAD* TO DO.
WHATEVER HE HAD TO DO.
NO MATTER WHAT IT COST HIM.

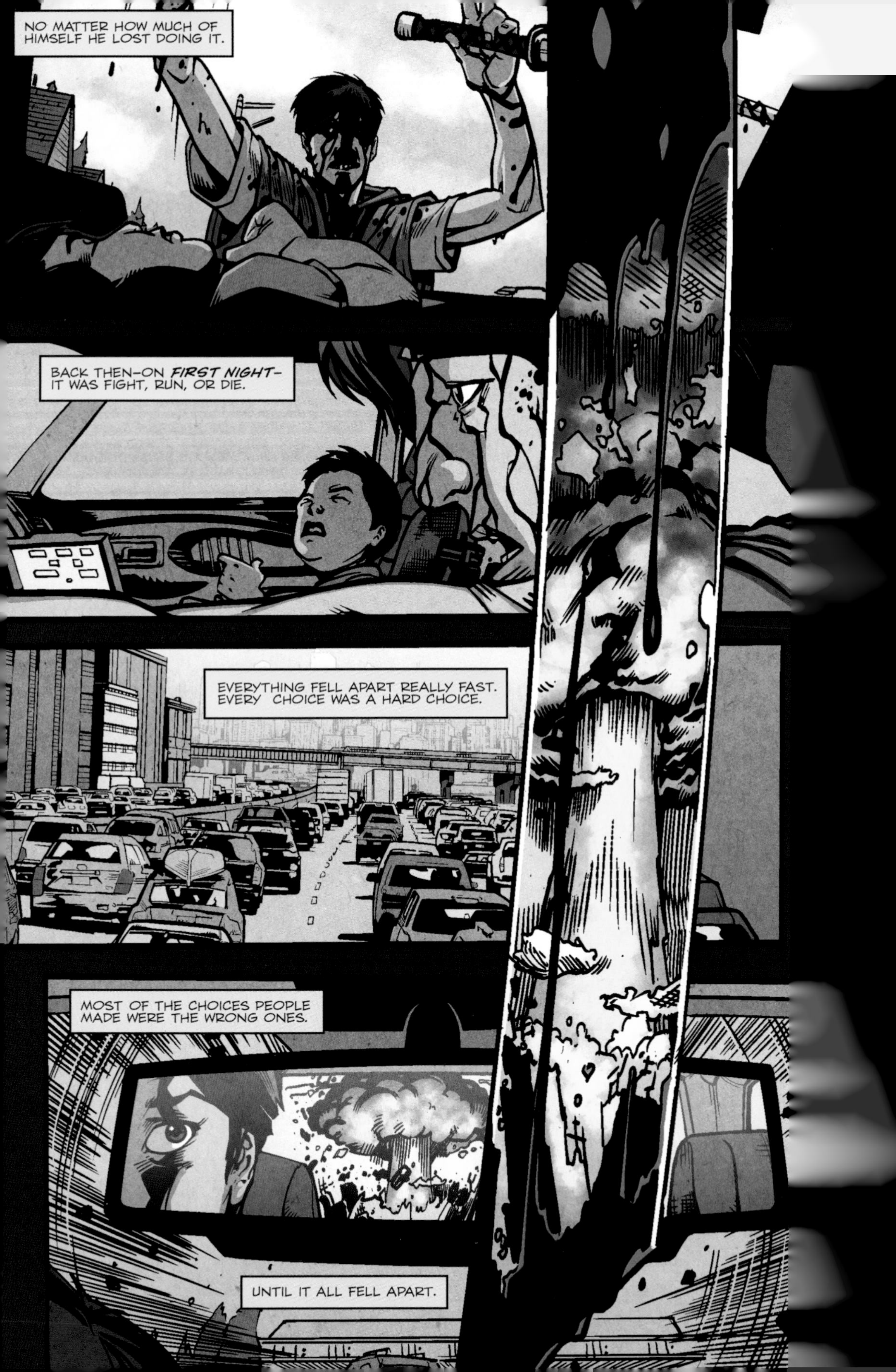

NO MATTER HOW MUCH OF HIMSELF HE LOST DOING IT.
BACK THEN—ON *FIRST NIGHT*—IT WAS FIGHT, RUN, OR DIE.
EVERYTHING FELL APART REALLY FAST. EVERY CHOICE WAS A HARD CHOICE.
MOST OF THE CHOICES PEOPLE MADE WERE THE WRONG ONES.
UNTIL IT ALL FELL APART.

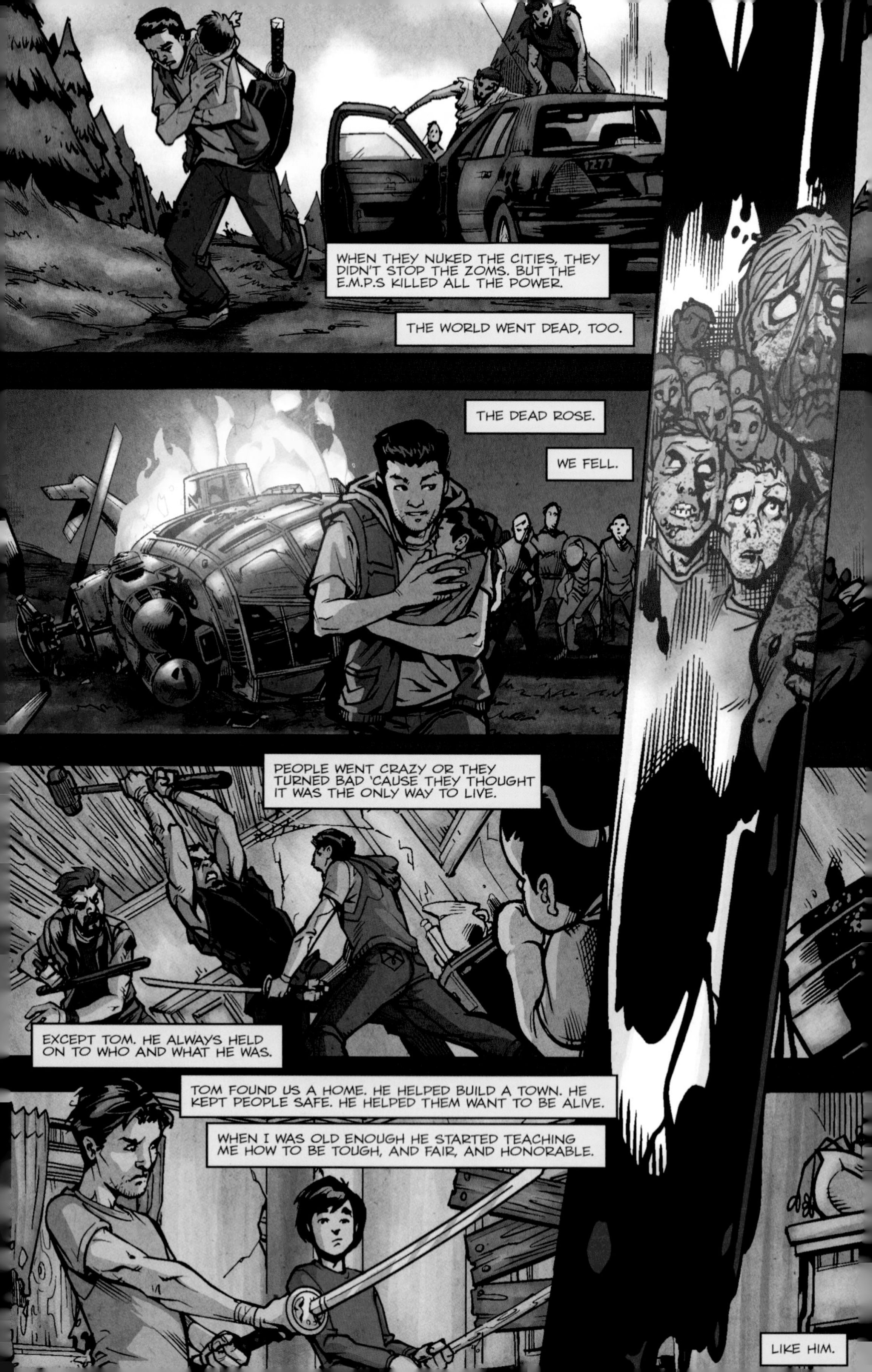
WHEN THEY NUKED THE CITIES, THEY DIDN'T STOP THE ZOMS. BUT THE E.M.P.S KILLED ALL THE POWER.
THE WORLD WENT DEAD, TOO.
THE DEAD ROSE.
WE FELL.
PEOPLE WENT CRAZY OR THEY TURNED BAD 'CAUSE THEY THOUGHT IT WAS THE ONLY WAY TO LIVE.
EXCEPT TOM. HE ALWAYS HELD ON TO WHO AND WHAT HE WAS.
TOM FOUND US A HOME. HE HELPED BUILD A TOWN. HE KEPT PEOPLE SAFE. HE HELPED THEM WANT TO BE ALIVE.
WHEN I WAS OLD ENOUGH HE STARTED TEACHING ME HOW TO BE TOUGH, AND FAIR, AND HONORABLE.
LIKE HIM.

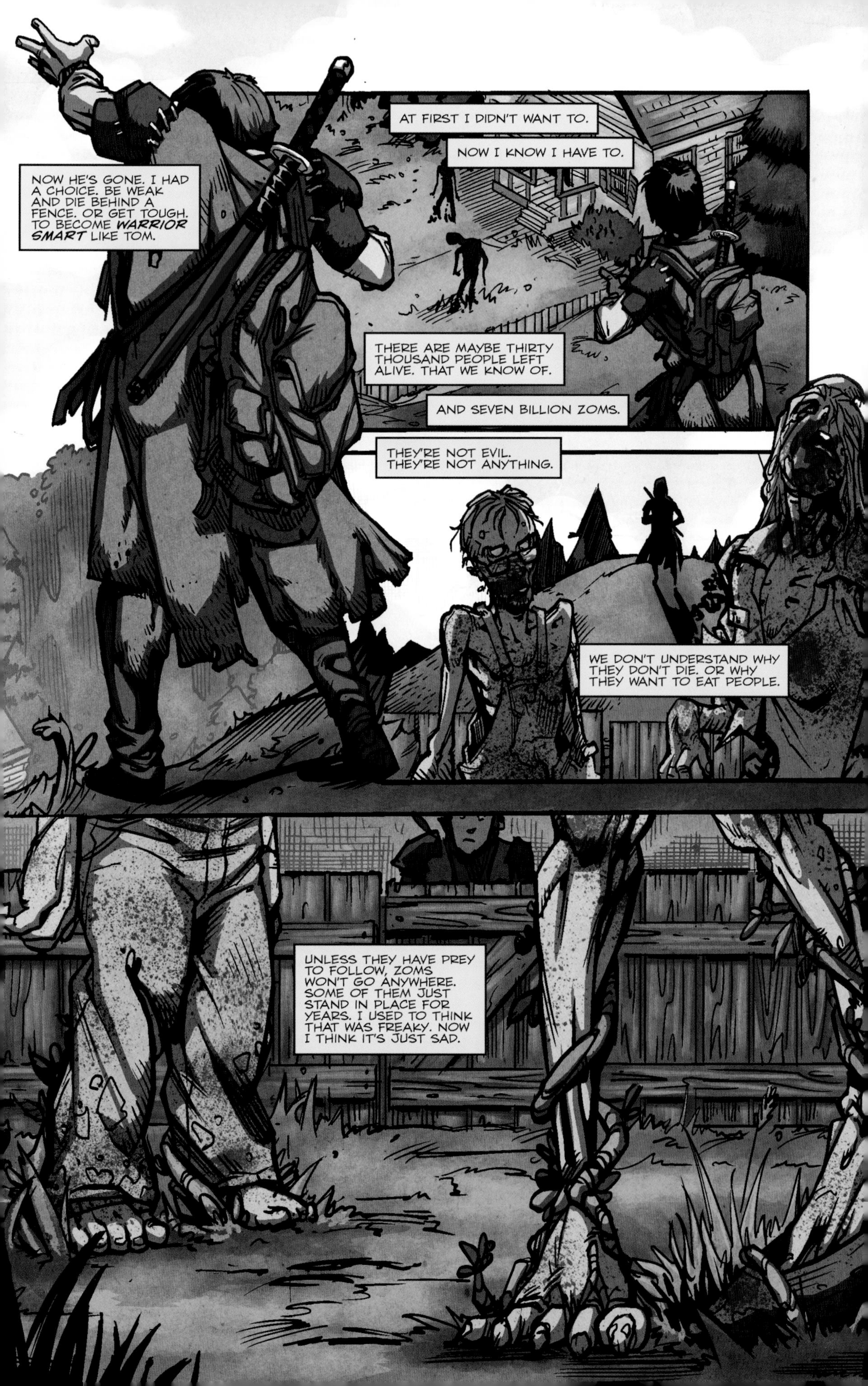
NOW HE'S GONE. I HAD A CHOICE. BE WEAK AND DIE BEHIND A FENCE. OR GET TOUGH. TO BECOME *WARRIOR SMART* LIKE TOM.
AT FIRST I DIDN'T WANT TO.
NOW I KNOW I HAVE TO.
THERE ARE MAYBE THIRTY THOUSAND PEOPLE LEFT ALIVE. THAT WE KNOW OF.
AND SEVEN BILLION ZOMS.
THEY'RE NOT EVIL. THEY'RE NOT ANYTHING.
WE DON'T UNDERSTAND WHY THEY DON'T DIE. OR WHY THEY WANT TO EAT PEOPLE.
UNLESS THEY HAVE PREY TO FOLLOW, ZOMS WON'T GO ANYWHERE. SOME OF THEM JUST STAND IN PLACE FOR YEARS. I USED TO THINK THAT WAS FREAKY. NOW I THINK IT'S JUST SAD.

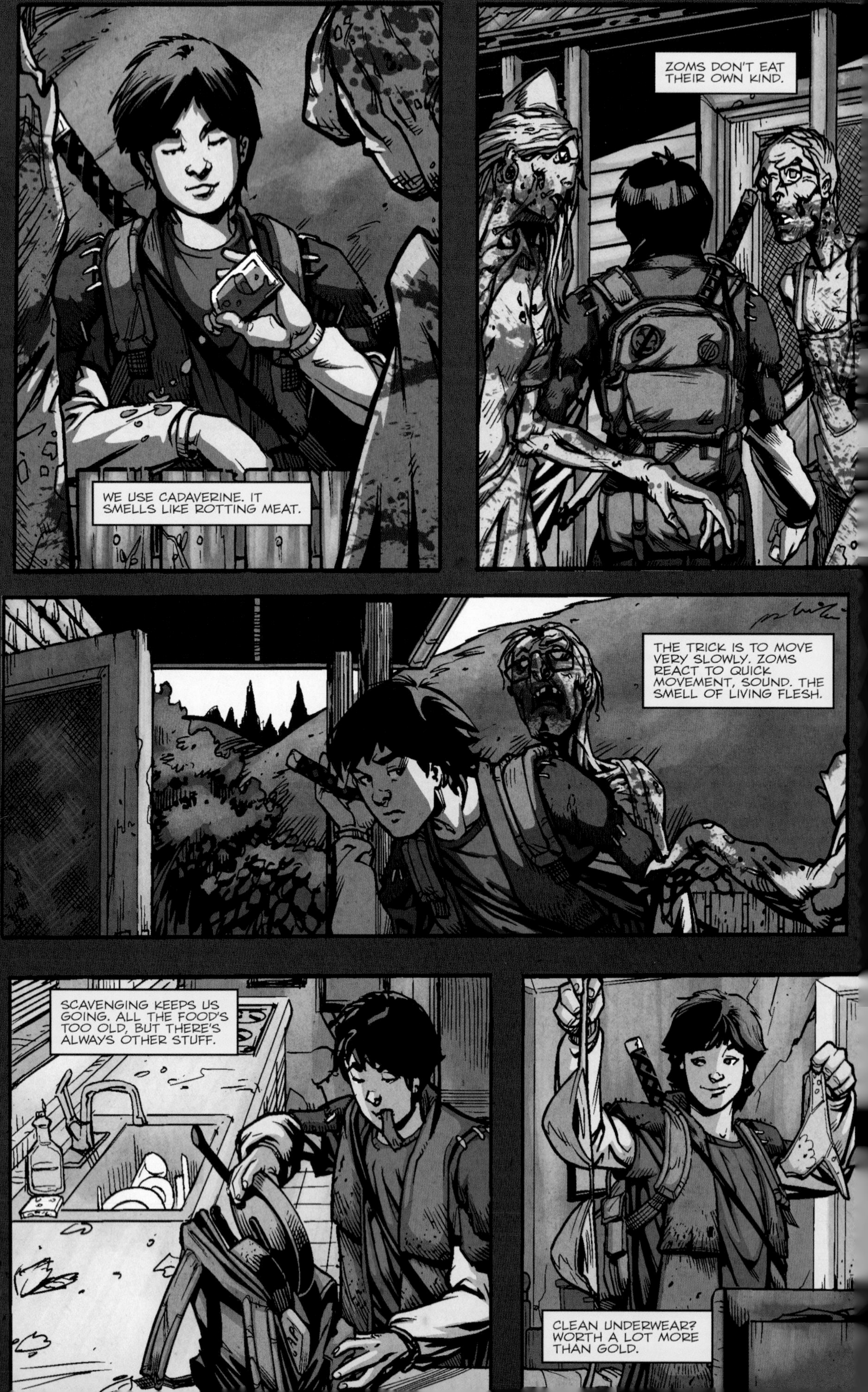
WE USE CADAVERINE. IT SMELLS LIKE ROTTING MEAT.
ZOMS DON'T EAT THEIR OWN KIND.
THE TRICK IS TO MOVE VERY SLOWLY. ZOMS REACT TO QUICK MOVEMENT, SOUND. THE SMELL OF LIVING FLESH.
SCAVENGING KEEPS US GOING. ALL THE FOOD'S TOO OLD, BUT THERE'S ALWAYS OTHER STUFF.
CLEAN UNDERWEAR? WORTH A LOT MORE THAN GOLD.

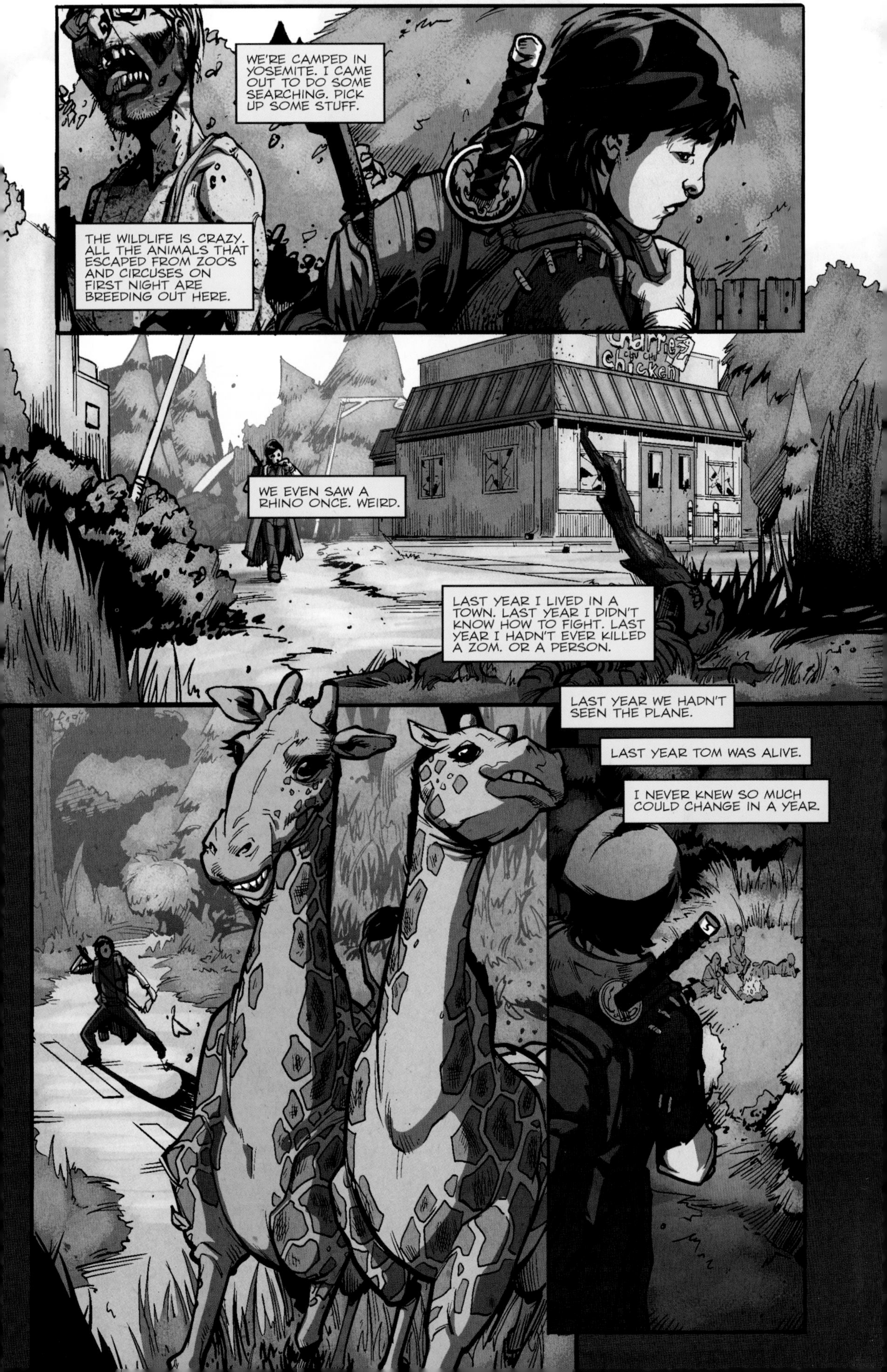
WE'RE CAMPED IN YOSEMITE. I CAME OUT TO DO SOME SEARCHING. PICK UP SOME STUFF.
THE WILDLIFE IS CRAZY. ALL THE ANIMALS THAT ESCAPED FROM ZOOS AND CIRCUSES ON FIRST NIGHT ARE BREEDING OUT HERE.
Charlie's Chicken
WE EVEN SAW A RHINO ONCE. WEIRD.
LAST YEAR I LIVED IN A TOWN. LAST YEAR I DIDN'T KNOW HOW TO FIGHT. LAST YEAR I HADN'T EVER KILLED A ZOM. OR A PERSON.
LAST YEAR WE HADN'T SEEN THE PLANE.
LAST YEAR TOM WAS ALIVE.
I NEVER KNEW SO MUCH COULD CHANGE IN A YEAR.

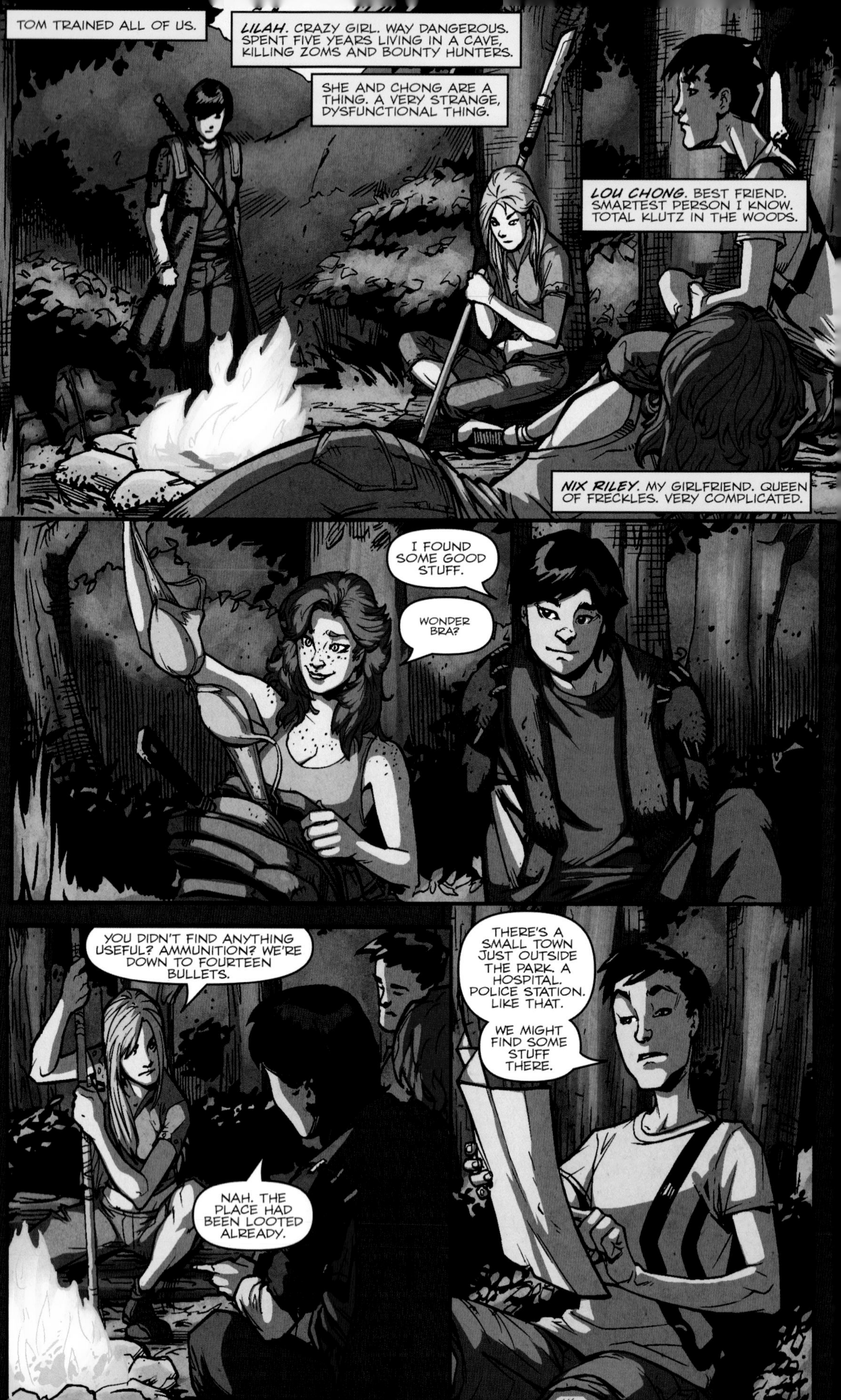
TOM TRAINED ALL OF US.
LILAH. CRAZY GIRL. WAY DANGEROUS. SPENT FIVE YEARS LIVING IN A CAVE, KILLING ZOMS AND BOUNTY HUNTERS.
SHE AND CHONG ARE A THING. A VERY STRANGE, DYSFUNCTIONAL THING.
LOU CHONG. BEST FRIEND. SMARTEST PERSON I KNOW. TOTAL KLUTZ IN THE WOODS.
NIX RILEY. MY GIRLFRIEND. QUEEN OF FRECKLES. VERY COMPLICATED.
I FOUND SOME GOOD STUFF.
WONDER BRA?
YOU DIDN'T FIND ANYTHING USEFUL? AMMUNITION? WE'RE DOWN TO FOURTEEN BULLETS.
NAH. THE PLACE HAD BEEN LOOTED ALREADY.
THERE'S A SMALL TOWN JUST OUTSIDE THE PARK. A HOSPITAL. POLICE STATION. LIKE THAT.
WE MIGHT FIND SOME STUFF THERE.

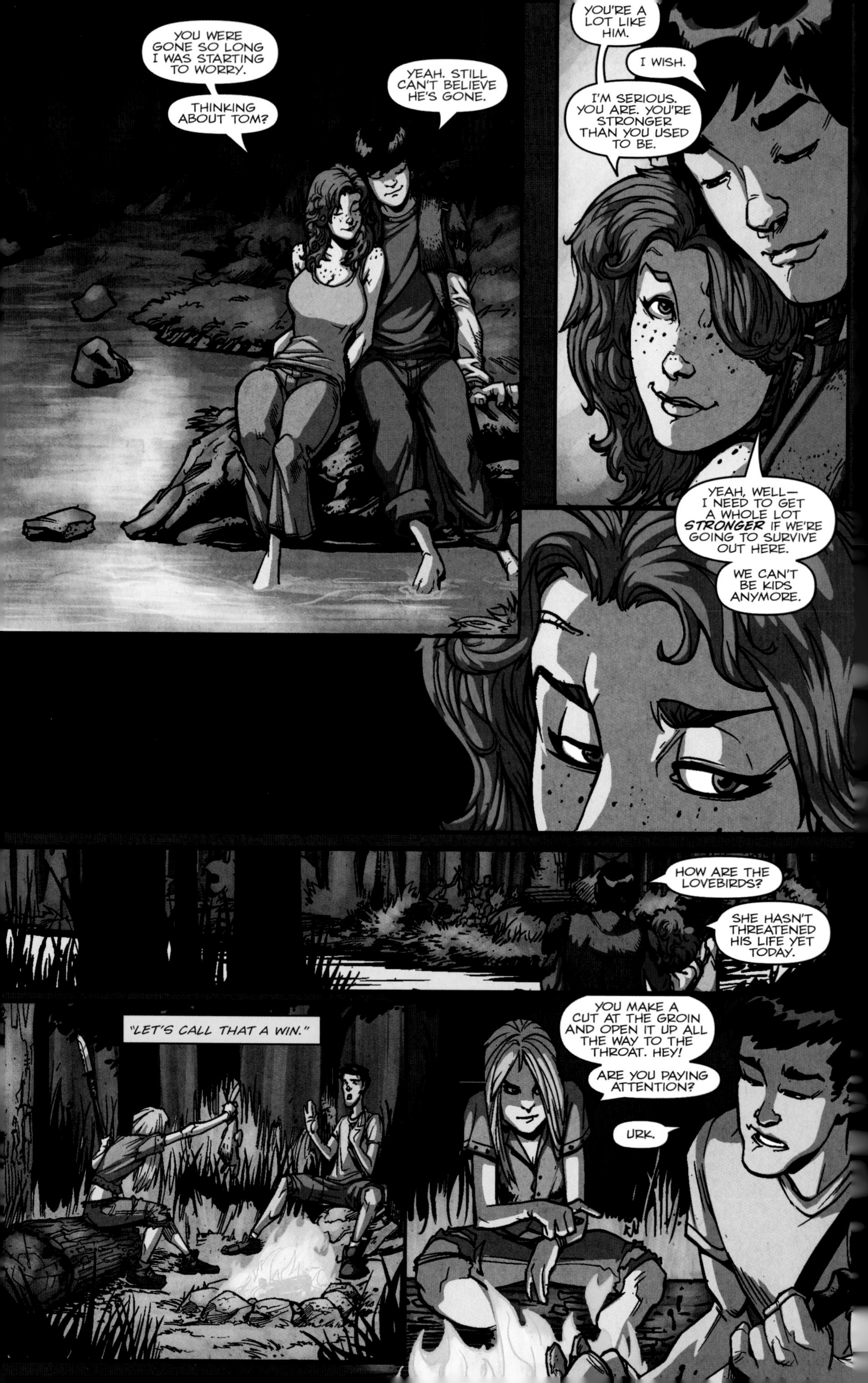
YOU WERE GONE SO LONG I WAS STARTING TO WORRY.
THINKING ABOUT TOM?
YEAH. STILL CAN'T BELIEVE HE'S GONE.
YOU'RE A LOT LIKE HIM.
I WISH.
I'M SERIOUS. YOU ARE. YOU'RE STRONGER THAN YOU USED TO BE.
YEAH, WELL— I NEED TO GET A WHOLE LOT STRONGER IF WE'RE GOING TO SURVIVE OUT HERE.
WE CAN'T BE KIDS ANYMORE.
HOW ARE THE LOVEBIRDS?
SHE HASN'T THREATENED HIS LIFE YET TODAY.
"LET'S CALL THAT A WIN."
YOU MAKE A CUT AT THE GROIN AND OPEN IT UP ALL THE WAY TO THE THROAT. HEY!
ARE YOU PAYING ATTENTION?
URK.

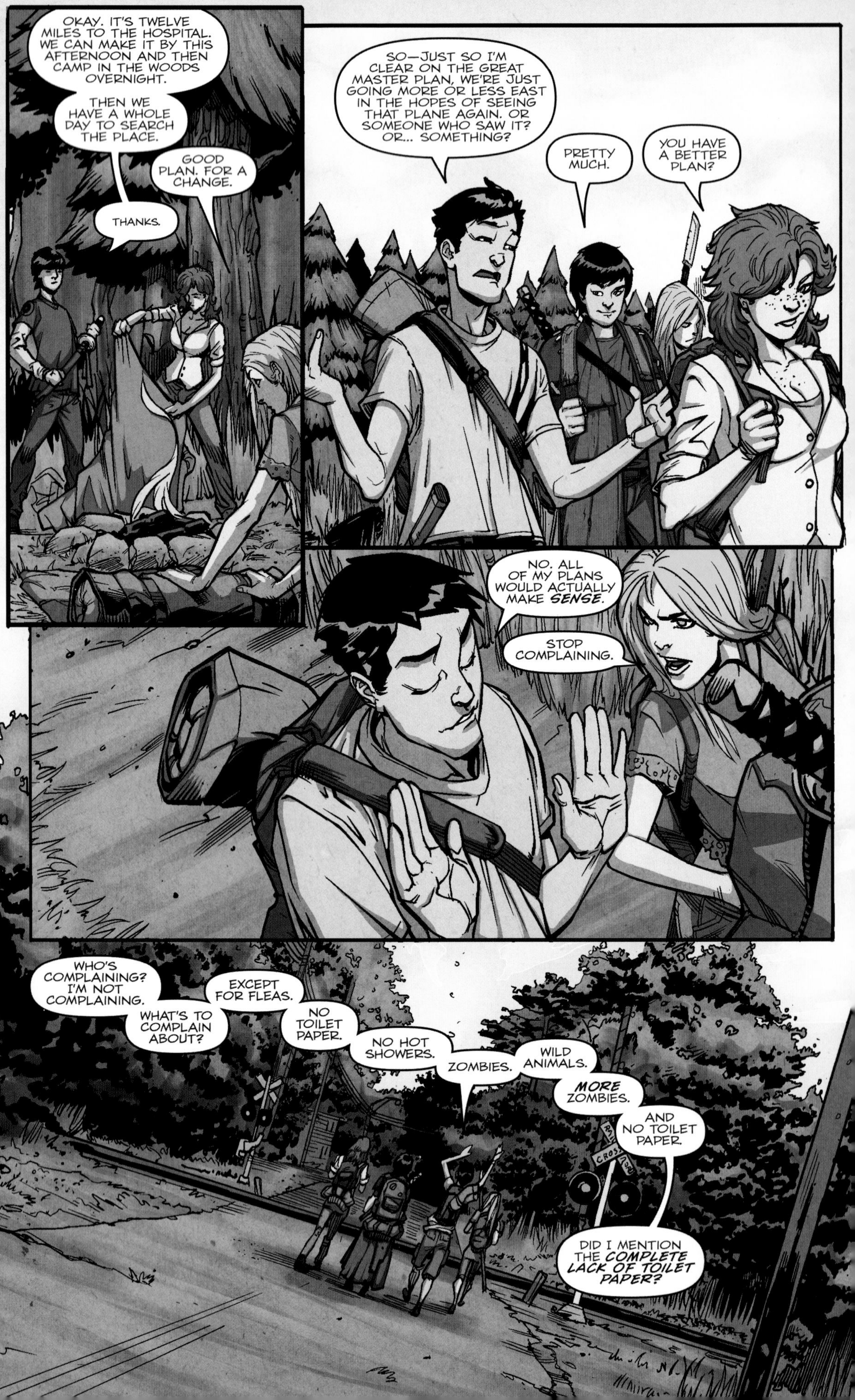
OKAY. IT'S TWELVE MILES TO THE HOSPITAL. WE CAN MAKE IT BY THIS AFTERNOON AND THEN CAMP IN THE WOODS OVERNIGHT.
THEN WE HAVE A WHOLE DAY TO SEARCH THE PLACE.
GOOD PLAN. FOR A CHANGE.
THANKS.
SO—JUST SO I'M CLEAR ON THE GREAT MASTER PLAN, WE'RE JUST GOING MORE OR LESS EAST IN THE HOPES OF SEEING THAT PLANE AGAIN. OR SOMEONE WHO SAW IT? OR... SOMETHING?
PRETTY MUCH.
YOU HAVE A BETTER PLAN?
NO. ALL OF MY PLANS WOULD ACTUALLY MAKE ***SENSE***.
STOP COMPLAINING.
WHO'S COMPLAINING? I'M NOT COMPLAINING.
WHAT'S TO COMPLAIN ABOUT?
EXCEPT FOR FLEAS.
NO TOILET PAPER.
NO HOT SHOWERS.
ZOMBIES.
WILD ANIMALS.
MORE ZOMBIES.
AND NO TOILET PAPER.
DID I MENTION THE ***COMPLETE LACK OF TOILET PAPER?***

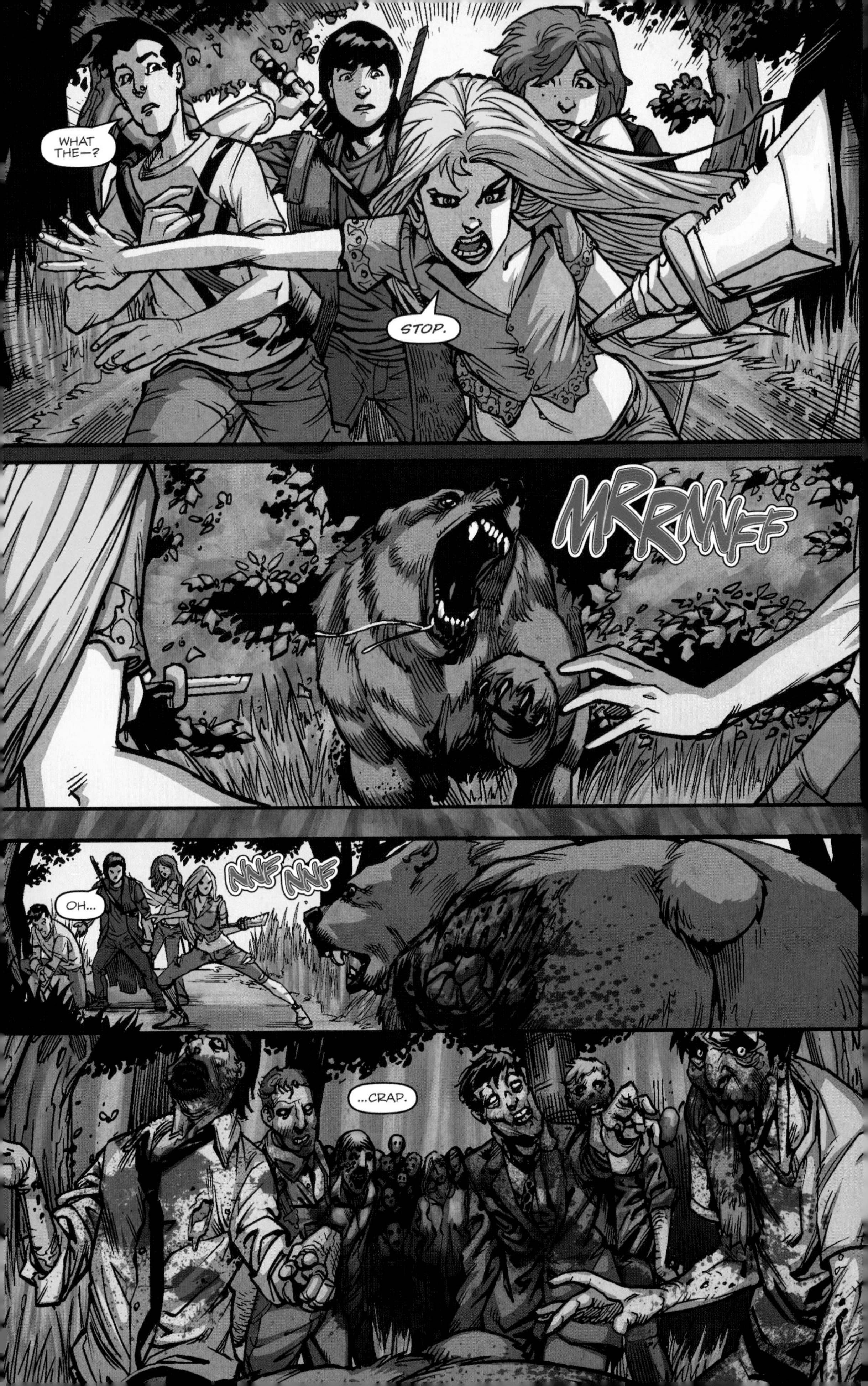
WHAT THE—?
STOP.
MRRNNFF
OH...
NNF NNF
...CRAP.

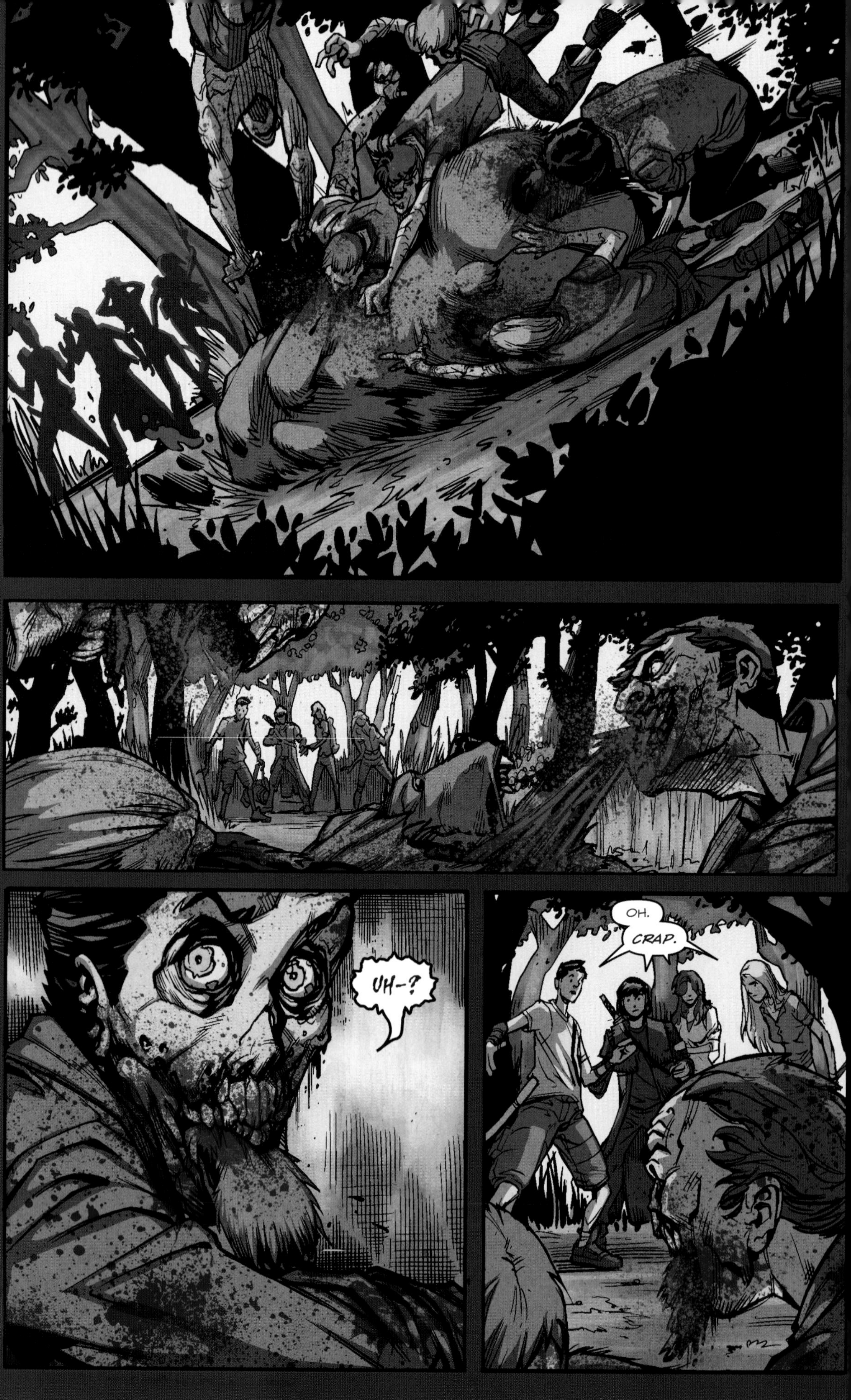
UH-?
OH.
CRAP.

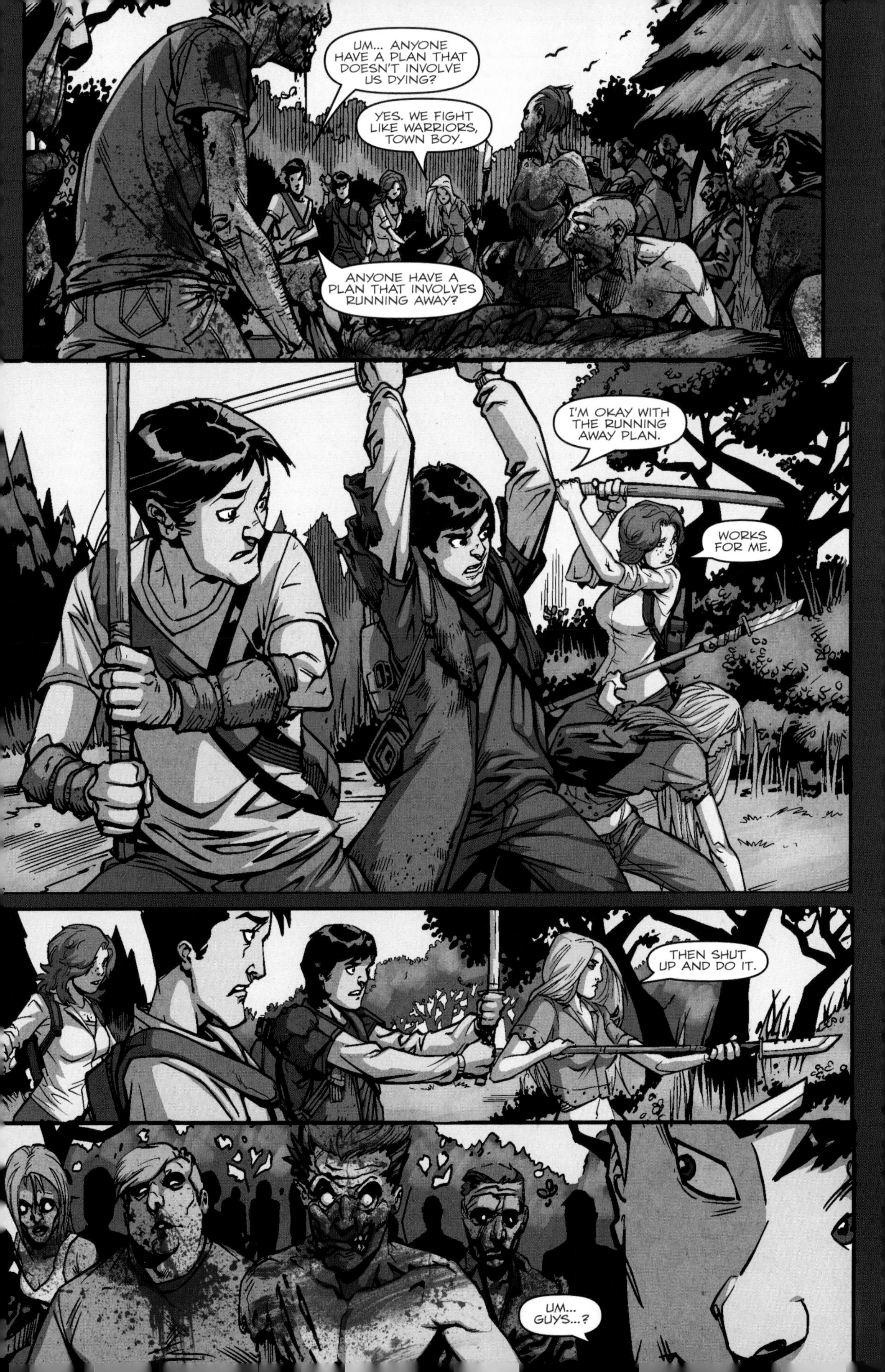
UM... ANYONE HAVE A PLAN THAT DOESN'T INVOLVE US DYING?
YES. WE FIGHT LIKE WARRIORS, TOWN BOY.
ANYONE HAVE A PLAN THAT INVOLVES RUNNING AWAY?
I'M OKAY WITH THE RUNNING AWAY PLAN.
WORKS FOR ME.
THEN SHUT UP AND DO IT.
UM... GUYS...?

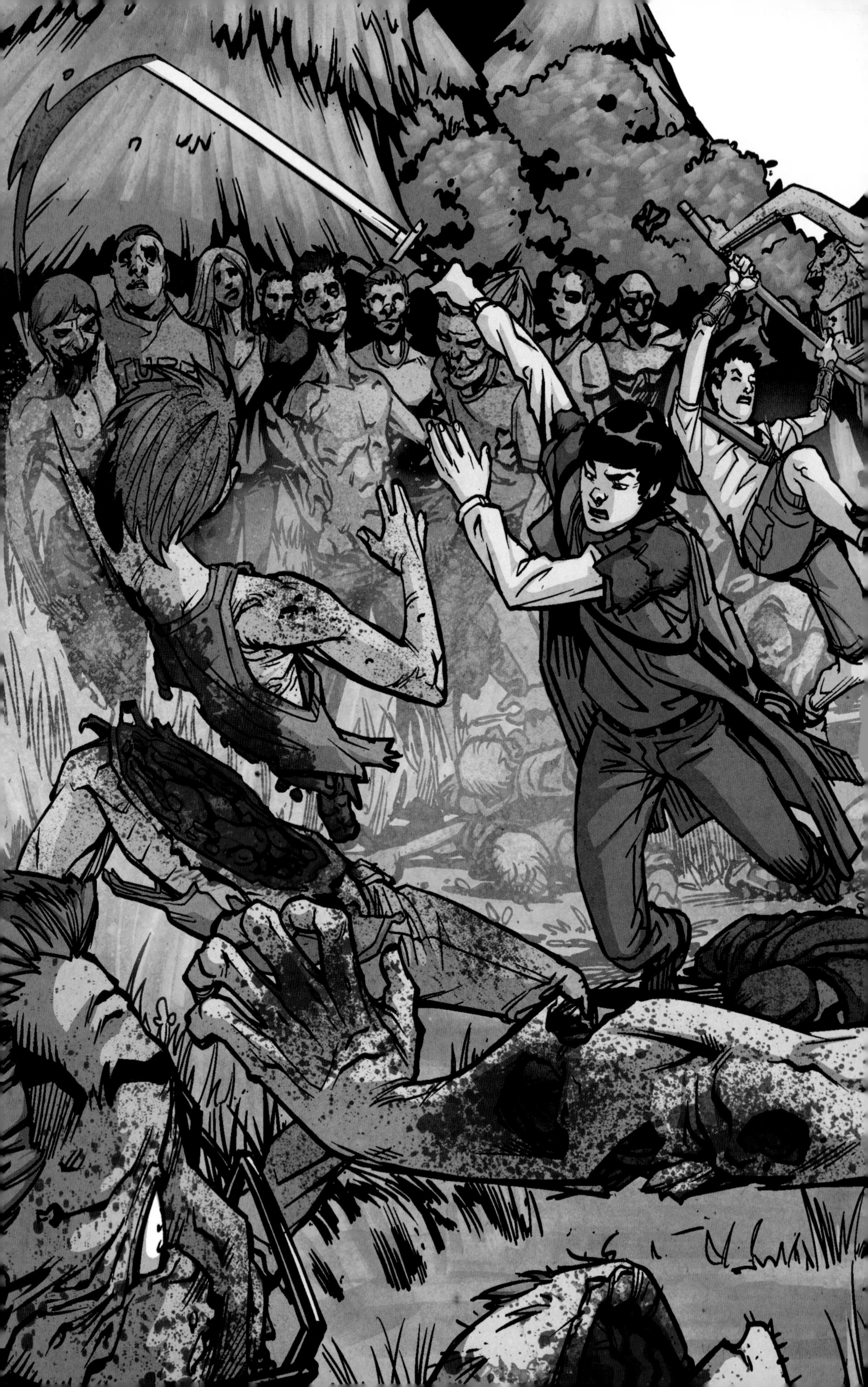

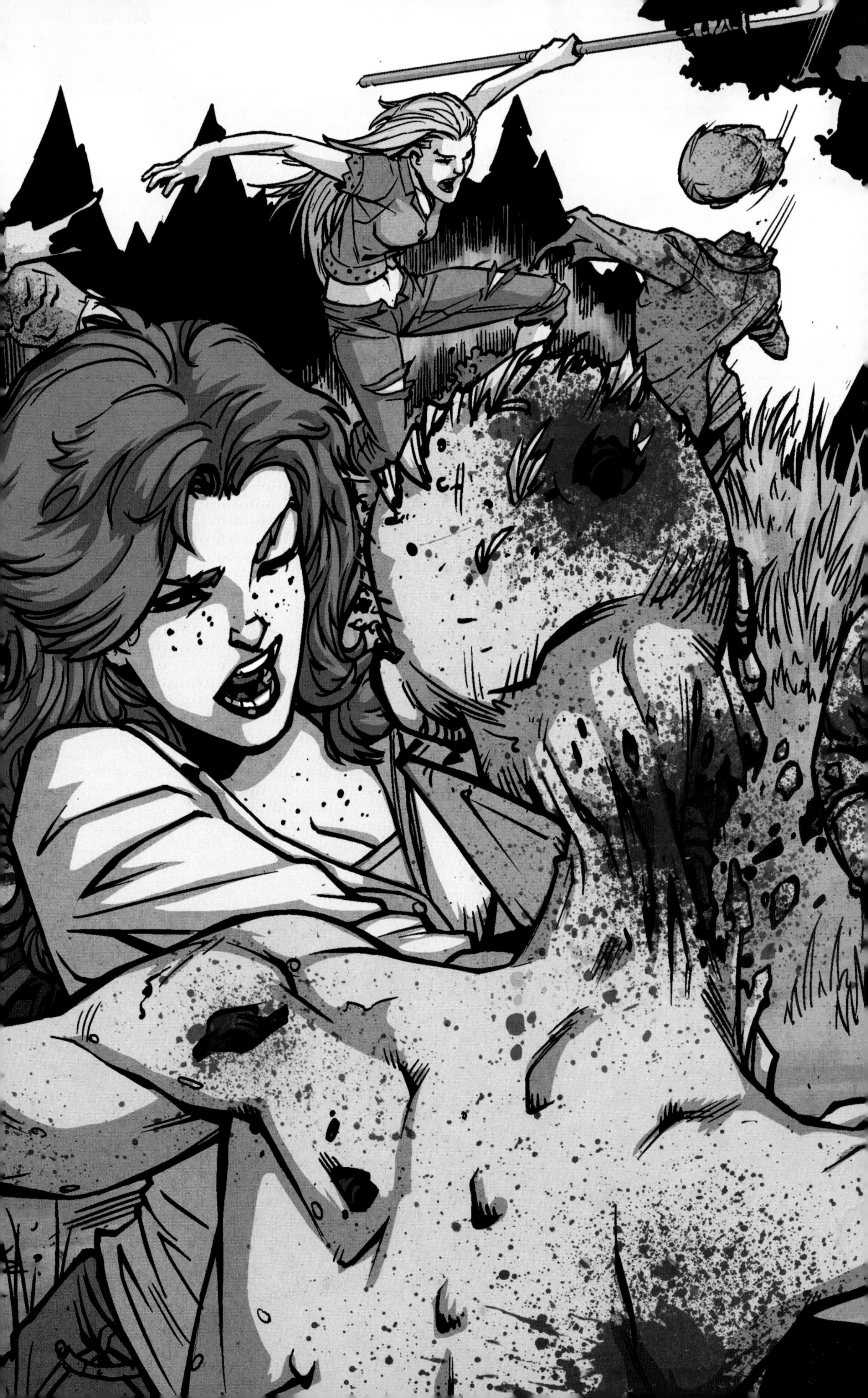

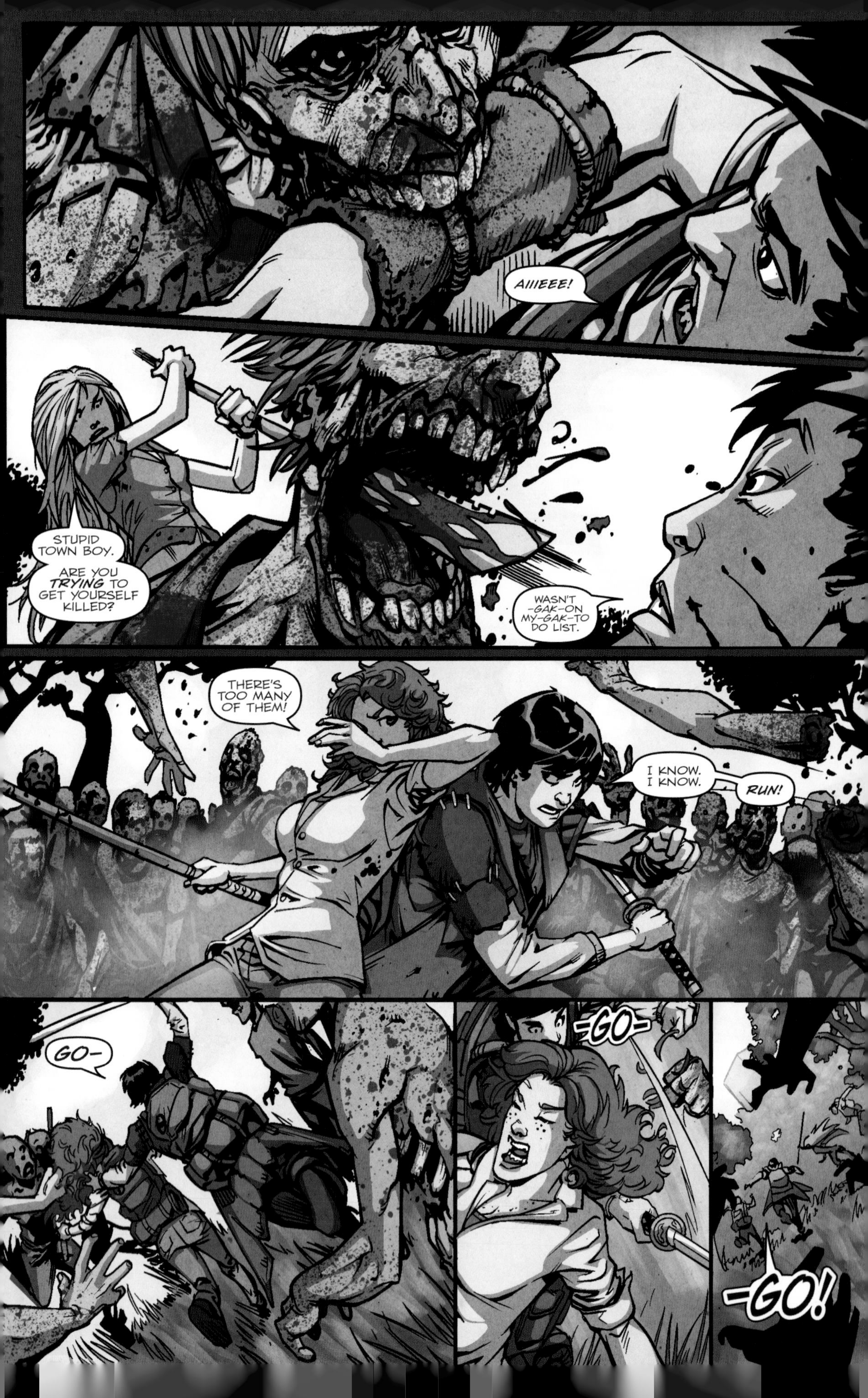
AIIIEEE!
STUPID TOWN BOY.
ARE YOU TRYING TO GET YOURSELF KILLED?
WASN'T -GAK-ON MY-GAK-TO DO LIST.
THERE'S TOO MANY OF THEM!
I KNOW. I KNOW.
RUN!
GO-
-GO-
-GO!

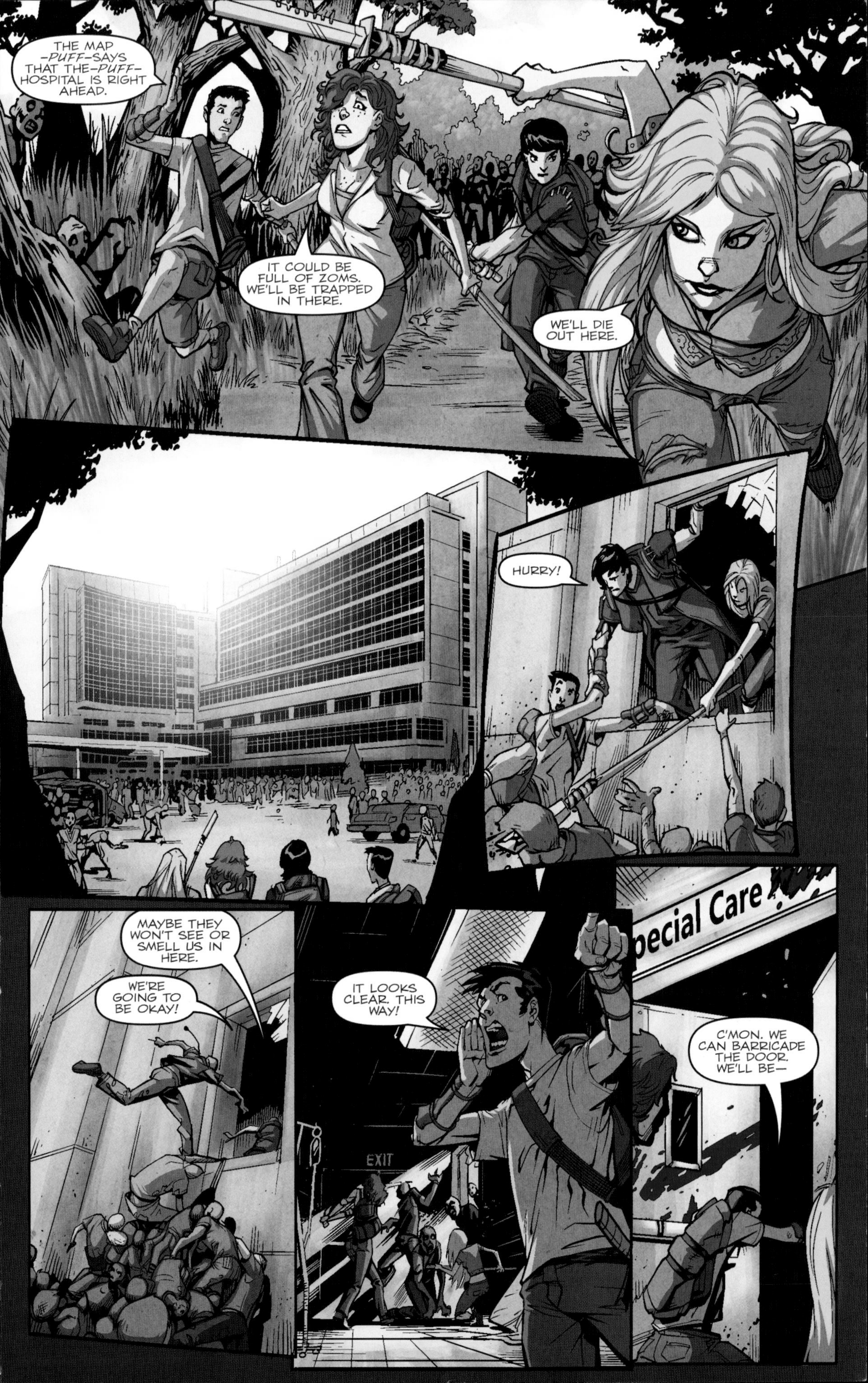
THE MAP -PUFF- SAYS THAT THE -PUFF- HOSPITAL IS RIGHT AHEAD.
IT COULD BE FULL OF ZOMS. WE'LL BE TRAPPED IN THERE.
WE'LL DIE OUT HERE.
HURRY!
MAYBE THEY WON'T SEE OR SMELL US IN HERE.
WE'RE GOING TO BE OKAY!
IT LOOKS CLEAR. THIS WAY!
EXIT
pecial Care
C'MON. WE CAN BARRICADE THE DOOR. WE'LL BE—

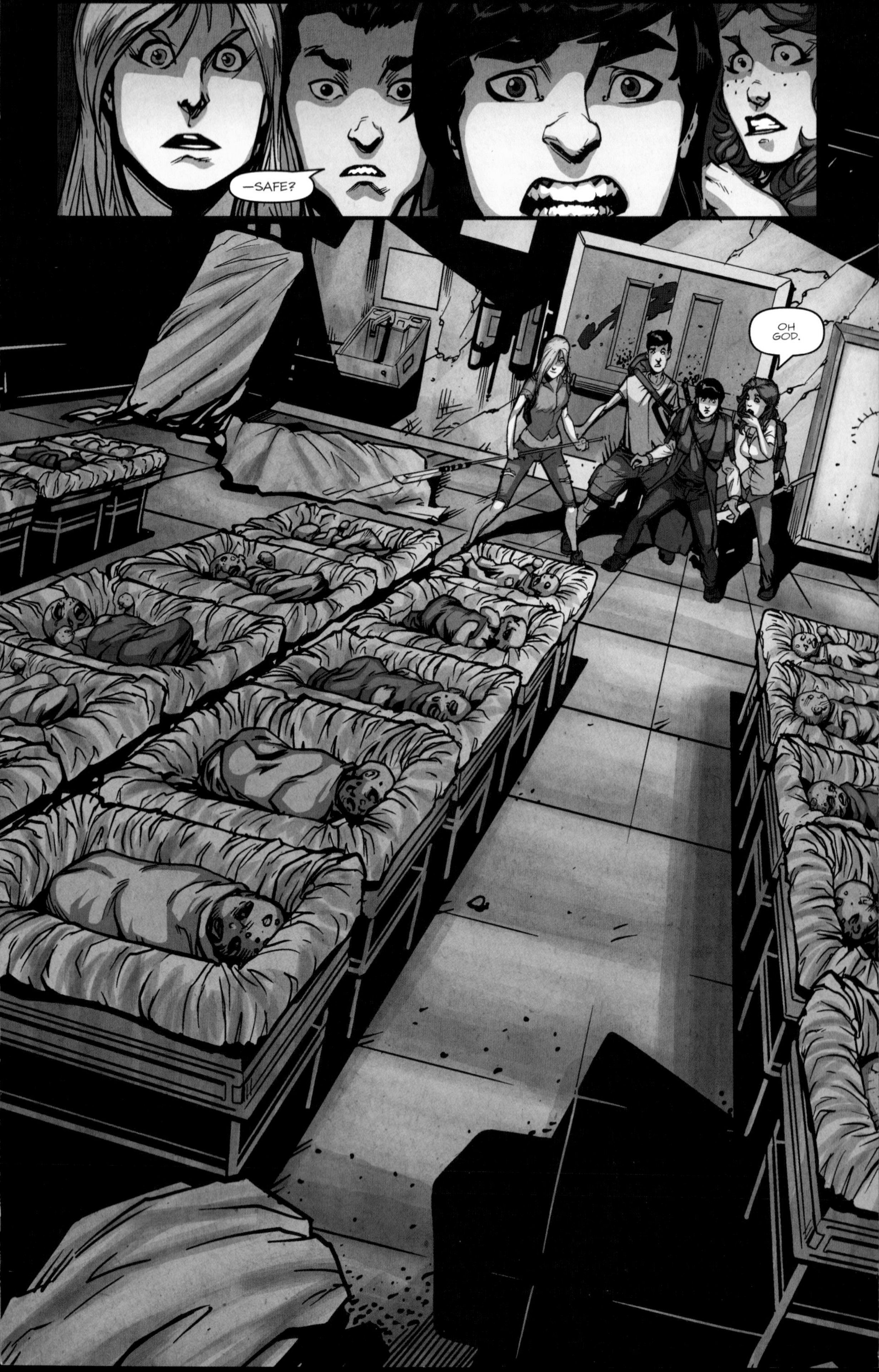
—SAFE?
OH GOD.

Art by Alex Ronald

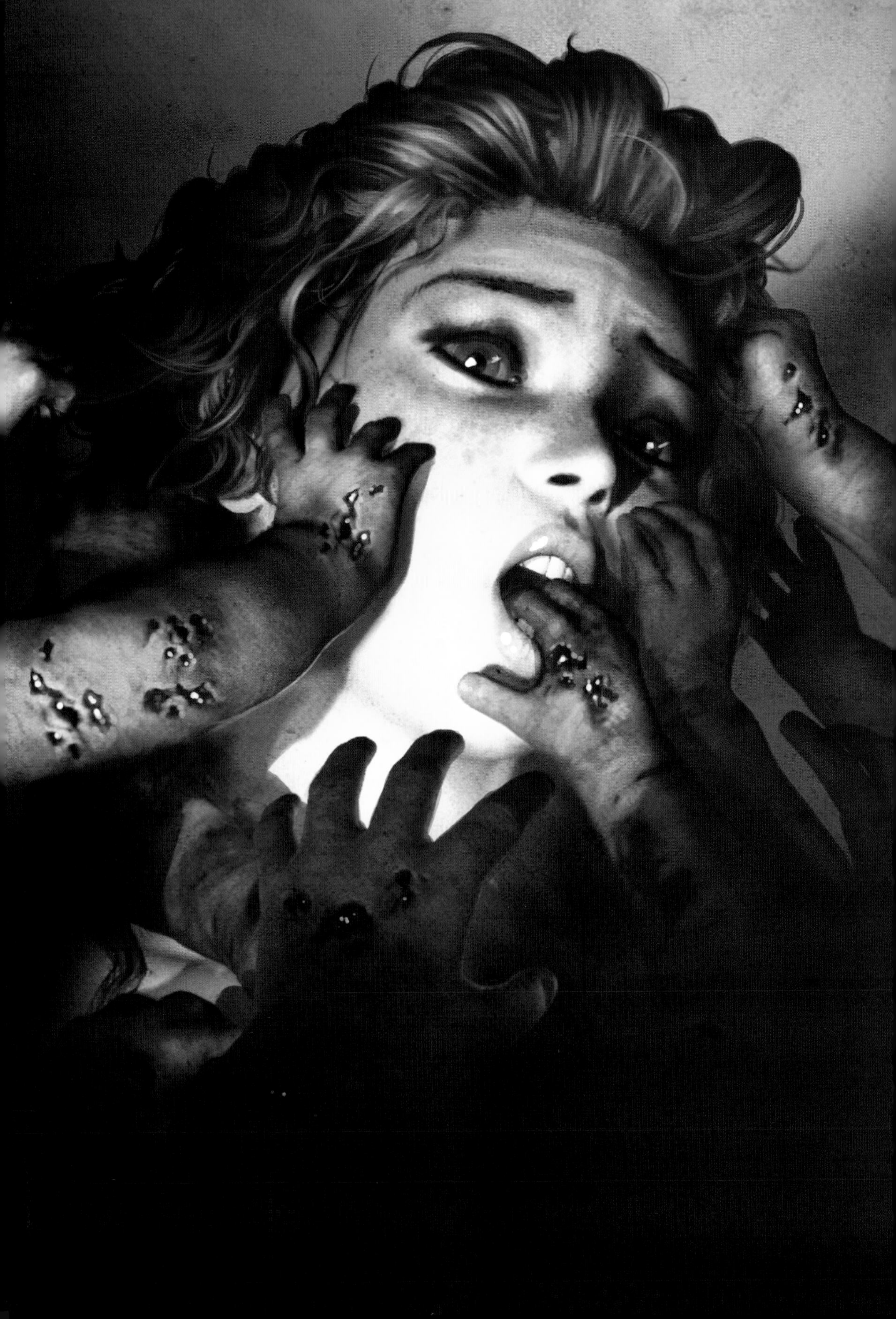

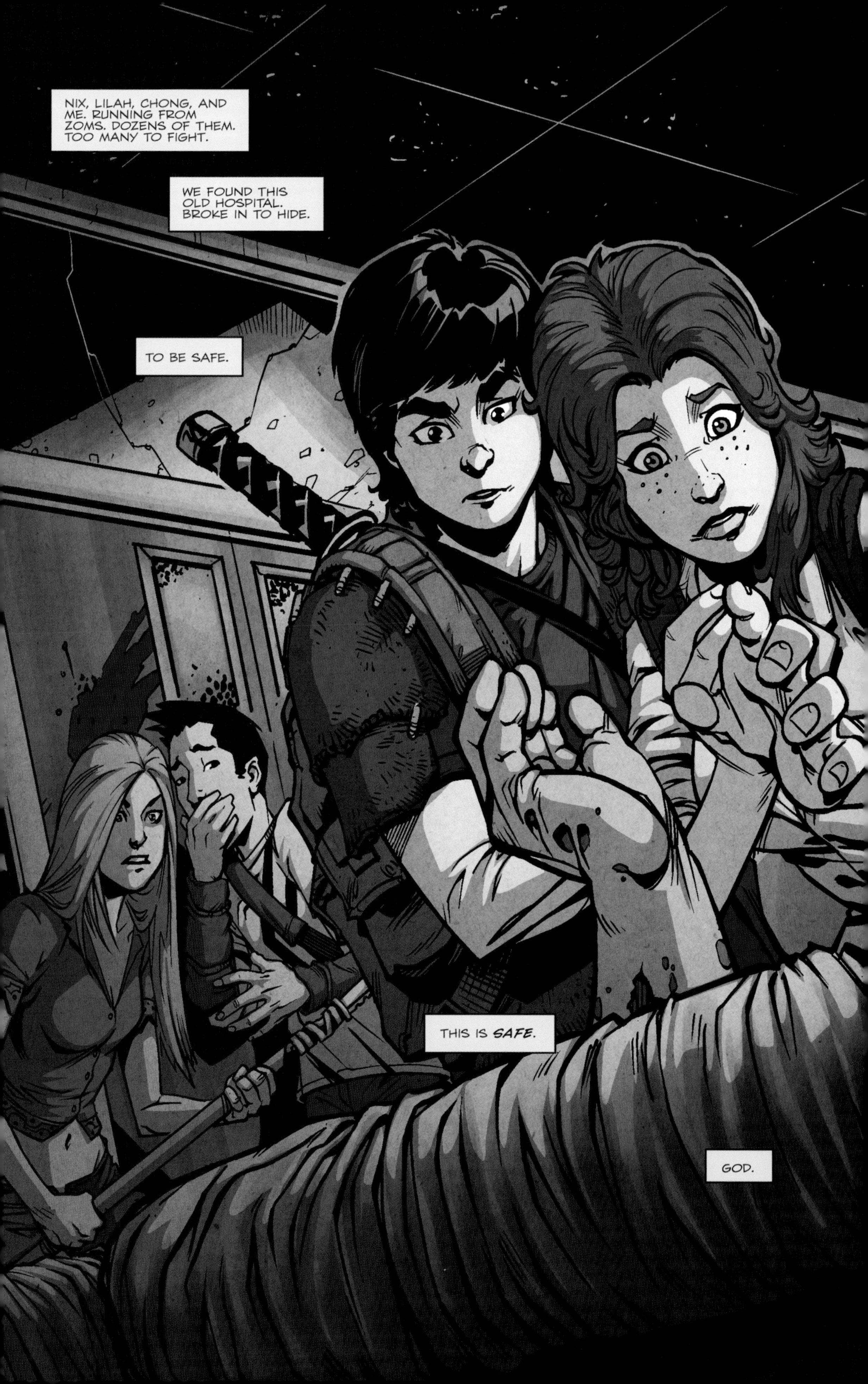
NIX, LILAH, CHONG, AND ME. RUNNING FROM ZOMS. DOZENS OF THEM. TOO MANY TO FIGHT.
WE FOUND THIS OLD HOSPITAL. BROKE IN TO HIDE.
TO BE SAFE.
THIS IS *SAFE*.
GOD.

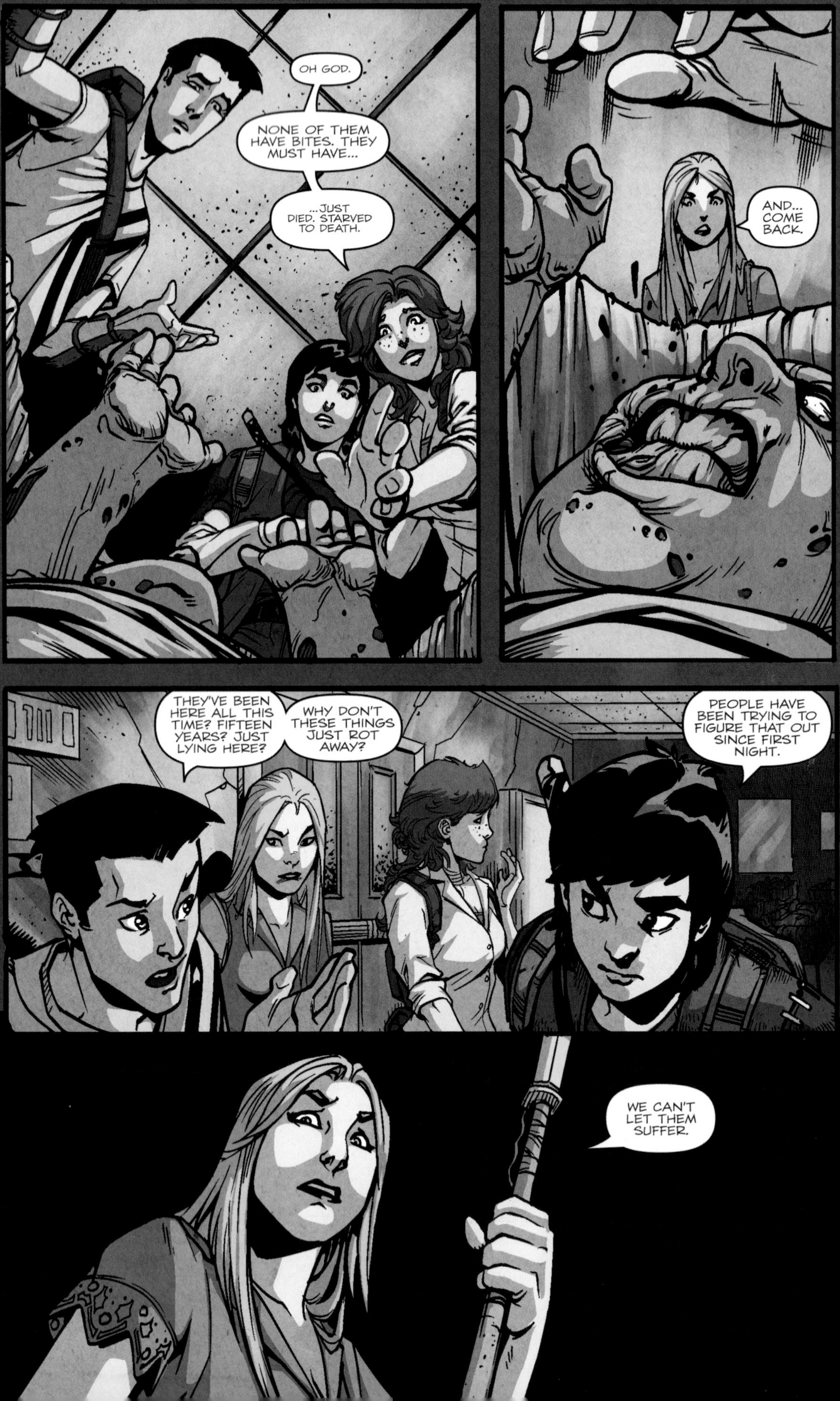
OH GOD.
NONE OF THEM HAVE BITES. THEY MUST HAVE...
...JUST DIED. STARVED TO DEATH.
AND... COME BACK.
THEY'VE BEEN HERE ALL THIS TIME? FIFTEEN YEARS? JUST LYING HERE?
WHY DON'T THESE THINGS JUST ROT AWAY?
PEOPLE HAVE BEEN TRYING TO FIGURE THAT OUT SINCE FIRST NIGHT.
WE CAN'T LET THEM SUFFER.

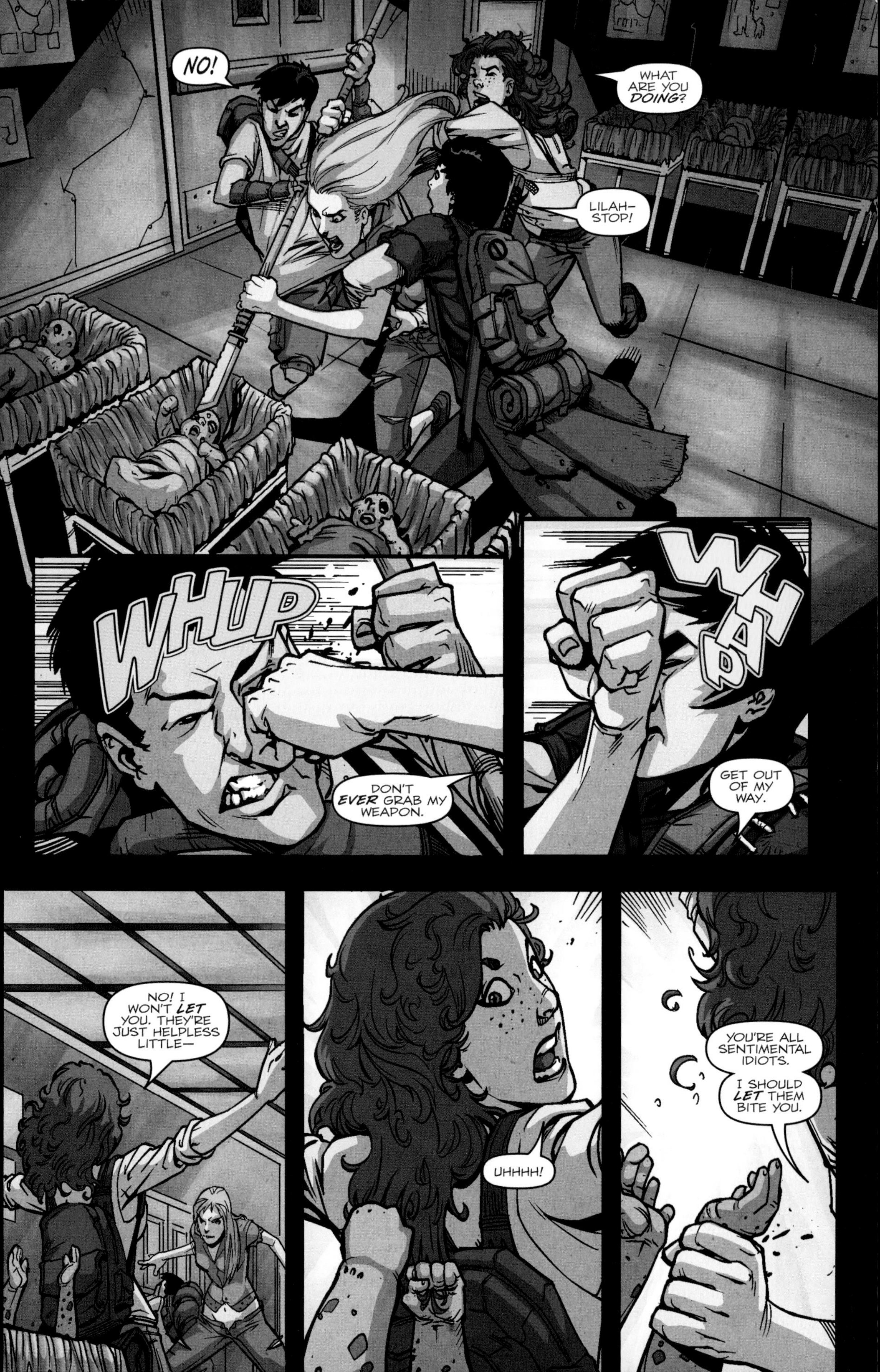
NO!
WHAT ARE YOU DOING?
LILAH- STOP!
WHUP
DON'T EVER GRAB MY WEAPON.
WHAP
GET OUT OF MY WAY.
NO! I WON'T LET YOU. THEY'RE JUST HELPLESS LITTLE—
UHHHH!
YOU'RE ALL SENTIMENTAL IDIOTS.
I SHOULD LET THEM BITE YOU.

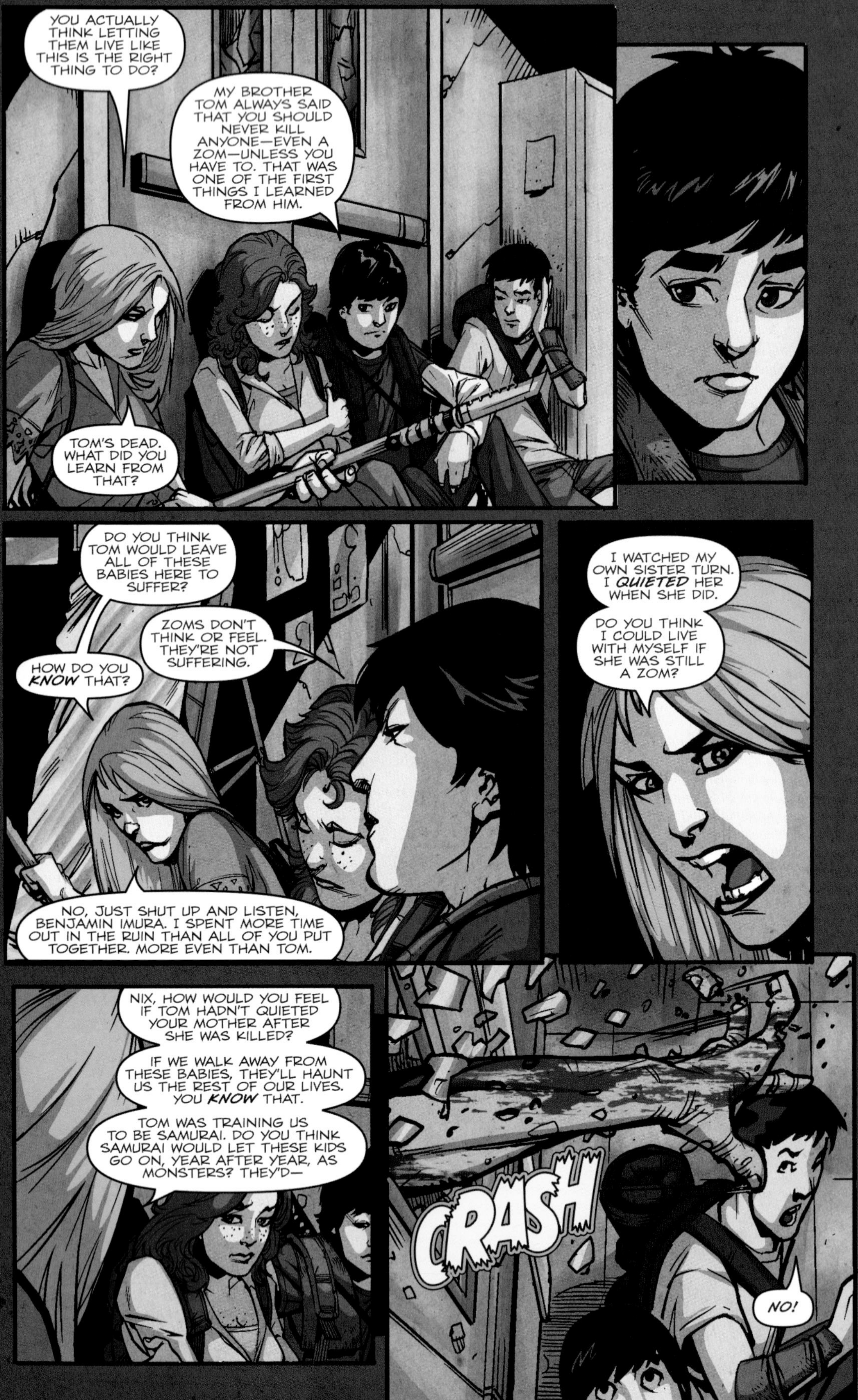
YOU ACTUALLY THINK LETTING THEM LIVE LIKE THIS IS THE RIGHT THING TO DO?
MY BROTHER TOM ALWAYS SAID THAT YOU SHOULD NEVER KILL ANYONE—EVEN A ZOM—UNLESS YOU HAVE TO. THAT WAS ONE OF THE FIRST THINGS I LEARNED FROM HIM.
TOM'S DEAD. WHAT DID YOU LEARN FROM THAT?
DO YOU THINK TOM WOULD LEAVE ALL OF THESE BABIES HERE TO SUFFER?
ZOMS DON'T THINK OR FEEL. THEY'RE NOT SUFFERING.
HOW DO YOU *KNOW* THAT?
NO, JUST SHUT UP AND LISTEN, BENJAMIN IMURA. I SPENT MORE TIME OUT IN THE RUIN THAN ALL OF YOU PUT TOGETHER. MORE EVEN THAN TOM.
I WATCHED MY OWN SISTER TURN. I ***QUIETED*** HER WHEN SHE DID.
DO YOU THINK I COULD LIVE WITH MYSELF IF SHE WAS STILL A ZOM?
NIX, HOW WOULD YOU FEEL IF TOM HADN'T QUIETED YOUR MOTHER AFTER SHE WAS KILLED?
IF WE WALK AWAY FROM THESE BABIES, THEY'LL HAUNT US THE REST OF OUR LIVES. YOU ***KNOW*** THAT.
TOM WAS TRAINING US TO BE SAMURAI. DO YOU THINK SAMURAI WOULD LET THESE KIDS GO ON, YEAR AFTER YEAR, AS MONSTERS? THEY'D—
CRASH
NO!

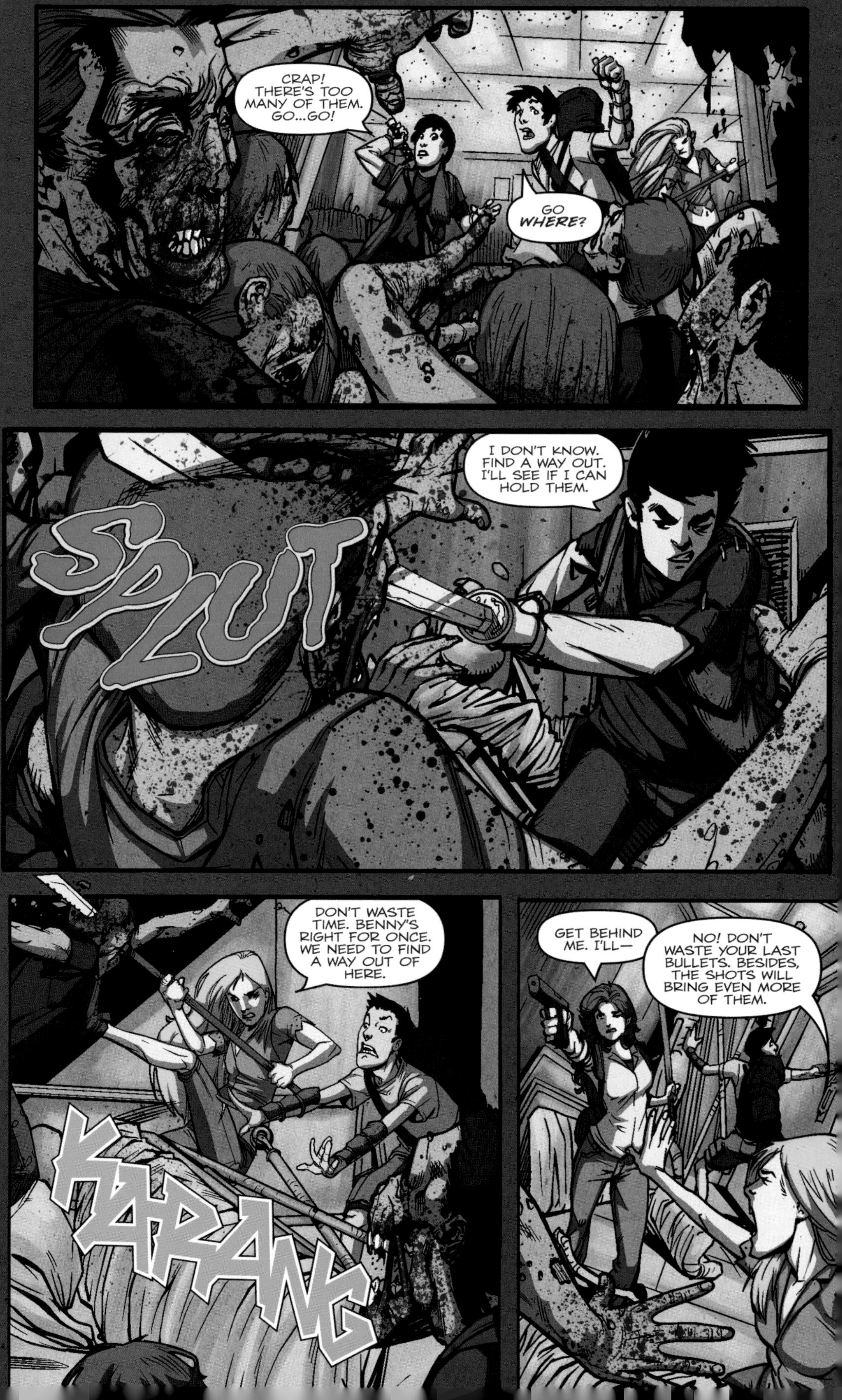
CRAP! THERE'S TOO MANY OF THEM. GO...GO!
GO WHERE?
I DON'T KNOW. FIND A WAY OUT. I'LL SEE IF I CAN HOLD THEM.
SPLUT
DON'T WASTE TIME. BENNY'S RIGHT FOR ONCE. WE NEED TO FIND A WAY OUT OF HERE.
KARANG
GET BEHIND ME. I'LL—
NO! DON'T WASTE YOUR LAST BULLETS. BESIDES, THE SHOTS WILL BRING EVEN MORE OF THEM.

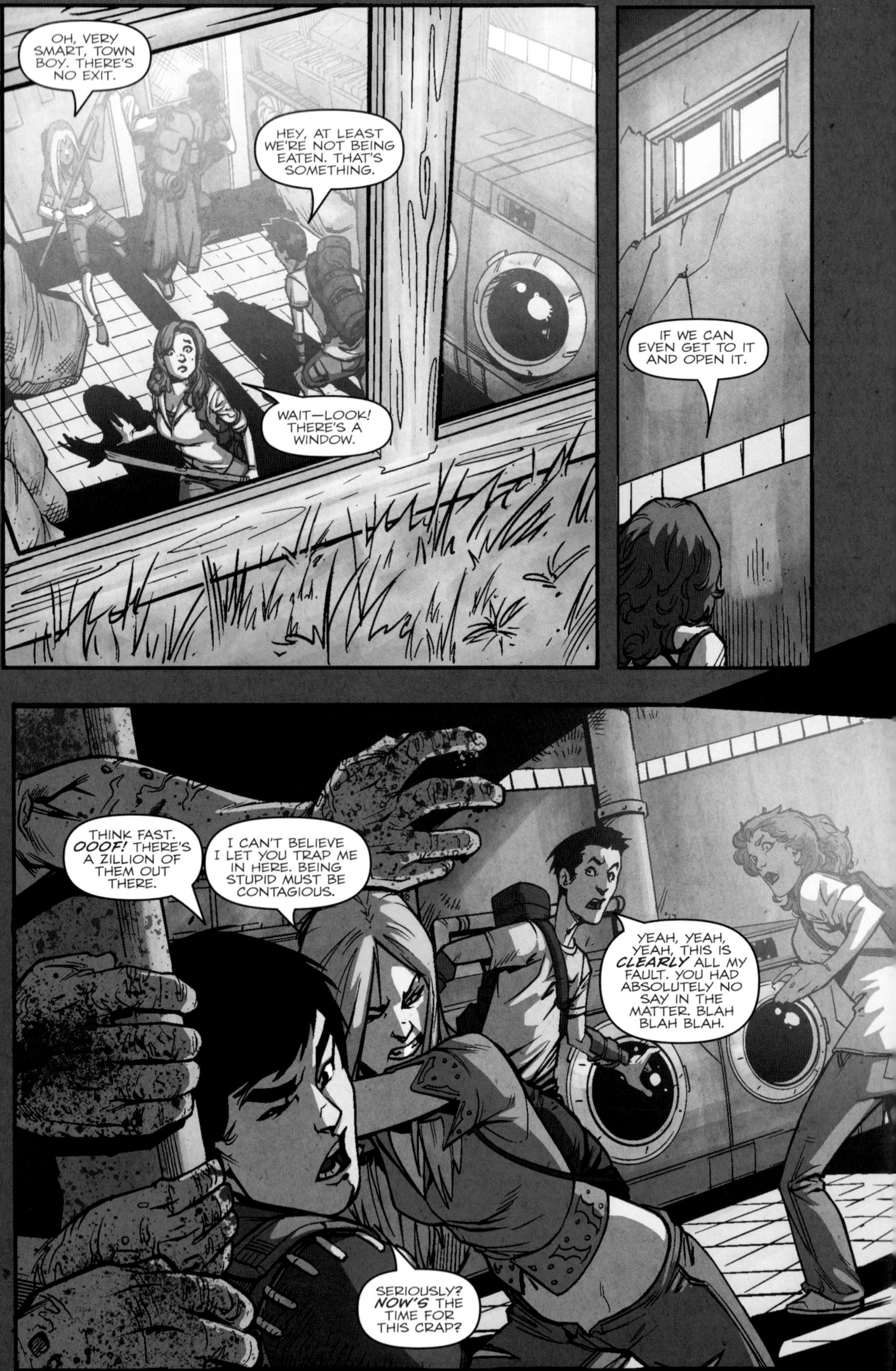
OH, VERY SMART, TOWN BOY. THERE'S NO EXIT.
HEY, AT LEAST WE'RE NOT BEING EATEN. THAT'S SOMETHING.
WAIT—LOOK! THERE'S A WINDOW.
IF WE CAN EVEN GET TO IT AND OPEN IT.
THINK FAST. OOOF! THERE'S A ZILLION OF THEM OUT THERE.
I CAN'T BELIEVE I LET YOU TRAP ME IN HERE. BEING STUPID MUST BE CONTAGIOUS.
YEAH, YEAH, YEAH, THIS IS CLEARLY ALL MY FAULT. YOU HAD ABSOLUTELY NO SAY IN THE MATTER. BLAH BLAH BLAH.
SERIOUSLY? NOW'S THE TIME FOR THIS CRAP?

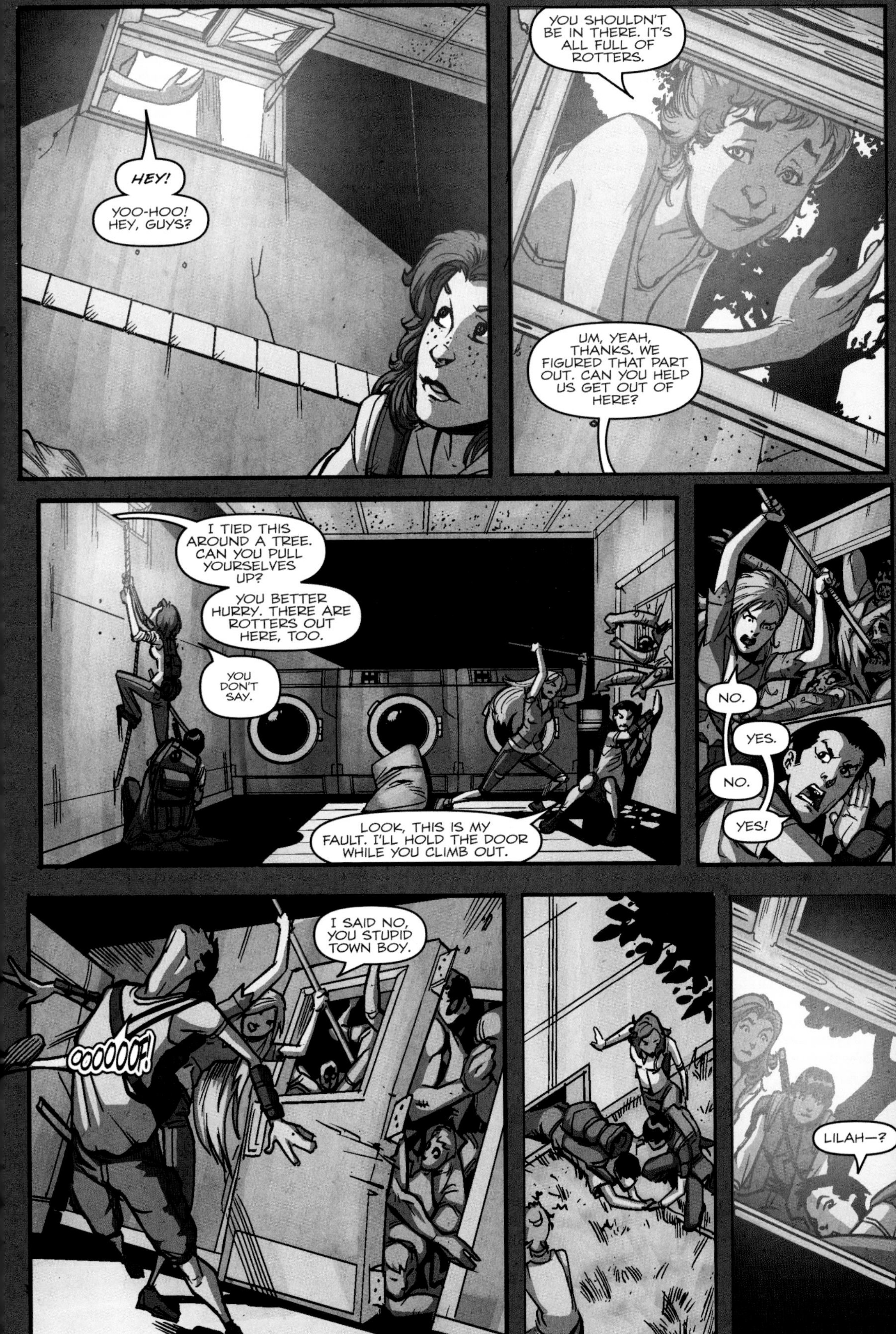
HEY!
YOO-HOO! HEY, GUYS?
YOU SHOULDN'T BE IN THERE. IT'S ALL FULL OF ROTTERS.
UM, YEAH, THANKS. WE FIGURED THAT PART OUT. CAN YOU HELP US GET OUT OF HERE?
I TIED THIS AROUND A TREE. CAN YOU PULL YOURSELVES UP?
YOU BETTER HURRY. THERE ARE ROTTERS OUT HERE, TOO.
YOU DON'T SAY.
LOOK, THIS IS MY FAULT. I'LL HOLD THE DOOR WHILE YOU CLIMB OUT.
NO.
YES.
NO.
YES!
I SAID NO, YOU STUPID TOWN BOY.
OOOOOOF!
LILAH—?

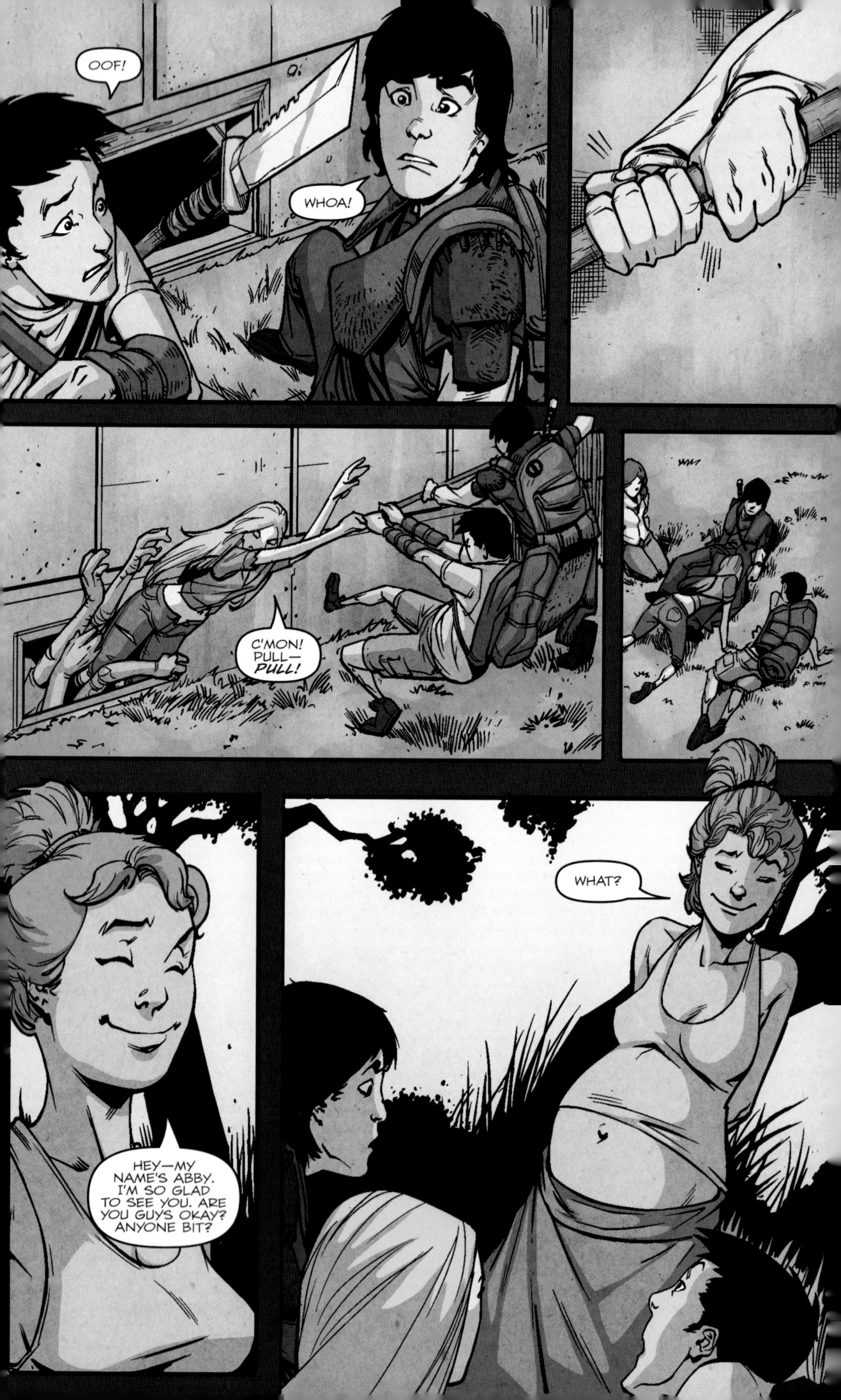
OOF!
WHOA!
C'MON! PULL— PULL!
HEY—MY NAME'S ABBY. I'M SO GLAD TO SEE YOU. ARE YOU GUYS OKAY? ANYONE BIT?
WHAT?

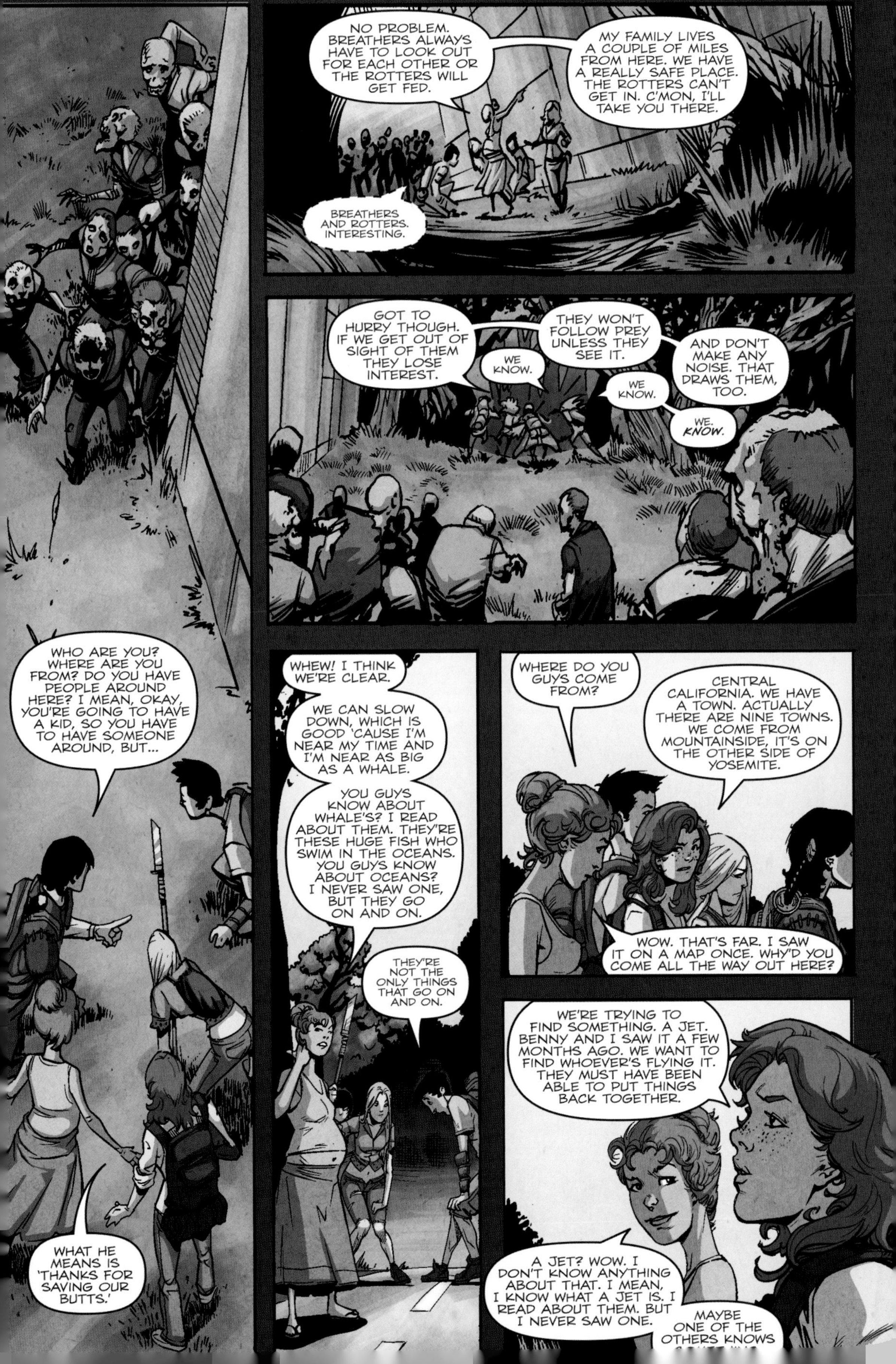

NO PROBLEM. BREATHERS ALWAYS HAVE TO LOOK OUT FOR EACH OTHER OR THE ROTTERS WILL GET FED.
MY FAMILY LIVES A COUPLE OF MILES FROM HERE. WE HAVE A REALLY SAFE PLACE. THE ROTTERS CAN'T GET IN. C'MON, I'LL TAKE YOU THERE.
BREATHERS AND ROTTERS. INTERESTING.
GOT TO HURRY THOUGH. IF WE GET OUT OF SIGHT OF THEM THEY LOSE INTEREST.
WE KNOW.
THEY WON'T FOLLOW PREY UNLESS THEY SEE IT.
WE KNOW.
AND DON'T MAKE ANY NOISE. THAT DRAWS THEM, TOO.
WE. *KNOW*.
WHO ARE YOU? WHERE ARE YOU FROM? DO YOU HAVE PEOPLE AROUND HERE? I MEAN, OKAY, YOU'RE GOING TO HAVE A KID, SO YOU HAVE TO HAVE SOMEONE AROUND, BUT...
WHAT HE MEANS IS 'THANKS FOR SAVING OUR BUTTS.'
WHEW! I THINK WE'RE CLEAR.
WE CAN SLOW DOWN, WHICH IS GOOD 'CAUSE I'M NEAR MY TIME AND I'M NEAR AS BIG AS A WHALE.
YOU GUYS KNOW ABOUT WHALE'S? I READ ABOUT THEM. THEY'RE THESE HUGE FISH WHO SWIM IN THE OCEANS. YOU GUYS KNOW ABOUT OCEANS? I NEVER SAW ONE, BUT THEY GO ON AND ON.
THEY'RE NOT THE ONLY THINGS THAT GO ON AND ON.
WHERE DO YOU GUYS COME FROM?
CENTRAL CALIFORNIA. WE HAVE A TOWN. ACTUALLY THERE ARE NINE TOWNS. WE COME FROM MOUNTAINSIDE, IT'S ON THE OTHER SIDE OF YOSEMITE.
WOW. THAT'S FAR. I SAW IT ON A MAP ONCE. WHY'D YOU COME ALL THE WAY OUT HERE?
WE'RE TRYING TO FIND SOMETHING. A JET. BENNY AND I SAW IT A FEW MONTHS AGO. WE WANT TO FIND WHOEVER'S FLYING IT. THEY MUST HAVE BEEN ABLE TO PUT THINGS BACK TOGETHER.
A JET? WOW. I DON'T KNOW ANYTHING ABOUT THAT. I MEAN, I KNOW WHAT A JET IS. I READ ABOUT THEM. BUT I NEVER SAW ONE.
MAYBE ONE OF THE OTHERS KNOWS

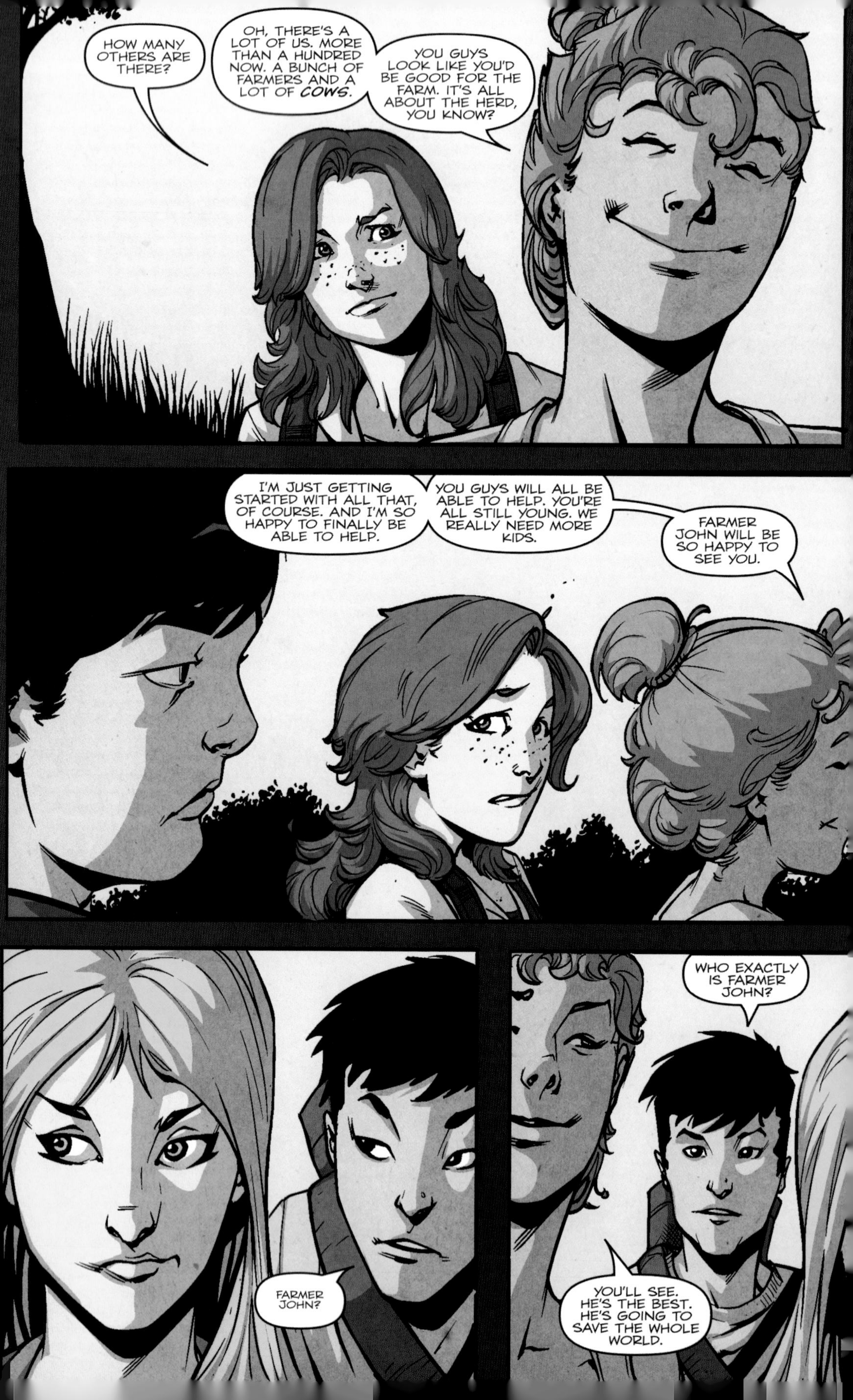
HOW MANY OTHERS ARE THERE?
OH, THERE'S A LOT OF US. MORE THAN A HUNDRED NOW. A BUNCH OF FARMERS AND A LOT OF COWS.
YOU GUYS LOOK LIKE YOU'D BE GOOD FOR THE FARM. IT'S ALL ABOUT THE HERD, YOU KNOW?
I'M JUST GETTING STARTED WITH ALL THAT, OF COURSE. AND I'M SO HAPPY TO FINALLY BE ABLE TO HELP.
YOU GUYS WILL ALL BE ABLE TO HELP. YOU'RE ALL STILL YOUNG. WE REALLY NEED MORE KIDS.
FARMER JOHN WILL BE SO HAPPY TO SEE YOU.
FARMER JOHN?
WHO EXACTLY IS FARMER JOHN?
YOU'LL SEE. HE'S THE BEST. HE'S GOING TO SAVE THE WHOLE WORLD.

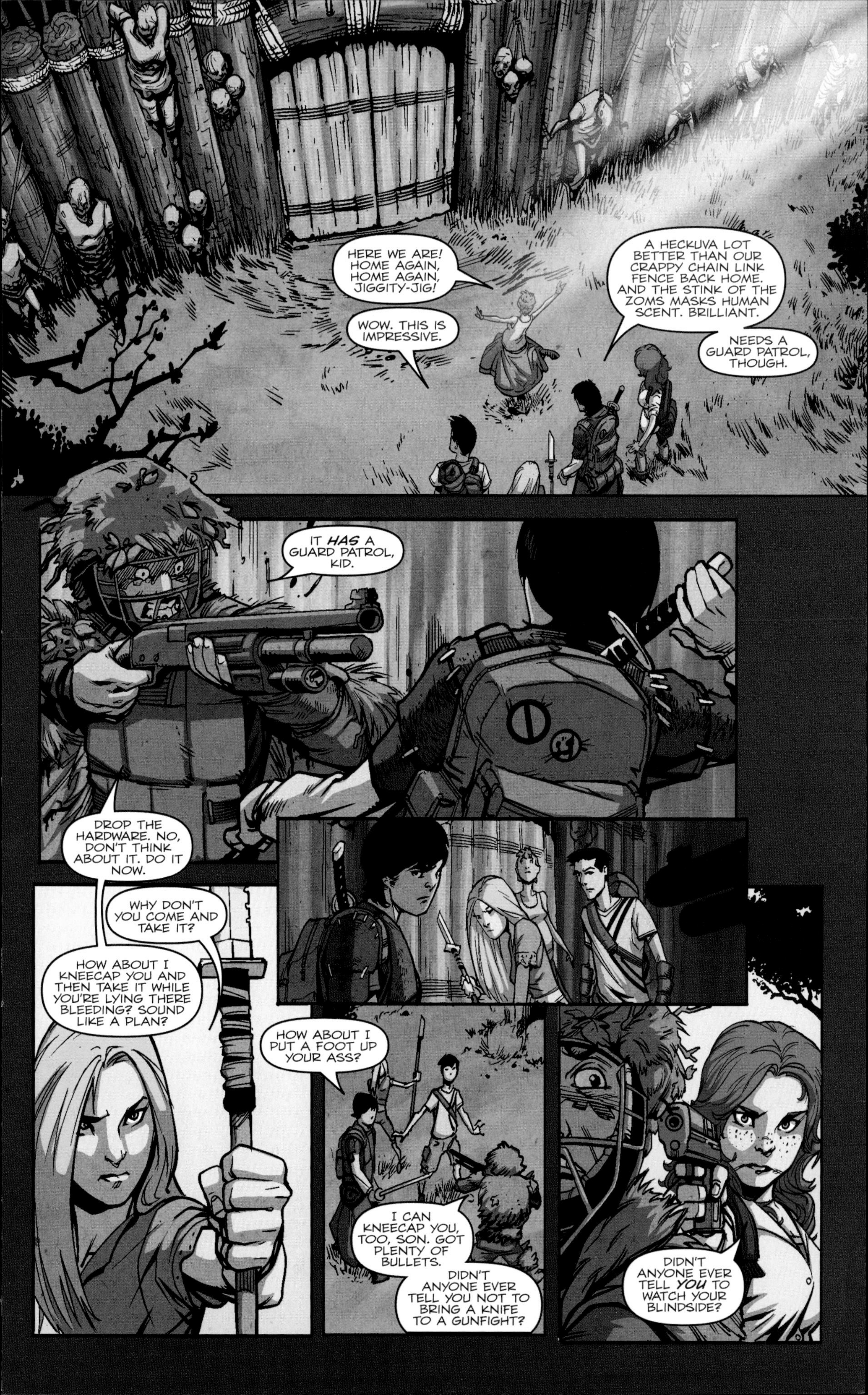
HERE WE ARE! HOME AGAIN, HOME AGAIN, JIGGITY-JIG!
WOW. THIS IS IMPRESSIVE.
A HECKUVA LOT BETTER THAN OUR CRAPPY CHAIN LINK FENCE BACK HOME. AND THE STINK OF THE ZOMS MASKS HUMAN SCENT. BRILLIANT.
NEEDS A GUARD PATROL, THOUGH.
IT HAS A GUARD PATROL, KID.
DROP THE HARDWARE. NO, DON'T THINK ABOUT IT. DO IT NOW.
WHY DON'T YOU COME AND TAKE IT?
HOW ABOUT I KNEECAP YOU AND THEN TAKE IT WHILE YOU'RE LYING THERE BLEEDING? SOUND LIKE A PLAN?
HOW ABOUT I PUT A FOOT UP YOUR ASS?
I CAN KNEECAP YOU, TOO, SON. GOT PLENTY OF BULLETS.
DIDN'T ANYONE EVER TELL YOU NOT TO BRING A KNIFE TO A GUNFIGHT?
DIDN'T ANYONE EVER TELL YOU TO WATCH YOUR BLINDSIDE?

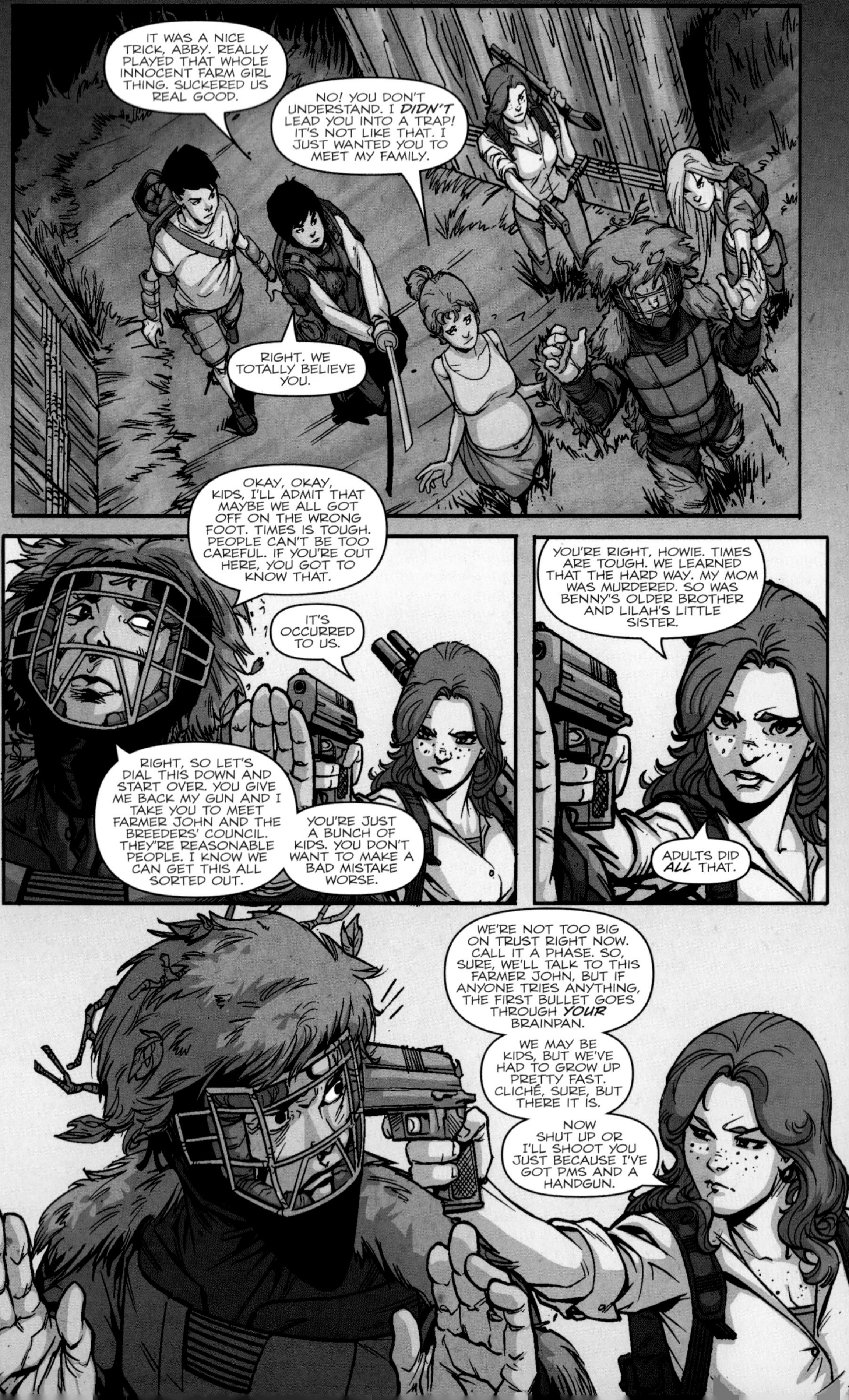

IT WAS A NICE TRICK, ABBY. REALLY PLAYED THAT WHOLE INNOCENT FARM GIRL THING. SUCKERED US REAL GOOD.
NO! YOU DON'T UNDERSTAND. I *DIDN'T* LEAD YOU INTO A TRAP! IT'S NOT LIKE THAT. I JUST WANTED YOU TO MEET MY FAMILY.
RIGHT. WE TOTALLY BELIEVE YOU.
OKAY, OKAY, KIDS, I'LL ADMIT THAT MAYBE WE ALL GOT OFF ON THE WRONG FOOT. TIMES IS TOUGH. PEOPLE CAN'T BE TOO CAREFUL. IF YOU'RE OUT HERE, YOU GOT TO KNOW THAT.
IT'S OCCURRED TO US.
RIGHT, SO LET'S DIAL THIS DOWN AND START OVER. YOU GIVE ME BACK MY GUN AND I TAKE YOU TO MEET FARMER JOHN AND THE BREEDERS' COUNCIL. THEY'RE REASONABLE PEOPLE. I KNOW WE CAN GET THIS ALL SORTED OUT.
YOU'RE JUST A BUNCH OF KIDS. YOU DON'T WANT TO MAKE A BAD MISTAKE WORSE.
YOU'RE RIGHT, HOWIE. TIMES ARE TOUGH. WE LEARNED THAT THE HARD WAY. MY MOM WAS MURDERED. SO WAS BENNY'S OLDER BROTHER AND LILAH'S LITTLE SISTER.
ADULTS DID *ALL* THAT.
WE'RE NOT TOO BIG ON TRUST RIGHT NOW. CALL IT A PHASE. SO, SURE, WE'LL TALK TO THIS FARMER JOHN, BUT IF ANYONE TRIES ANYTHING, THE FIRST BULLET GOES THROUGH *YOUR* BRAINPAN.
WE MAY BE KIDS, BUT WE'VE HAD TO GROW UP PRETTY FAST. CLICHÉ, SURE, BUT THERE IT IS.
NOW SHUT UP OR I'LL SHOOT YOU JUST BECAUSE I'VE GOT PMS AND A HANDGUN.

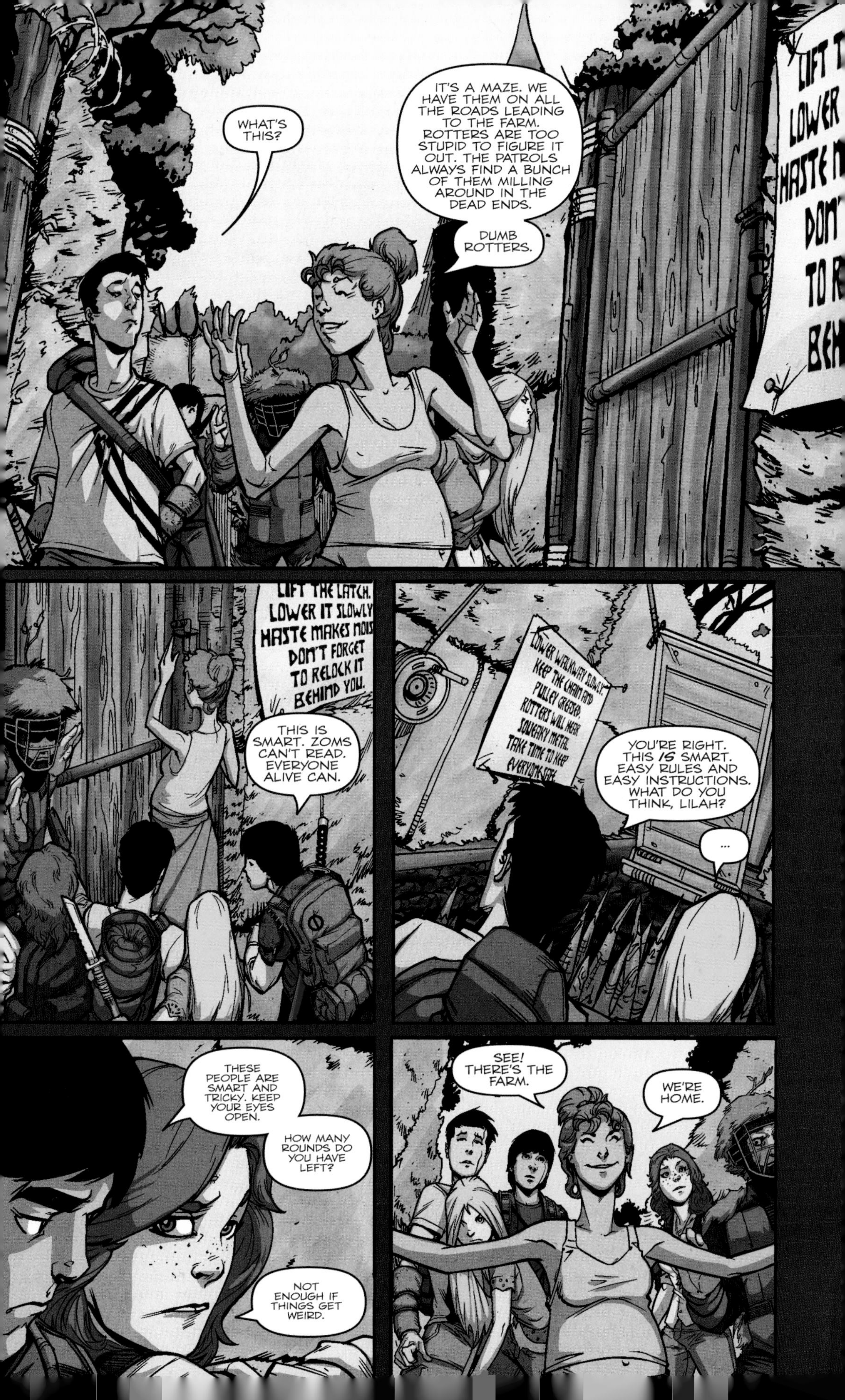
WHAT'S THIS?
IT'S A MAZE. WE HAVE THEM ON ALL THE ROADS LEADING TO THE FARM. ROTTERS ARE TOO STUPID TO FIGURE IT OUT. THE PATROLS ALWAYS FIND A BUNCH OF THEM MILLING AROUND IN THE DEAD ENDS.
DUMB ROTTERS.
LIFT THE LATCH. LOWER IT SLOWLY HASTE MAKES NOIS DON'T FORGET TO RELOCK IT BEHIND YOU.
THIS IS SMART. ZOMS CAN'T READ. EVERYONE ALIVE CAN.
LOWER WALKWAY SLOWLY. KEEP THE CHAIN AND PULLEY GREASED. ROTTERS WILL HEAR SQUEAKY METAL. TAKE TIME TO KEEP EVERYONE SAFE.
YOU'RE RIGHT. THIS *IS* SMART. EASY RULES AND EASY INSTRUCTIONS. WHAT DO YOU THINK, LILAH?
...
THESE PEOPLE ARE SMART AND TRICKY. KEEP YOUR EYES OPEN.
HOW MANY ROUNDS DO YOU HAVE LEFT?
NOT ENOUGH IF THINGS GET WEIRD.
SEE! THERE'S THE FARM.
WE'RE HOME.

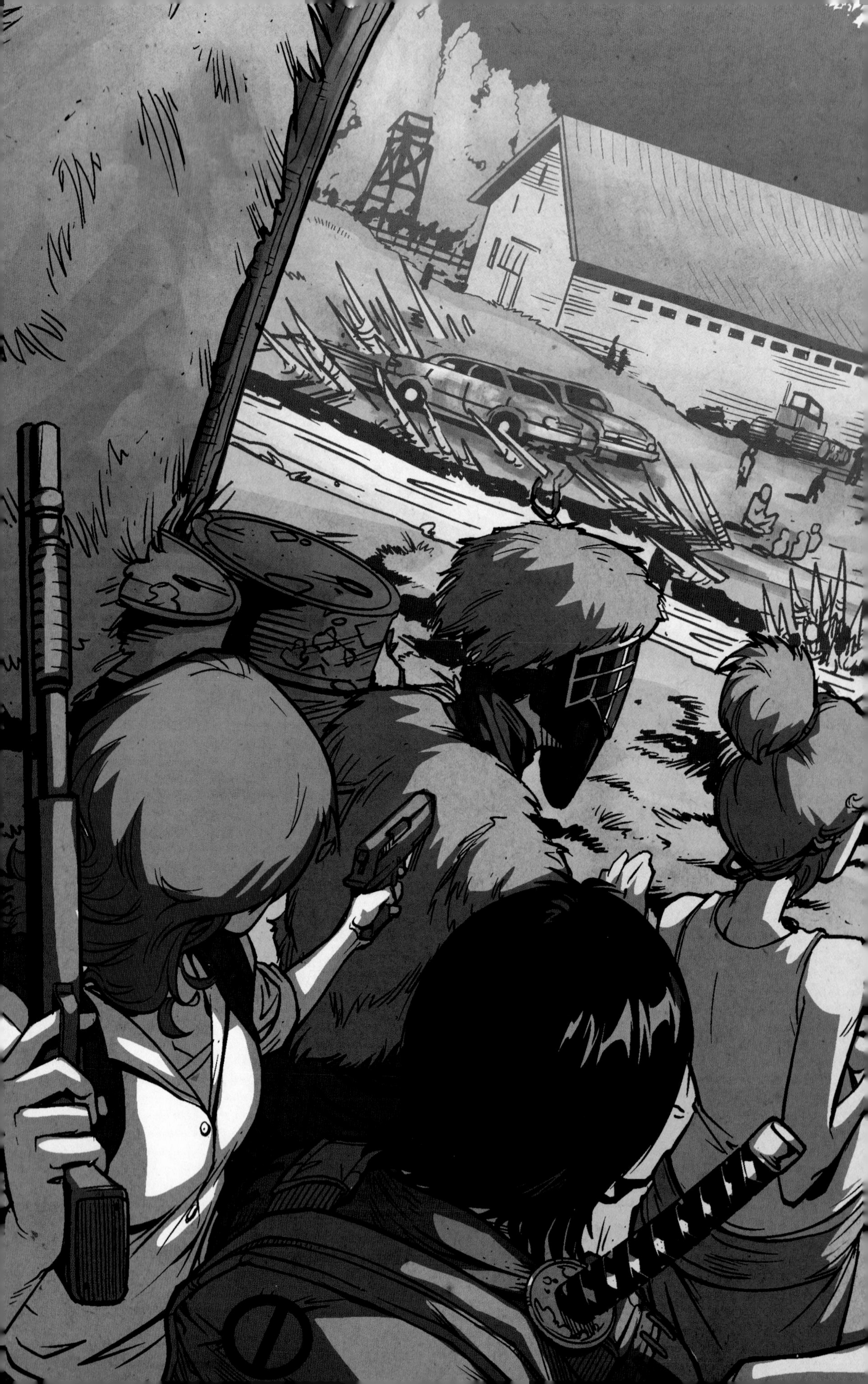

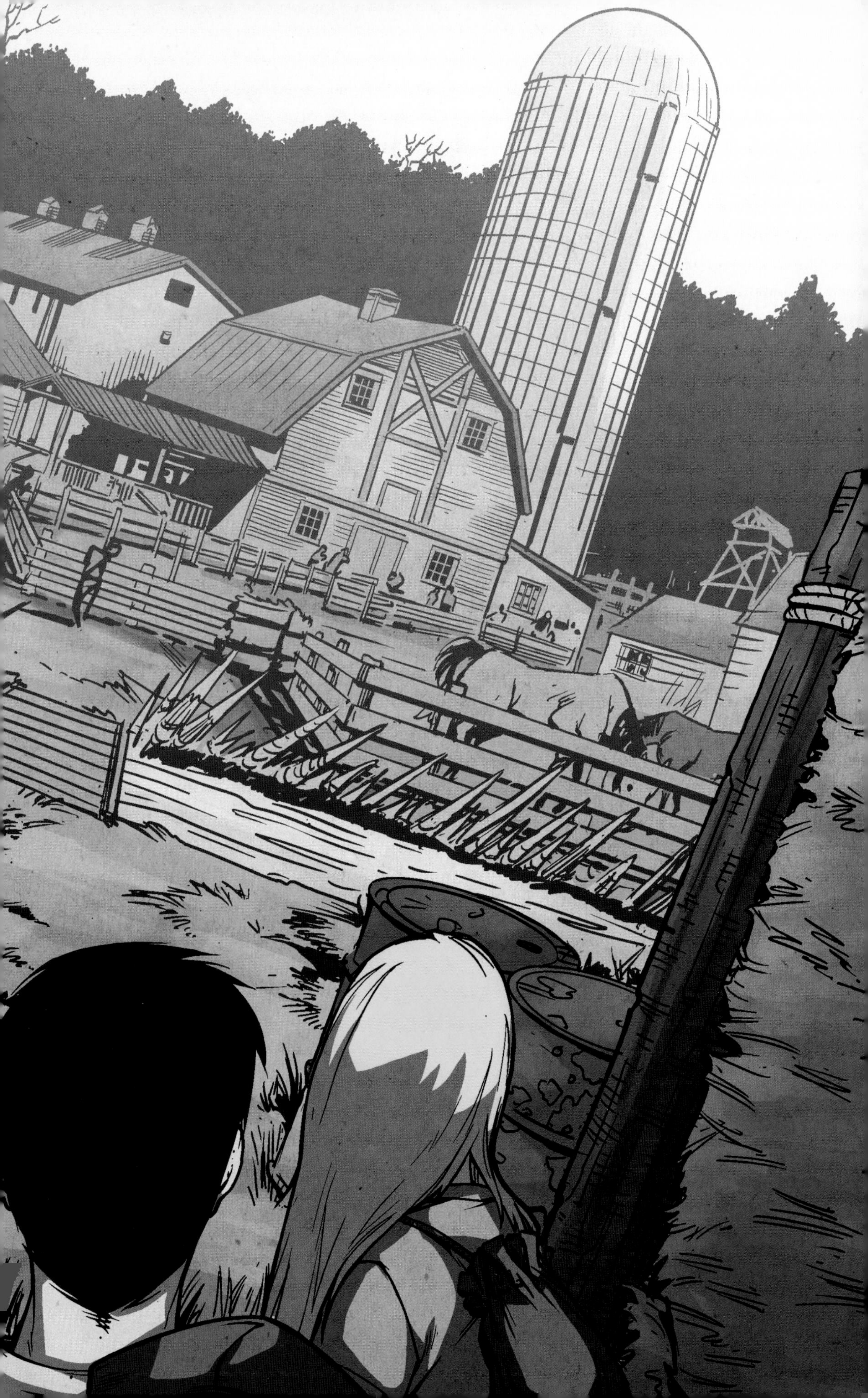

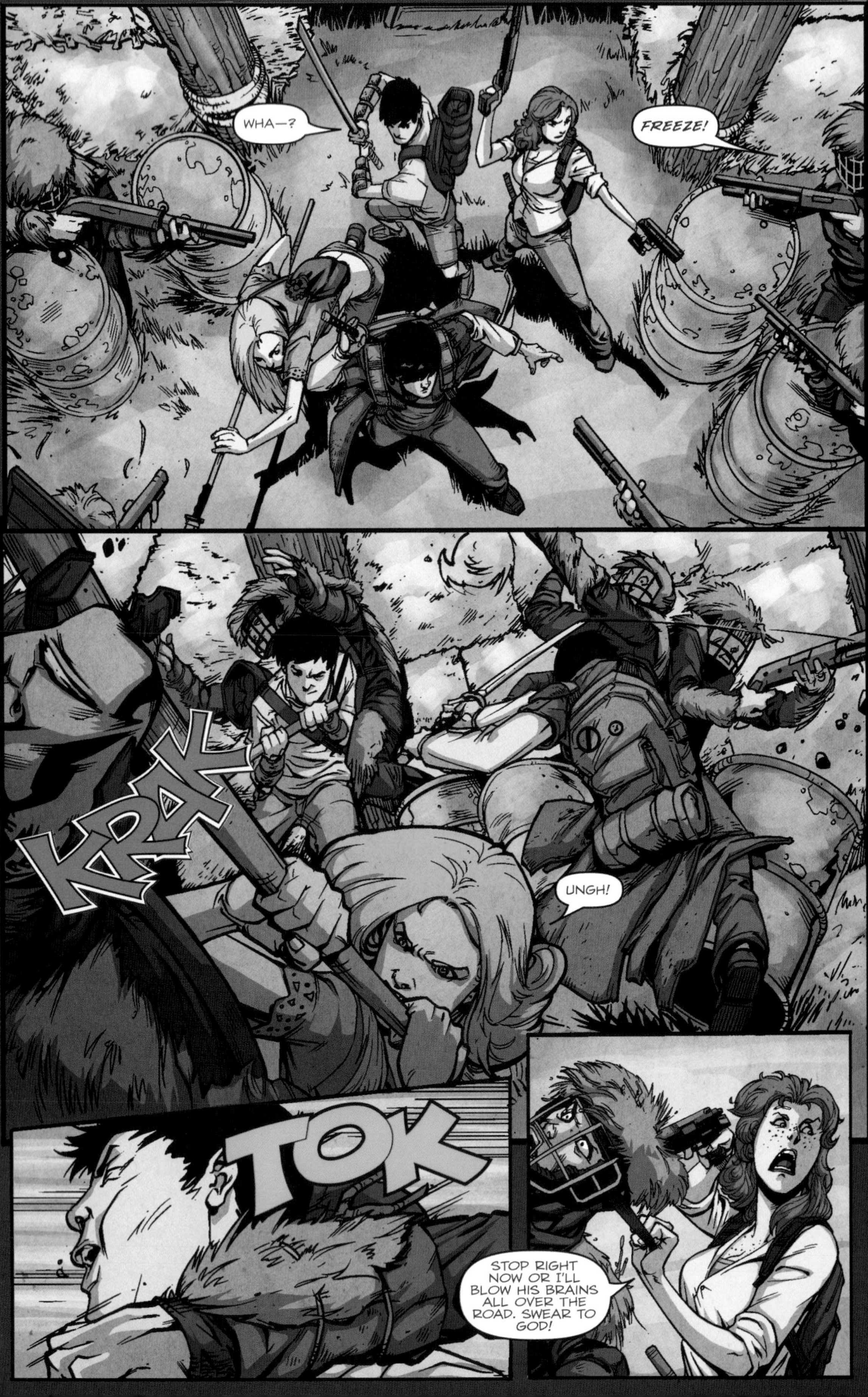
WHA—?
FREEZE!
KRAK
UNGH!
TOK
STOP RIGHT NOW OR I'LL BLOW HIS BRAINS ALL OVER THE ROAD. SWEAR TO GOD!

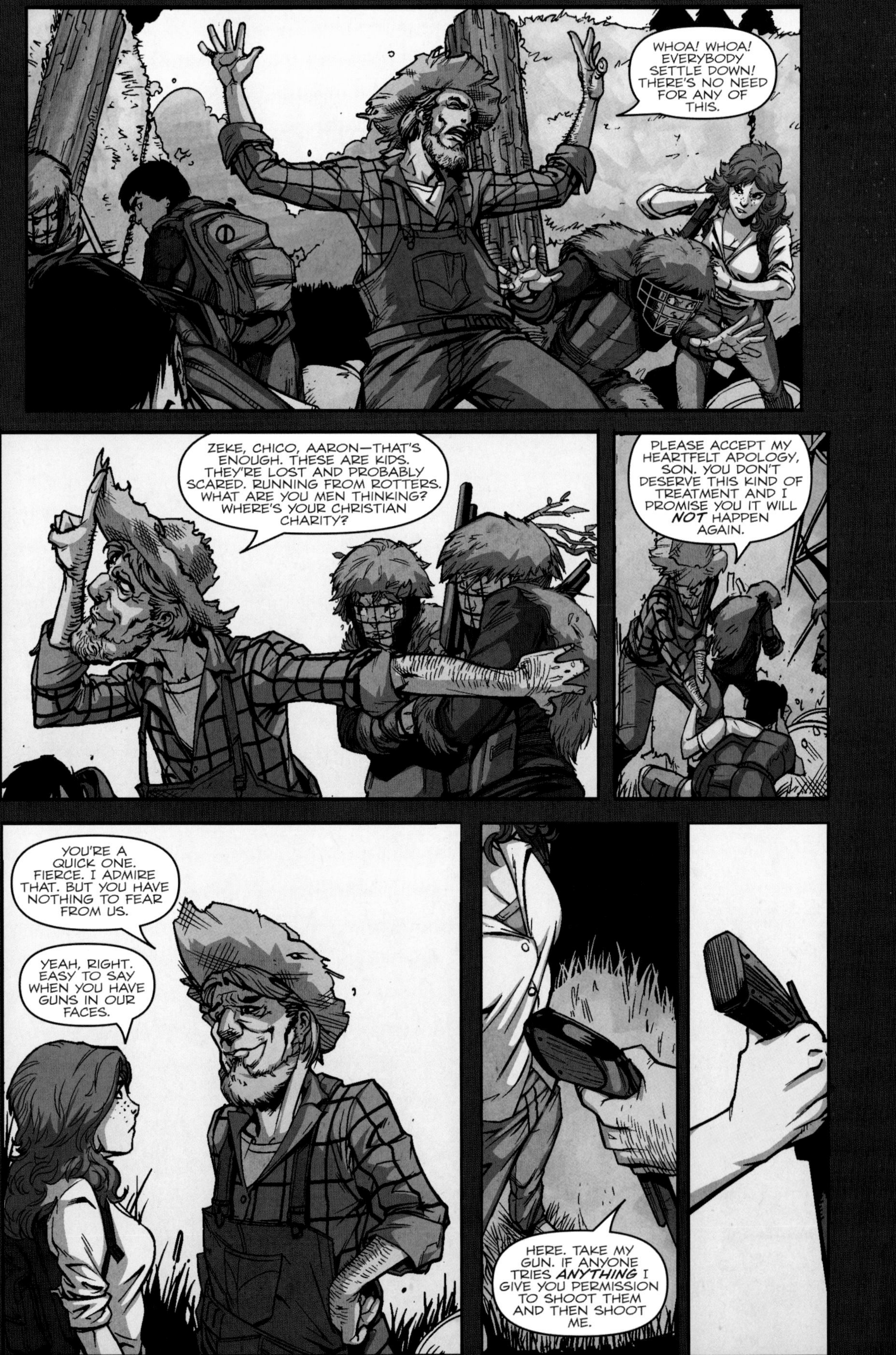
WHOA! WHOA! EVERYBODY SETTLE DOWN! THERE'S NO NEED FOR ANY OF THIS.
ZEKE, CHICO, AARON—THAT'S ENOUGH. THESE ARE KIDS. THEY'RE LOST AND PROBABLY SCARED. RUNNING FROM ROTTERS. WHAT ARE YOU MEN THINKING? WHERE'S YOUR CHRISTIAN CHARITY?
PLEASE ACCEPT MY HEARTFELT APOLOGY, SON. YOU DON'T DESERVE THIS KIND OF TREATMENT AND I PROMISE YOU IT WILL ***NOT*** HAPPEN AGAIN.
YOU'RE A QUICK ONE. FIERCE. I ADMIRE THAT. BUT YOU HAVE NOTHING TO FEAR FROM US.
YEAH, RIGHT. EASY TO SAY WHEN YOU HAVE GUNS IN OUR FACES.
HERE. TAKE MY GUN. IF ANYONE TRIES ***ANYTHING*** I GIVE YOU PERMISSION TO SHOOT THEM AND THEN SHOOT ME.

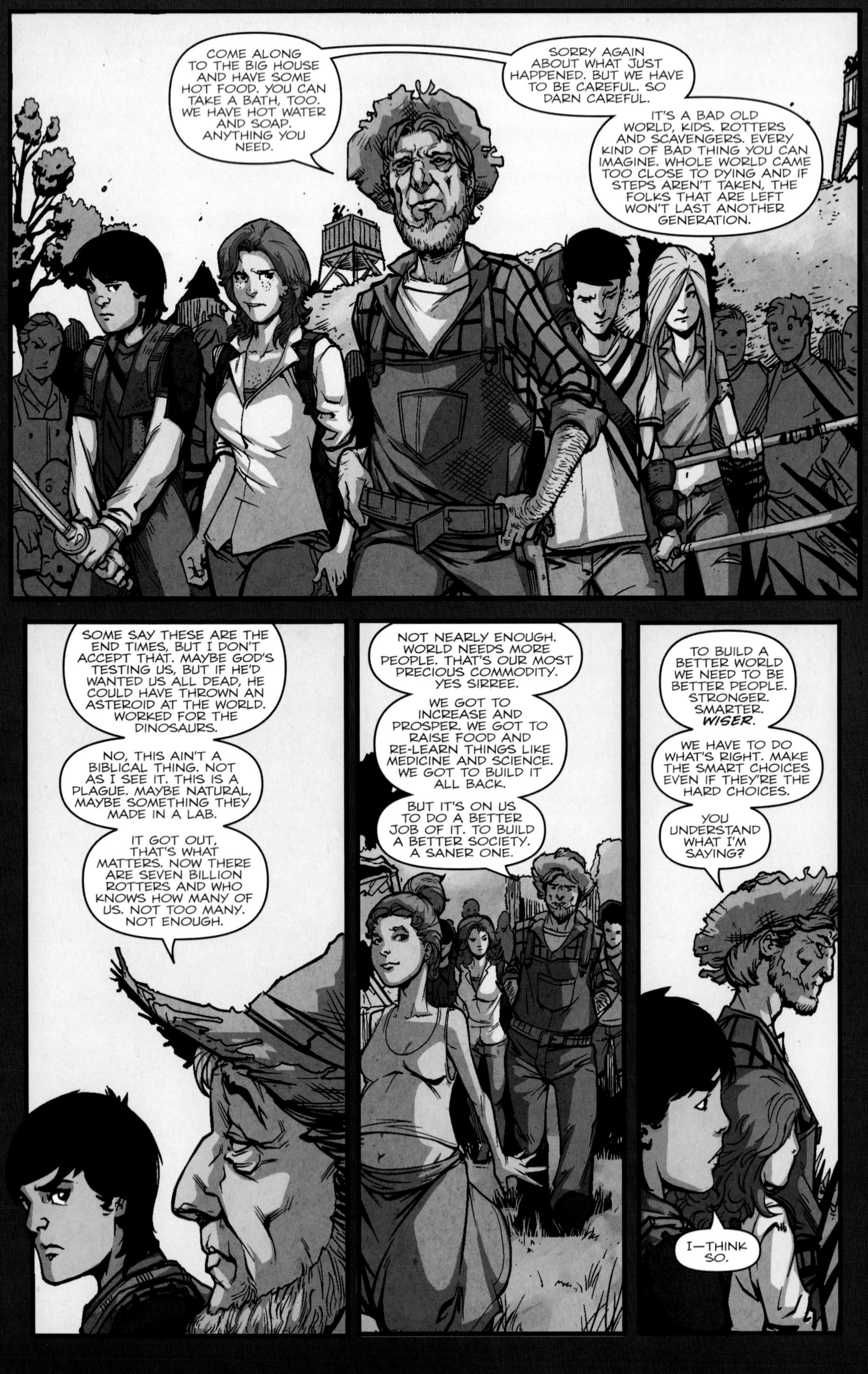
COME ALONG TO THE BIG HOUSE AND HAVE SOME HOT FOOD. YOU CAN TAKE A BATH, TOO. WE HAVE HOT WATER AND SOAP. ANYTHING YOU NEED.
SORRY AGAIN ABOUT WHAT JUST HAPPENED. BUT WE HAVE TO BE CAREFUL. SO DARN CAREFUL.
IT'S A BAD OLD WORLD, KIDS. ROTTERS AND SCAVENGERS. EVERY KIND OF BAD THING YOU CAN IMAGINE. WHOLE WORLD CAME TOO CLOSE TO DYING AND IF STEPS AREN'T TAKEN, THE FOLKS THAT ARE LEFT WON'T LAST ANOTHER GENERATION.
SOME SAY THESE ARE THE END TIMES, BUT I DON'T ACCEPT THAT. MAYBE GOD'S TESTING US, BUT IF HE'D WANTED US ALL DEAD, HE COULD HAVE THROWN AN ASTEROID AT THE WORLD. WORKED FOR THE DINOSAURS.
NO, THIS AIN'T A BIBLICAL THING. NOT AS I SEE IT. THIS IS A PLAGUE. MAYBE NATURAL, MAYBE SOMETHING THEY MADE IN A LAB.
IT GOT OUT, THAT'S WHAT MATTERS. NOW THERE ARE SEVEN BILLION ROTTERS AND WHO KNOWS HOW MANY OF US. NOT TOO MANY. NOT ENOUGH.
NOT NEARLY ENOUGH. WORLD NEEDS MORE PEOPLE. THAT'S OUR MOST PRECIOUS COMMODITY. YES SIRREE.
WE GOT TO INCREASE AND PROSPER. WE GOT TO RAISE FOOD AND RE-LEARN THINGS LIKE MEDICINE AND SCIENCE. WE GOT TO BUILD IT ALL BACK.
BUT IT'S ON US TO DO A BETTER JOB OF IT. TO BUILD A BETTER SOCIETY. A SANER ONE.
TO BUILD A BETTER WORLD WE NEED TO BE BETTER PEOPLE. STRONGER. SMARTER. *WISER*.
WE HAVE TO DO WHAT'S RIGHT. MAKE THE SMART CHOICES EVEN IF THEY'RE THE HARD CHOICES.
YOU UNDERSTAND WHAT I'M SAYING?
I—THINK SO.

YOU HAVEN'T ASKED ANYTHING ABOUT US. WHERE WE COME FROM. WHERE OUR PEOPLE ARE. NONE OF THAT.

DON'T BELIEVE IT'S ANY OF MY BUSINESS. A MAN'S GOT ENOUGH TO WORRY ABOUT WITH HIS OWN LIFE WITHOUT PRYING INTO SOMEONE ELSE'S.

IF YOU WANT TO TELL ME, YOU WILL. IF YOU DON'T, YOU WON'T.

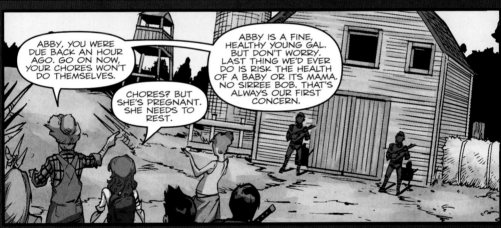

ABBY, YOU WERE DUE BACK AN HOUR AGO. GO ON NOW, YOUR CHORES WON'T DO THEMSELVES.

CHORES? BUT SHE'S PREGNANT. SHE NEEDS TO REST.

ABBY IS A FINE, HEALTHY YOUNG GAL. BUT DON'T WORRY. LAST THING WE'D EVER DO IS RISK THE HEALTH OF A BABY OR ITS MAMA. NO SIRREE BOB. THAT'S ALWAYS OUR FIRST CONCERN.

WHAT'S IN THERE?

COWS, OF COURSE. THAT'S WHAT WE'RE DOING HERE. BREEDING HEALTHY STOCK.

YOU HAVE ARMED GUARDS OUTSIDE A BARN?

YES, WE DO. GUARDS INSIDE AND OUT.

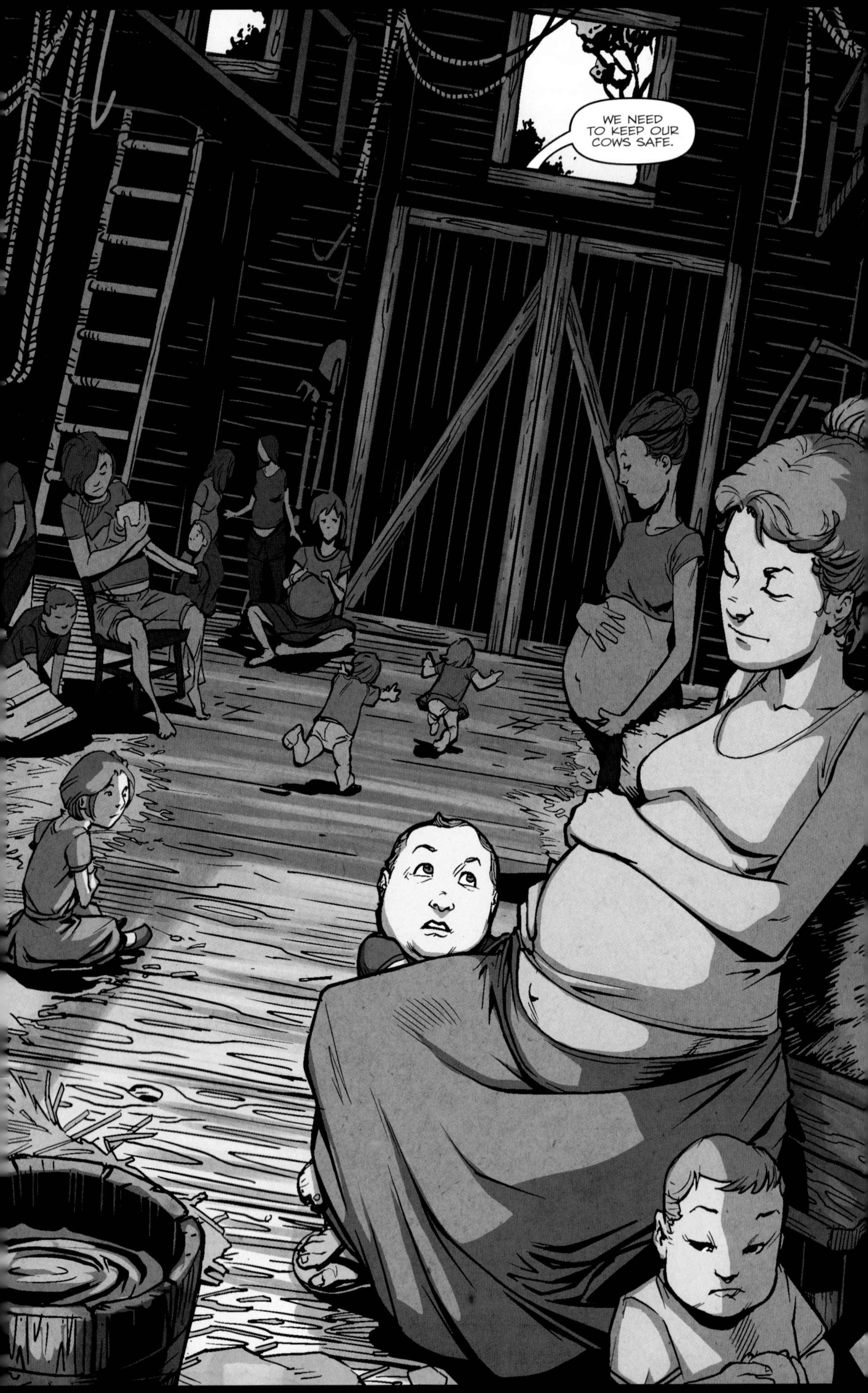
WE NEED TO KEEP OUR COWS SAFE.

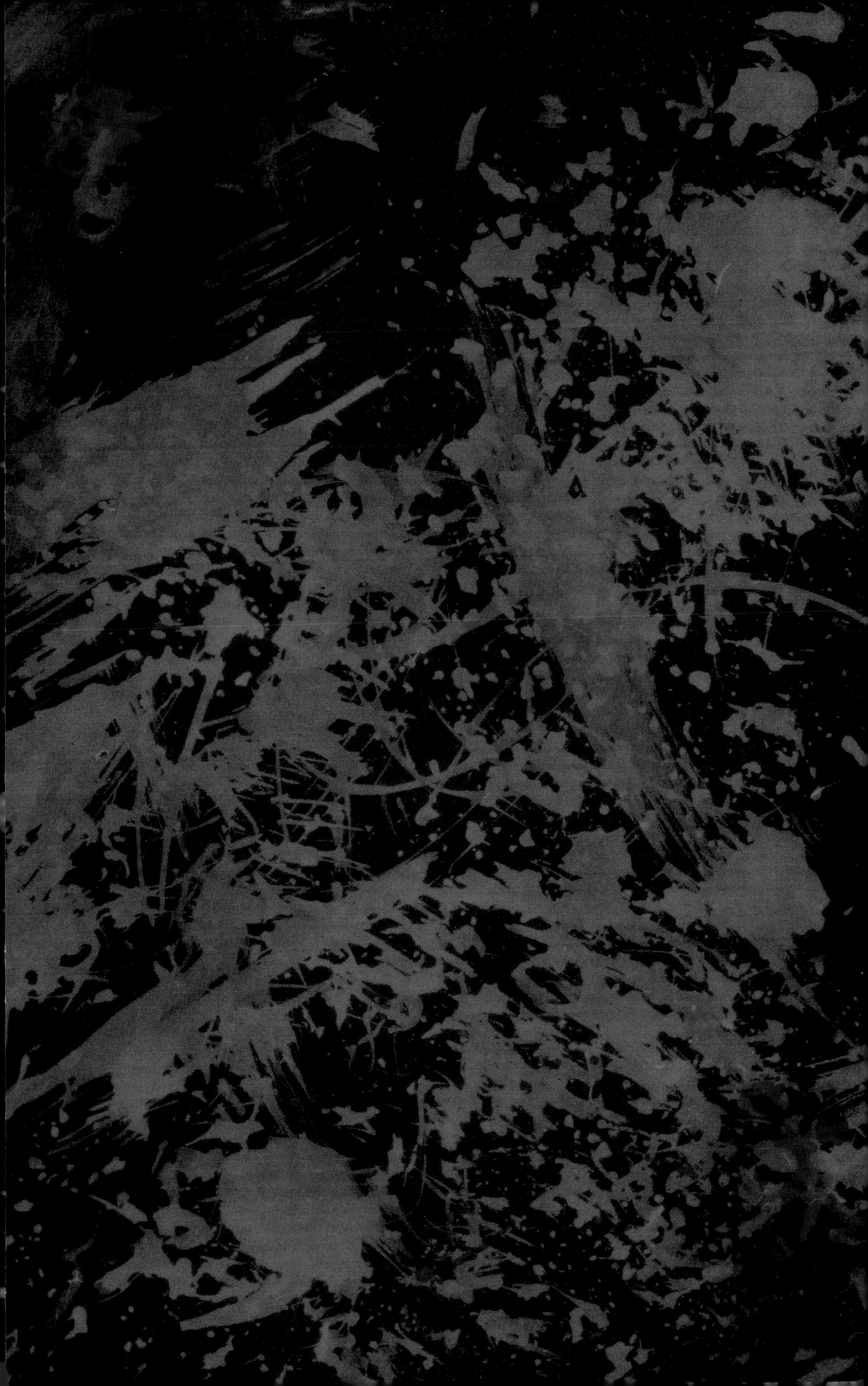

Art by Alex Ronald

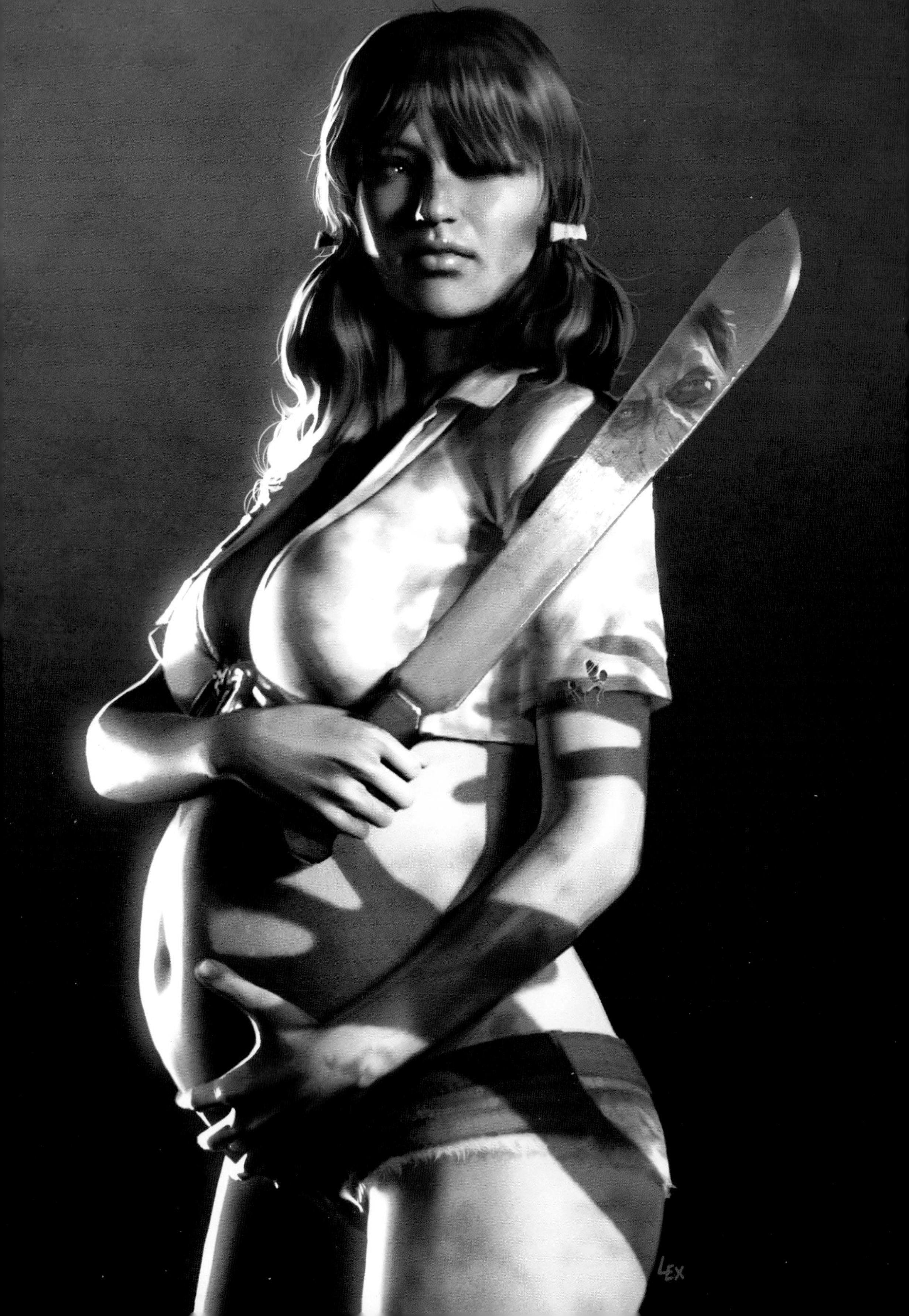
LEX

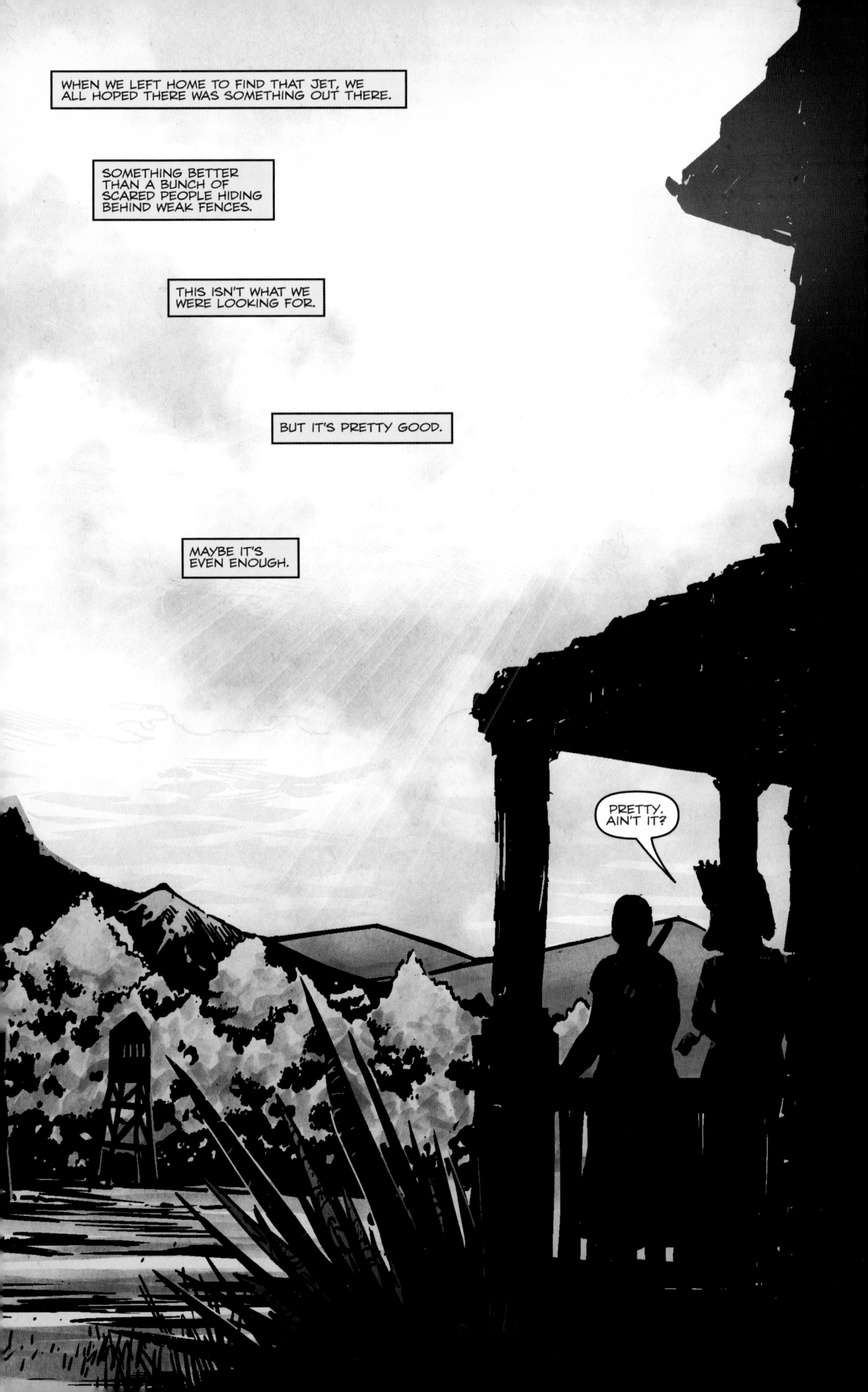
WHEN WE LEFT HOME TO FIND THAT JET, WE ALL HOPED THERE WAS SOMETHING OUT THERE.
SOMETHING BETTER THAN A BUNCH OF SCARED PEOPLE HIDING BEHIND WEAK FENCES.
THIS ISN'T WHAT WE WERE LOOKING FOR.
BUT IT'S PRETTY GOOD.
MAYBE IT'S EVEN ENOUGH.
PRETTY. AIN'T IT?

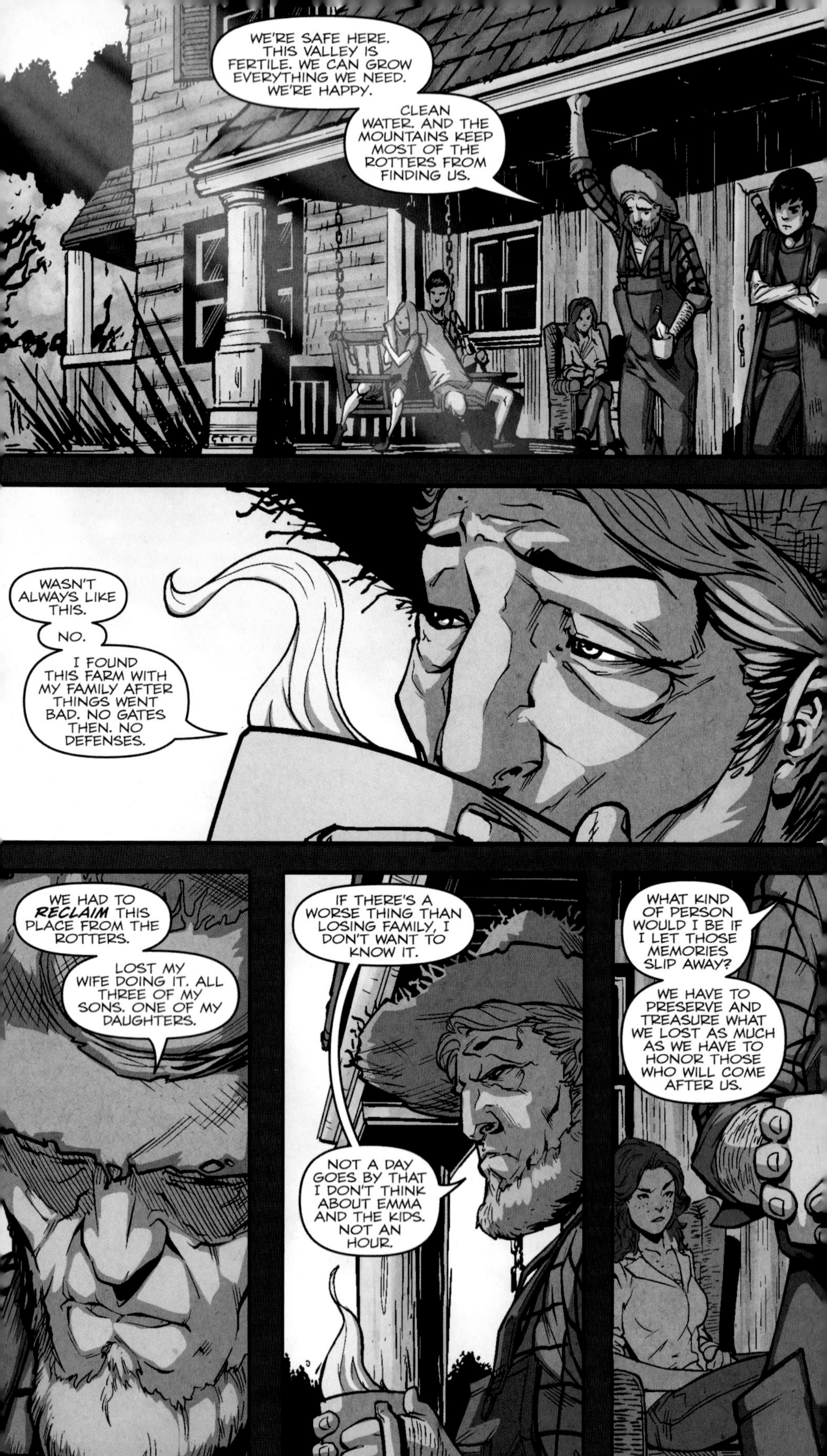
WE'RE SAFE HERE. THIS VALLEY IS FERTILE. WE CAN GROW EVERYTHING WE NEED. WE'RE HAPPY.
CLEAN WATER. AND THE MOUNTAINS KEEP MOST OF THE ROTTERS FROM FINDING US.
WASN'T ALWAYS LIKE THIS.
NO.
I FOUND THIS FARM WITH MY FAMILY AFTER THINGS WENT BAD. NO GATES THEN. NO DEFENSES.
WE HAD TO *RECLAIM* THIS PLACE FROM THE ROTTERS.
LOST MY WIFE DOING IT. ALL THREE OF MY SONS. ONE OF MY DAUGHTERS.
IF THERE'S A WORSE THING THAN LOSING FAMILY, I DON'T WANT TO KNOW IT.
NOT A DAY GOES BY THAT I DON'T THINK ABOUT EMMA AND THE KIDS. NOT AN HOUR.
WHAT KIND OF PERSON WOULD I BE IF I LET THOSE MEMORIES SLIP AWAY?
WE HAVE TO PRESERVE AND TREASURE WHAT WE LOST AS MUCH AS WE HAVE TO HONOR THOSE WHO WILL COME AFTER US.

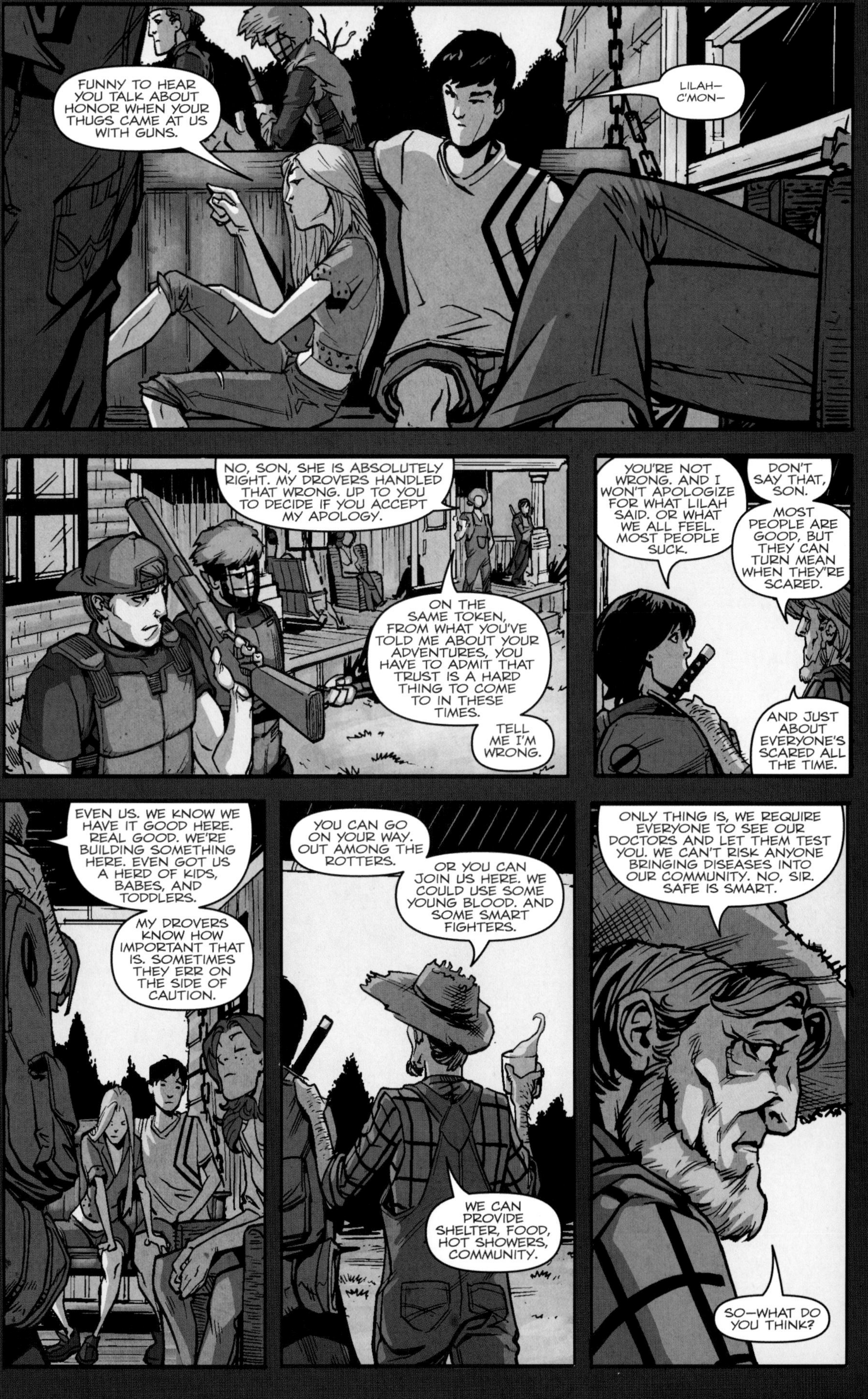
FUNNY TO HEAR YOU TALK ABOUT HONOR WHEN YOUR THUGS CAME AT US WITH GUNS.
LILAH— C'MON—
NO, SON, SHE IS ABSOLUTELY RIGHT. MY DROVERS HANDLED THAT WRONG. UP TO YOU TO DECIDE IF YOU ACCEPT MY APOLOGY.
ON THE SAME TOKEN, FROM WHAT YOU'VE TOLD ME ABOUT YOUR ADVENTURES, YOU HAVE TO ADMIT THAT TRUST IS A HARD THING TO COME TO IN THESE TIMES.
TELL ME I'M WRONG.
YOU'RE NOT WRONG. AND I WON'T APOLOGIZE FOR WHAT LILAH SAID. OR WHAT WE ALL FEEL. MOST PEOPLE SUCK.
DON'T SAY THAT, SON.
MOST PEOPLE ARE GOOD, BUT THEY CAN TURN MEAN WHEN THEY'RE SCARED.
AND JUST ABOUT EVERYONE'S SCARED ALL THE TIME.
EVEN US. WE KNOW WE HAVE IT GOOD HERE. REAL GOOD. WE'RE BUILDING SOMETHING HERE. EVEN GOT US A HERD OF KIDS, BABES, AND TODDLERS.
MY DROVERS KNOW HOW IMPORTANT THAT IS. SOMETIMES THEY ERR ON THE SIDE OF CAUTION.
YOU CAN GO ON YOUR WAY. OUT AMONG THE ROTTERS.
OR YOU CAN JOIN US HERE. WE COULD USE SOME YOUNG BLOOD. AND SOME SMART FIGHTERS.
WE CAN PROVIDE SHELTER, FOOD, HOT SHOWERS, COMMUNITY.
ONLY THING IS, WE REQUIRE EVERYONE TO SEE OUR DOCTORS AND LET THEM TEST YOU. WE CAN'T RISK ANYONE BRINGING DISEASES INTO OUR COMMUNITY. NO, SIR. SAFE IS SMART.
SO—WHAT DO YOU THINK?

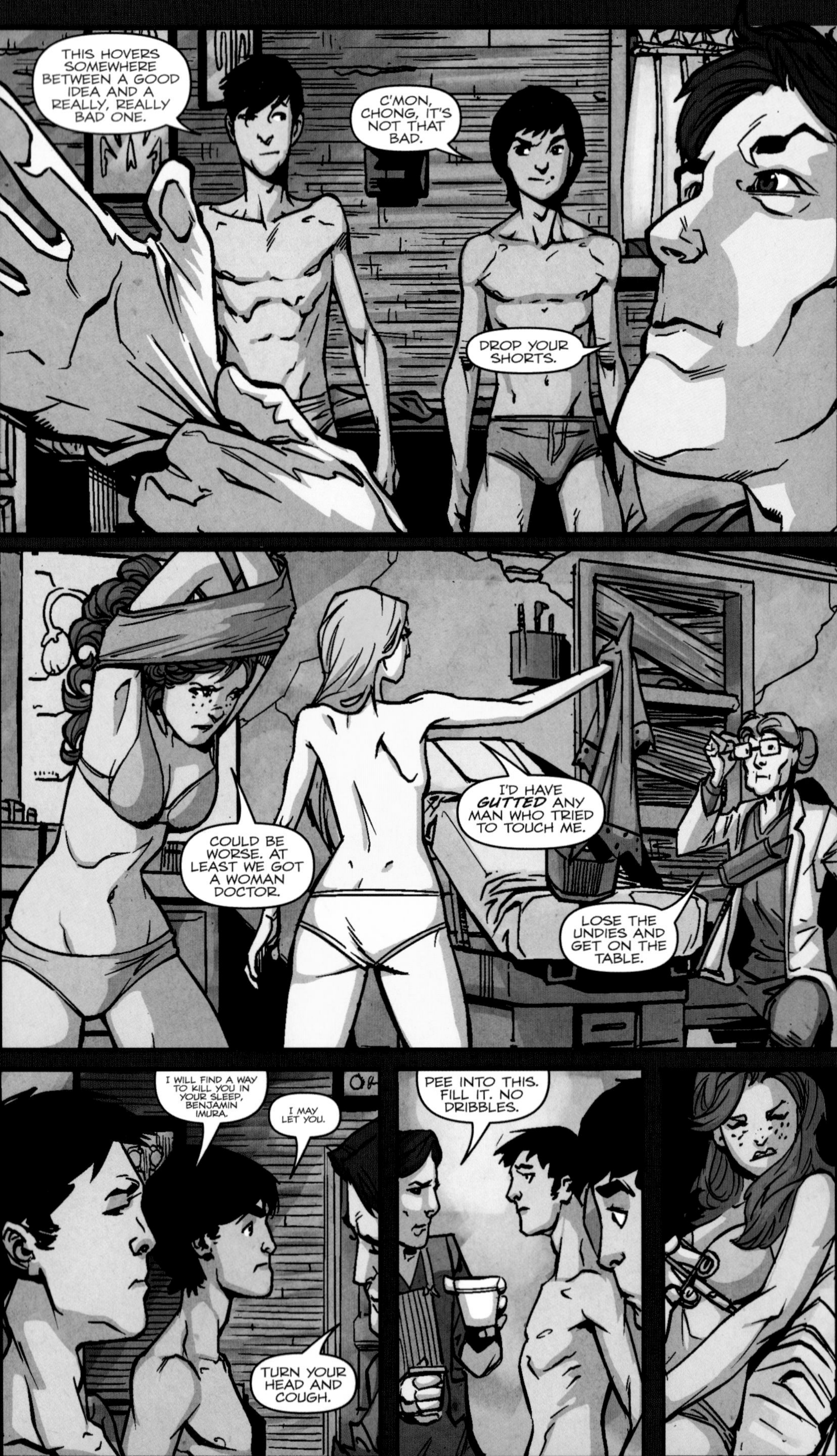
THIS HOVERS SOMEWHERE BETWEEN A GOOD IDEA AND A REALLY, REALLY BAD ONE.
C'MON, CHONG, IT'S NOT THAT BAD.
DROP YOUR SHORTS.
COULD BE WORSE. AT LEAST WE GOT A WOMAN DOCTOR.
I'D HAVE GUTTED ANY MAN WHO TRIED TO TOUCH ME.
LOSE THE UNDIES AND GET ON THE TABLE.
I WILL FIND A WAY TO KILL YOU IN YOUR SLEEP, BENJAMIN IMURA.
I MAY LET YOU.
TURN YOUR HEAD AND COUGH.
PEE INTO THIS. FILL IT. NO DRIBBLES.

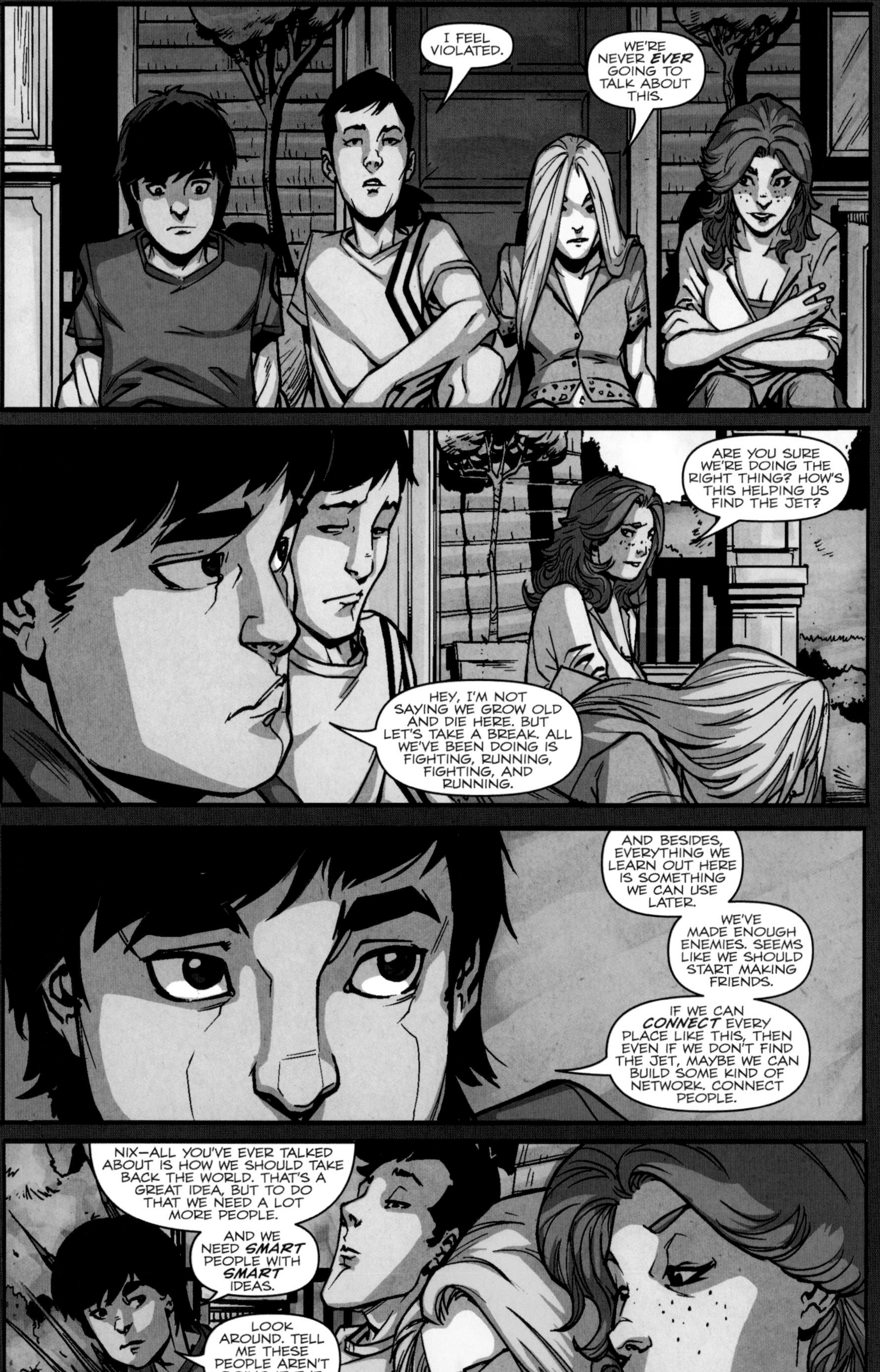
I FEEL VIOLATED.
WE'RE NEVER *EVER* GOING TO TALK ABOUT THIS.
ARE YOU SURE WE'RE DOING THE RIGHT THING? HOW'S THIS HELPING US FIND THE JET?
HEY, I'M NOT SAYING WE GROW OLD AND DIE HERE. BUT LET'S TAKE A BREAK. ALL WE'VE BEEN DOING IS FIGHTING, RUNNING, FIGHTING, AND RUNNING.
AND BESIDES, EVERYTHING WE LEARN OUT HERE IS SOMETHING WE CAN USE LATER.
WE'VE MADE ENOUGH ENEMIES. SEEMS LIKE WE SHOULD START MAKING FRIENDS.
IF WE CAN *CONNECT* EVERY PLACE LIKE THIS, THEN EVEN IF WE DON'T FIND THE JET, MAYBE WE CAN BUILD SOME KIND OF NETWORK. CONNECT PEOPLE.
NIX—ALL YOU'VE EVER TALKED ABOUT IS HOW WE SHOULD TAKE BACK THE WORLD. THAT'S A GREAT IDEA, BUT TO DO THAT WE NEED A LOT MORE PEOPLE.
AND WE NEED *SMART* PEOPLE WITH *SMART* IDEAS.
LOOK AROUND. TELL ME THESE PEOPLE AREN'T DOING IT THE RIGHT WAY.

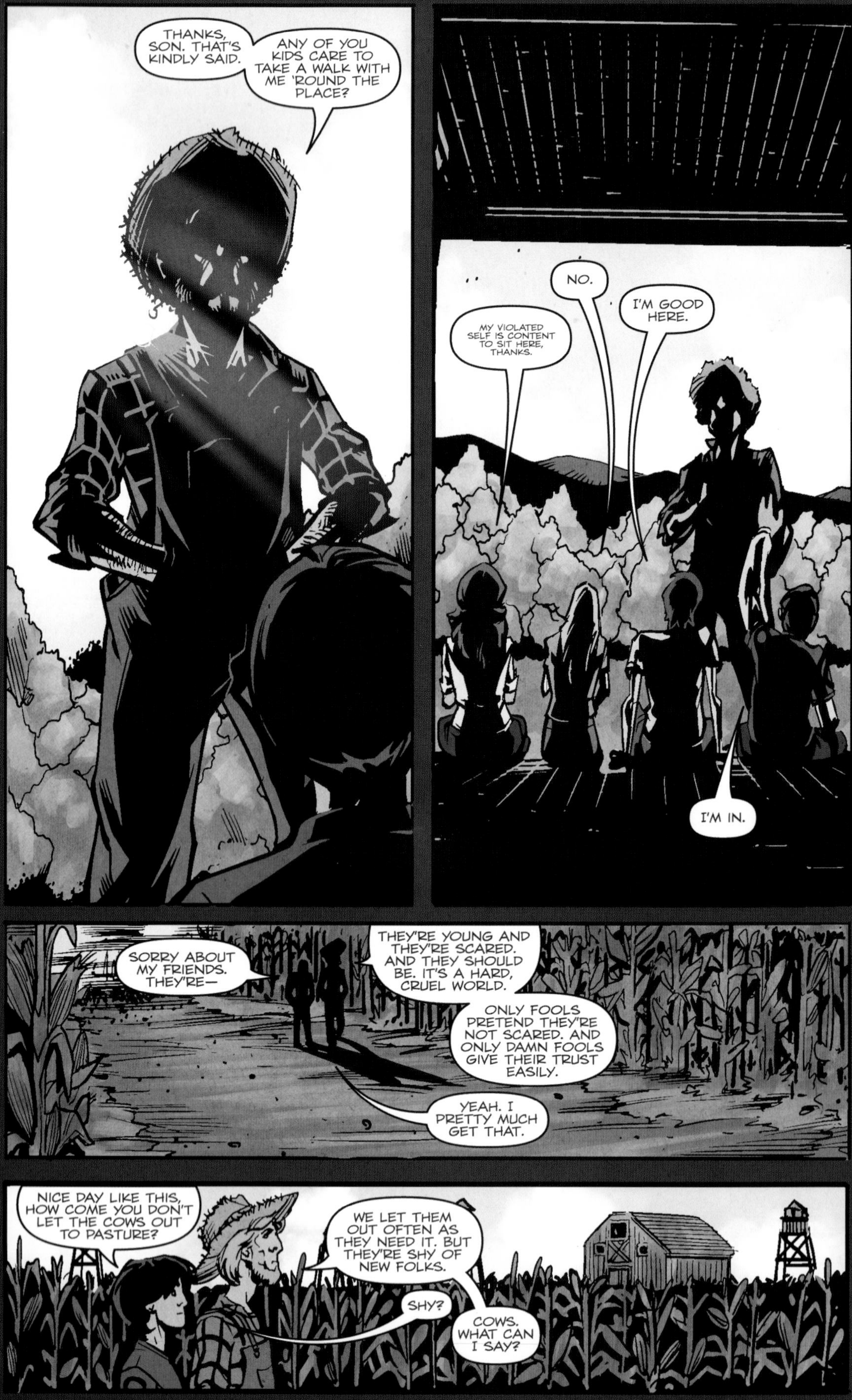
THANKS, SON. THAT'S KINDLY SAID.
ANY OF YOU KIDS CARE TO TAKE A WALK WITH ME 'ROUND THE PLACE?
MY VIOLATED SELF IS CONTENT TO SIT HERE, THANKS.
NO.
I'M GOOD HERE.
I'M IN.
SORRY ABOUT MY FRIENDS. THEY'RE—
THEY'RE YOUNG AND THEY'RE SCARED. AND THEY SHOULD BE. IT'S A HARD, CRUEL WORLD.
ONLY FOOLS PRETEND THEY'RE NOT SCARED. AND ONLY DAMN FOOLS GIVE THEIR TRUST EASILY.
YEAH. I PRETTY MUCH GET THAT.
NICE DAY LIKE THIS, HOW COME YOU DON'T LET THE COWS OUT TO PASTURE?
WE LET THEM OUT OFTEN AS THEY NEED IT. BUT THEY'RE SHY OF NEW FOLKS.
SHY?
COWS. WHAT CAN I SAY?

WOW. YOU HAVE *SO* MANY KIDS. IT'S GREAT.

THEY'RE OUR MOST PRECIOUS RESOURCE, AS I'M SURE YOU'LL UNDERSTAND. YOU BEING A SMART YOUNG MAN.

WHEN THE DEAD ROSE, TOO DARN MANY PEOPLE DIED. IT THINNED THE GENE POOL. TO REBUILD THE WORLD, WE NEED PEOPLE, AND LOTS OF 'EM.

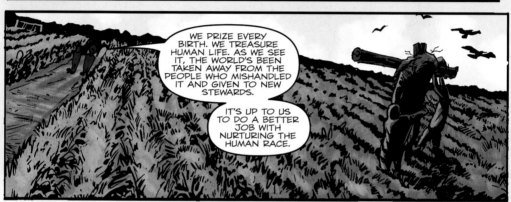

WE PRIZE EVERY BIRTH. WE TREASURE HUMAN LIFE. AS WE SEE IT, THE WORLD'S BEEN TAKEN AWAY FROM THE PEOPLE WHO MISHANDLED IT AND GIVEN TO NEW STEWARDS.

IT'S UP TO US TO DO A BETTER JOB WITH NURTURING THE HUMAN RACE.

LOOK, ABOUT THIS MORNING WITH US AND YOUR GUARD. WHAT WAS HIS NAME?

HOWIE. A DISAPPOINTING MAN.

WE DIDN'T MEAN TO HUMILIATE HIM LIKE THAT. HE JUST SURPRISED US.

DON'T SWEAT IT, SON. THESE THINGS HAPPEN.

WE DECIDED TO TAKE THAT AS A TEACHABLE MOMENT. WE'LL ALL LEARN FROM IT.

HOWIE MORGAN
HE FAILED TO PROTECT THE HERD.

I'M SORRY. I'M SORRY. OH GOD, I'M SORRY.

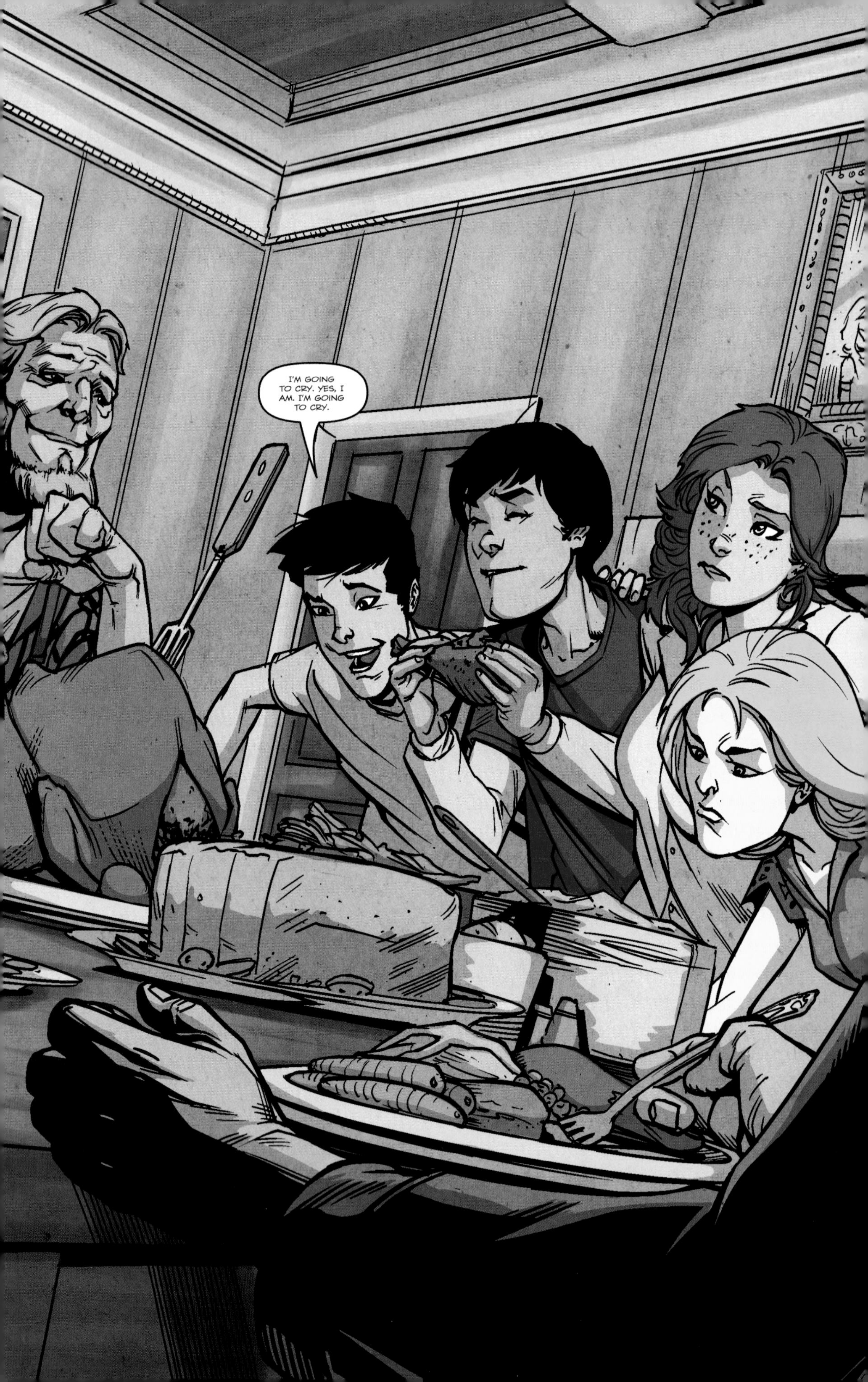
I'M GOING TO CRY. YES, I AM. I'M GOING TO CRY.

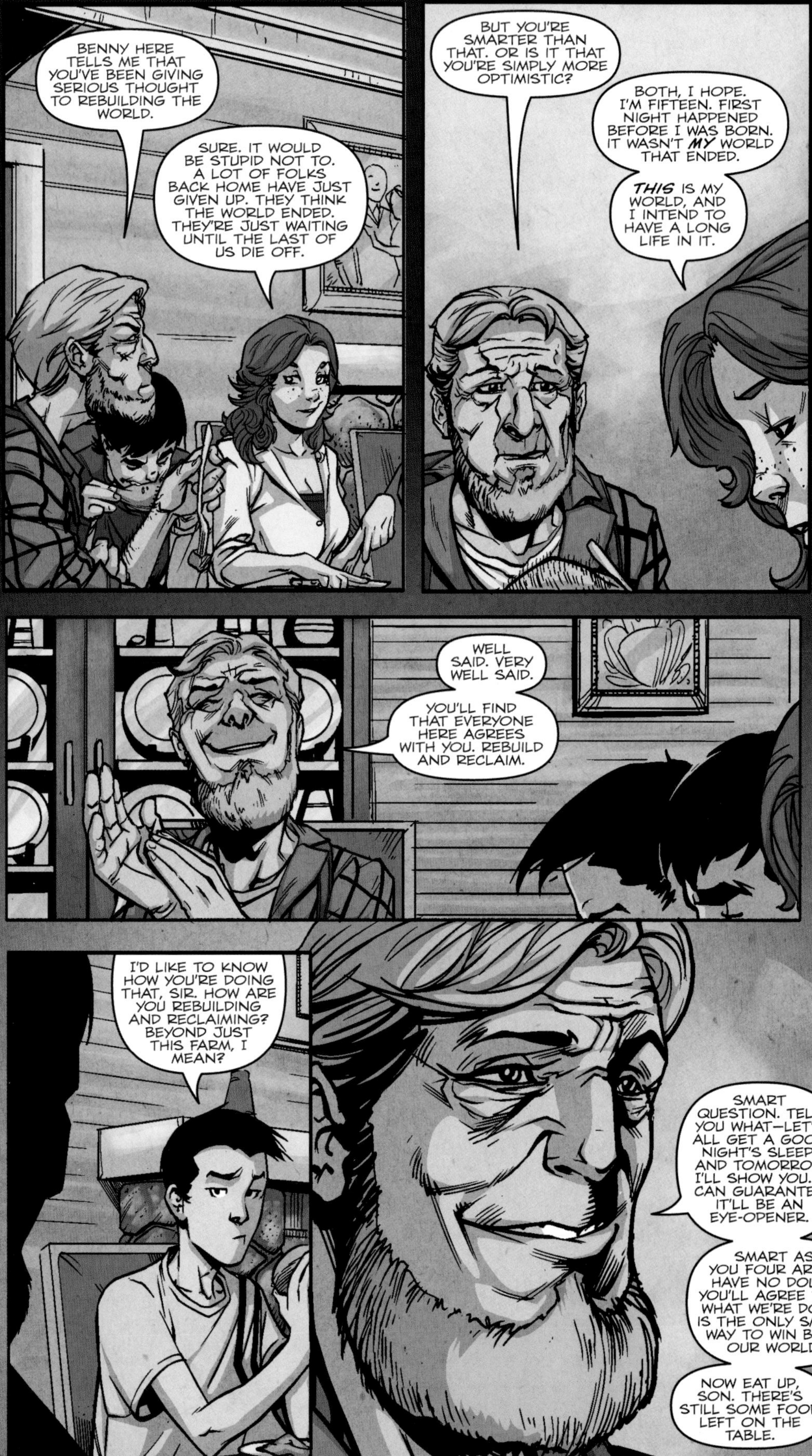
BENNY HERE TELLS ME THAT YOU'VE BEEN GIVING SERIOUS THOUGHT TO REBUILDING THE WORLD.
SURE. IT WOULD BE STUPID NOT TO. A LOT OF FOLKS BACK HOME HAVE JUST GIVEN UP. THEY THINK THE WORLD ENDED. THEY'RE JUST WAITING UNTIL THE LAST OF US DIE OFF.
BUT YOU'RE SMARTER THAN THAT. OR IS IT THAT YOU'RE SIMPLY MORE OPTIMISTIC?
BOTH, I HOPE. I'M FIFTEEN. FIRST NIGHT HAPPENED BEFORE I WAS BORN. IT WASN'T MY WORLD THAT ENDED.
THIS IS MY WORLD, AND I INTEND TO HAVE A LONG LIFE IN IT.
WELL SAID. VERY WELL SAID.
YOU'LL FIND THAT EVERYONE HERE AGREES WITH YOU. REBUILD AND RECLAIM.
I'D LIKE TO KNOW HOW YOU'RE DOING THAT, SIR. HOW ARE YOU REBUILDING AND RECLAIMING? BEYOND JUST THIS FARM, I MEAN?
SMART QUESTION. TELL YOU WHAT—LET'S ALL GET A GOOD NIGHT'S SLEEP, AND TOMORROW I'LL SHOW YOU. I CAN GUARANTEE IT'LL BE AN EYE-OPENER.
SMART AS YOU FOUR ARE—I HAVE NO DOUBT YOU'LL AGREE THAT WHAT WE'RE DOING IS THE ONLY SMART WAY TO WIN BACK OUR WORLD.
NOW EAT UP, SON. THERE'S STILL SOME FOOD LEFT ON THE TABLE.

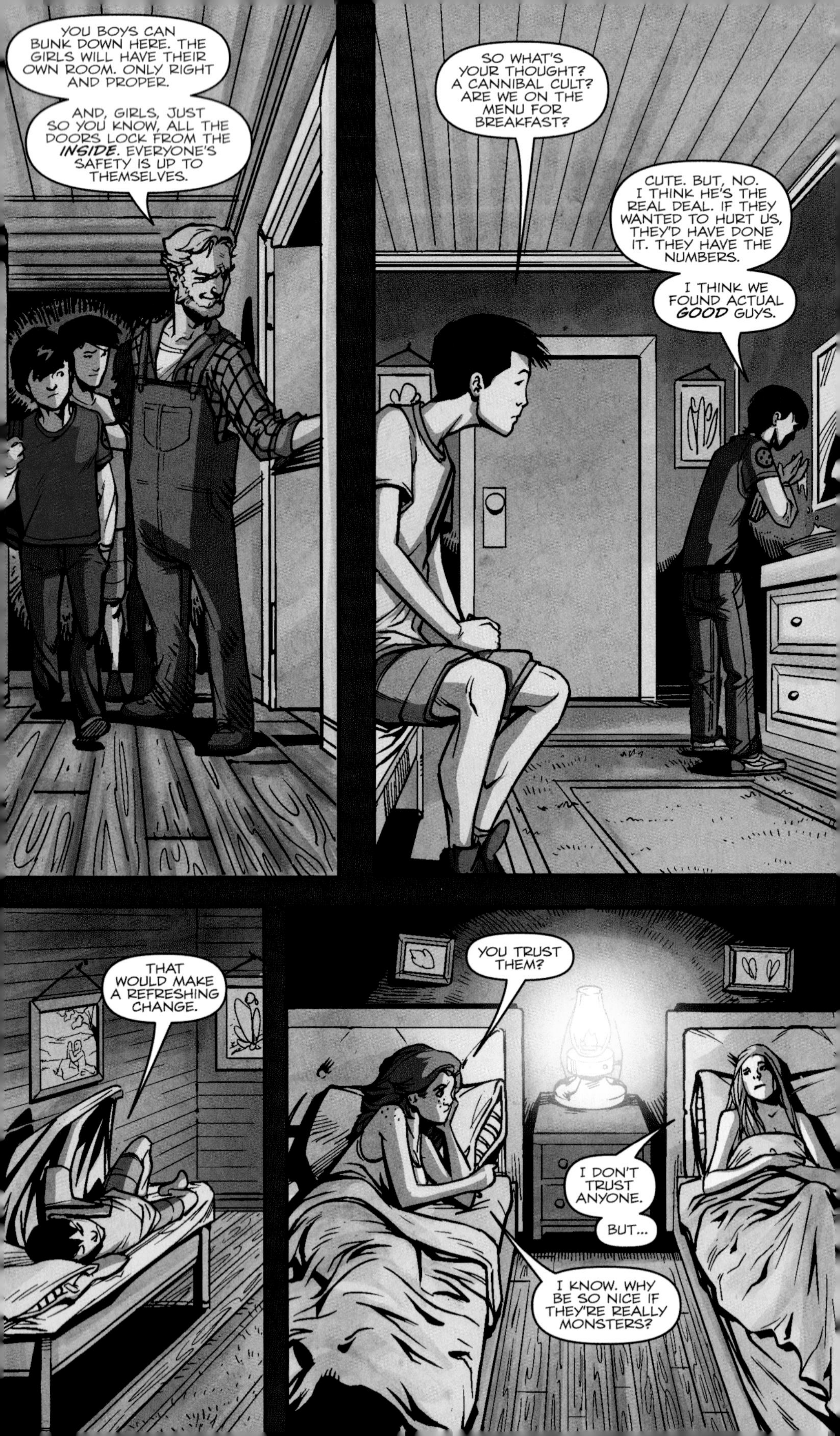
YOU BOYS CAN BUNK DOWN HERE. THE GIRLS WILL HAVE THEIR OWN ROOM. ONLY RIGHT AND PROPER.
AND, GIRLS, JUST SO YOU KNOW, ALL THE DOORS LOCK FROM THE *INSIDE*. EVERYONE'S SAFETY IS UP TO THEMSELVES.
SO WHAT'S YOUR THOUGHT? A CANNIBAL CULT? ARE WE ON THE MENU FOR BREAKFAST?
CUTE. BUT, NO. I THINK HE'S THE REAL DEAL. IF THEY WANTED TO HURT US, THEY'D HAVE DONE IT. THEY HAVE THE NUMBERS.
I THINK WE FOUND ACTUAL *GOOD* GUYS.
THAT WOULD MAKE A REFRESHING CHANGE.
YOU TRUST THEM?
I DON'T TRUST ANYONE.
BUT...
I KNOW. WHY BE SO NICE IF THEY'RE REALLY MONSTERS?

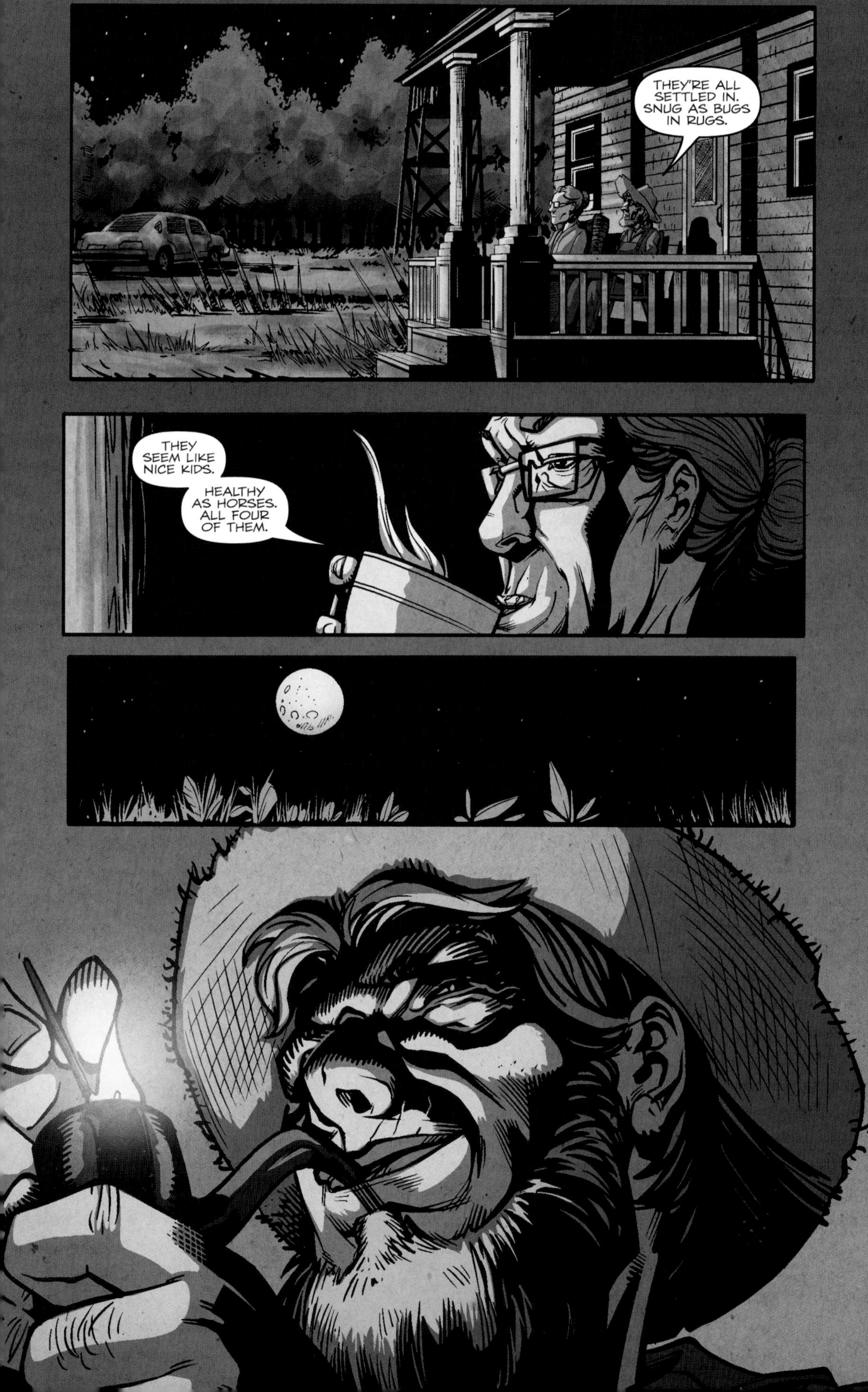
THEY'RE ALL SETTLED IN. SNUG AS BUGS IN RUGS.
THEY SEEM LIKE NICE KIDS.
HEALTHY AS HORSES. ALL FOUR OF THEM.

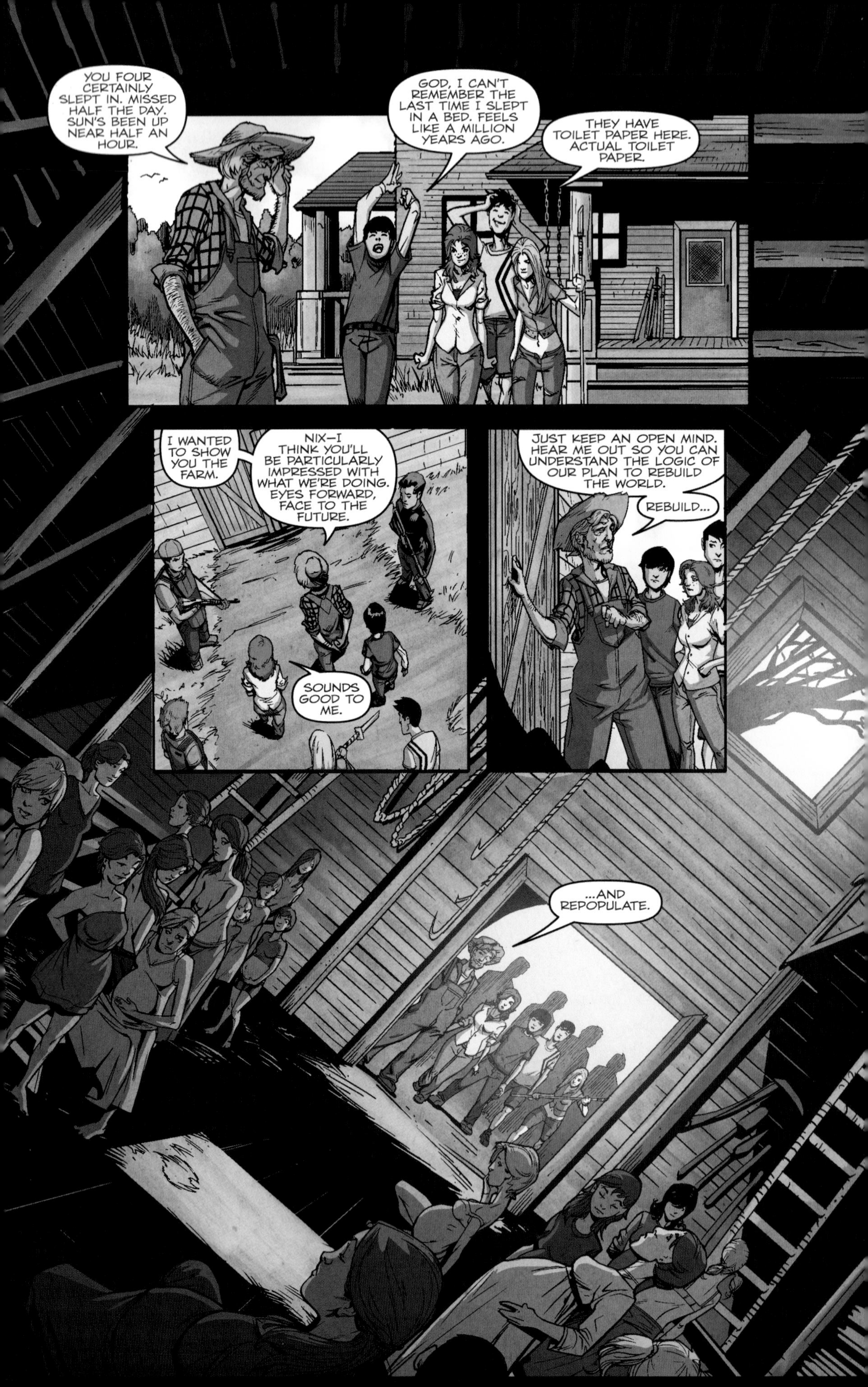
YOU FOUR CERTAINLY SLEPT IN. MISSED HALF THE DAY. SUN'S BEEN UP NEAR HALF AN HOUR.
GOD, I CAN'T REMEMBER THE LAST TIME I SLEPT IN A BED. FEELS LIKE A MILLION YEARS AGO.
THEY HAVE TOILET PAPER HERE. ACTUAL TOILET PAPER.
I WANTED TO SHOW YOU THE FARM.
NIX--I THINK YOU'LL BE PARTICULARLY IMPRESSED WITH WHAT WE'RE DOING. EYES FORWARD, FACE TO THE FUTURE.
SOUNDS GOOD TO ME.
JUST KEEP AN OPEN MIND. HEAR ME OUT SO YOU CAN UNDERSTAND THE LOGIC OF OUR PLAN TO REBUILD THE WORLD.
REBUILD...
...AND REPOPULATE.

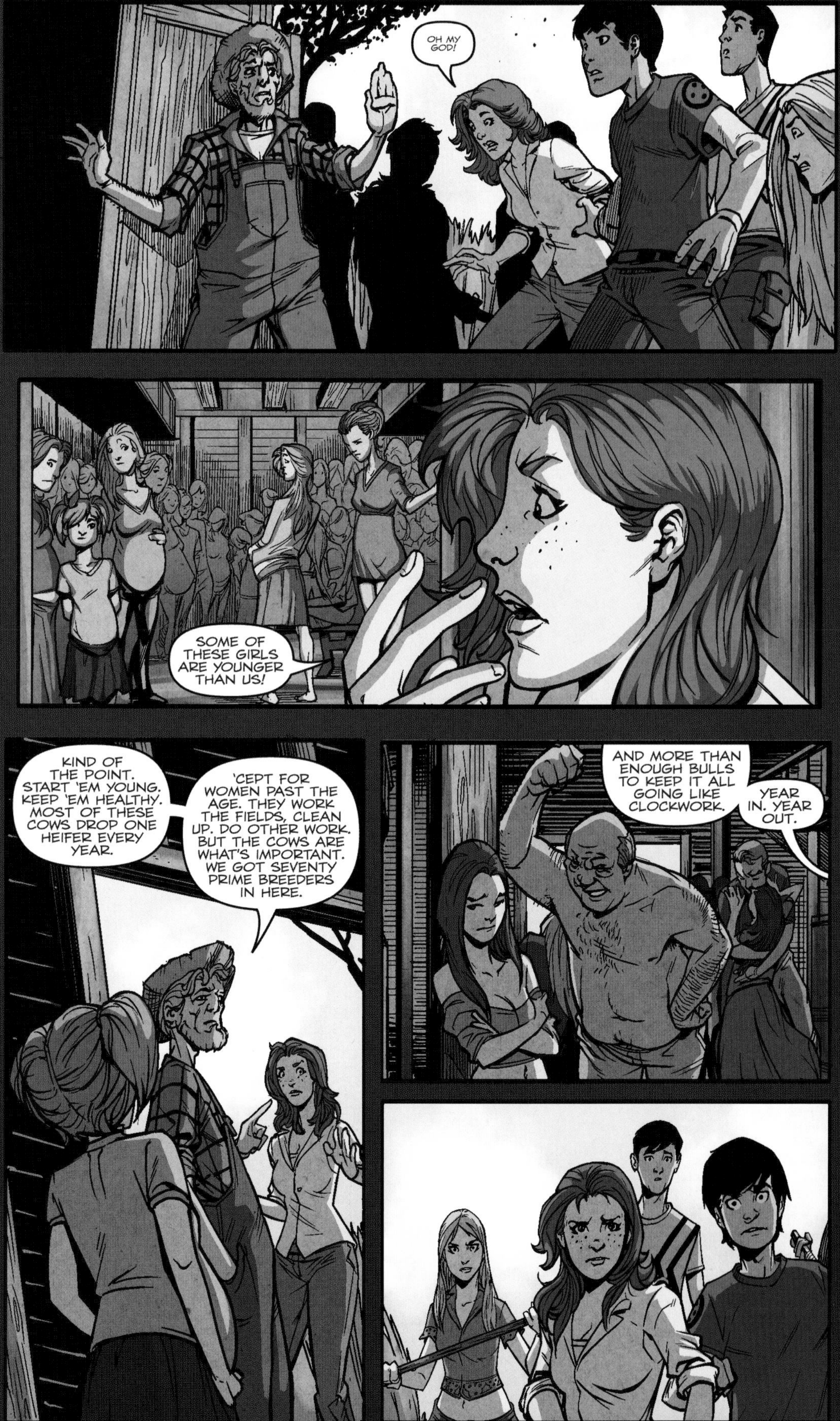
OH MY GOD!
SOME OF THESE GIRLS ARE YOUNGER THAN US!
KIND OF THE POINT. START 'EM YOUNG. KEEP 'EM HEALTHY. MOST OF THESE COWS DROP ONE HEIFER EVERY YEAR.
'CEPT FOR WOMEN PAST THE AGE. THEY WORK THE FIELDS, CLEAN UP. DO OTHER WORK. BUT THE COWS ARE WHAT'S IMPORTANT. WE GOT SEVENTY PRIME BREEDERS IN HERE.
AND MORE THAN ENOUGH BULLS TO KEEP IT ALL GOING LIKE CLOCKWORK.
YEAR IN. YEAR OUT.

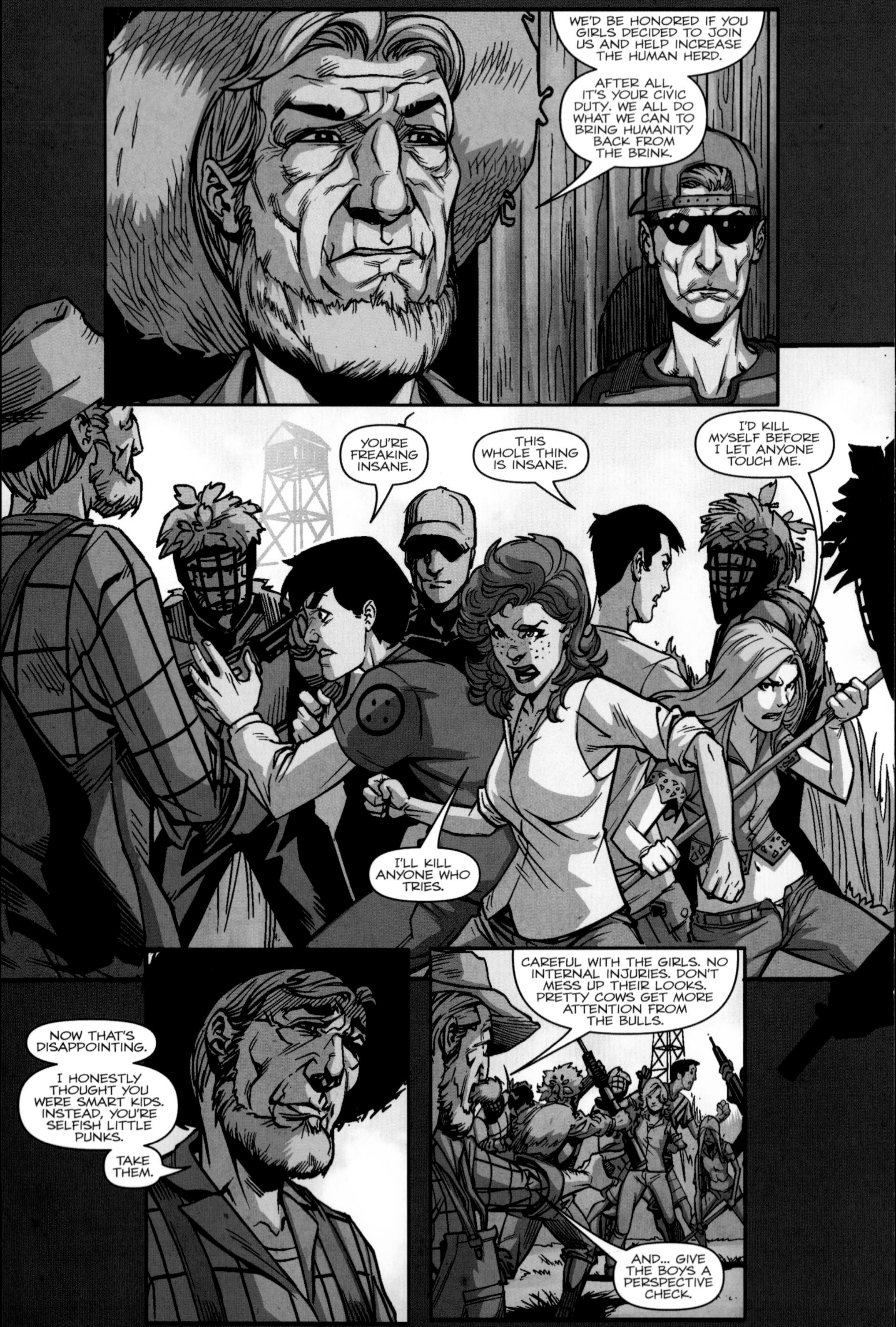
WE'D BE HONORED IF YOU GIRLS DECIDED TO JOIN US AND HELP INCREASE THE HUMAN HERD.
AFTER ALL, IT'S YOUR CIVIC DUTY. WE ALL DO WHAT WE CAN TO BRING HUMANITY BACK FROM THE BRINK.
YOU'RE FREAKING INSANE.
THIS WHOLE THING IS INSANE.
I'D KILL MYSELF BEFORE I LET ANYONE TOUCH ME.
I'LL KILL ANYONE WHO TRIES.
NOW THAT'S DISAPPOINTING.
I HONESTLY THOUGHT YOU WERE SMART KIDS. INSTEAD, YOU'RE SELFISH LITTLE PUNKS.
TAKE THEM.
CAREFUL WITH THE GIRLS. NO INTERNAL INJURIES. DON'T MESS UP THEIR LOOKS. PRETTY COWS GET MORE ATTENTION FROM THE BULLS.
AND... GIVE THE BOYS A PERSPECTIVE CHECK.

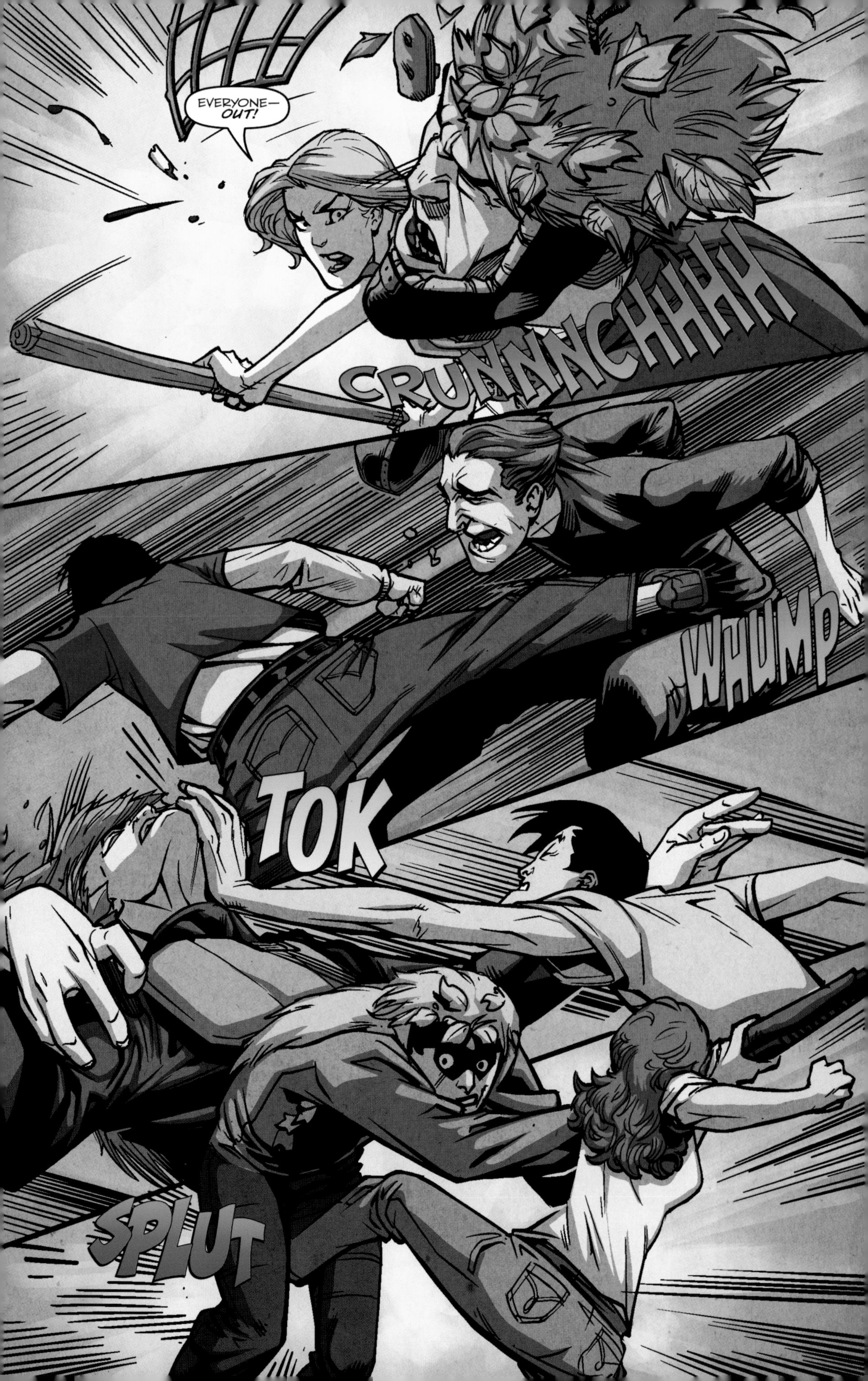
EVERYONE—
OUT!
CRUNNNCHHHH
WHUMP
TOK
SPLUT

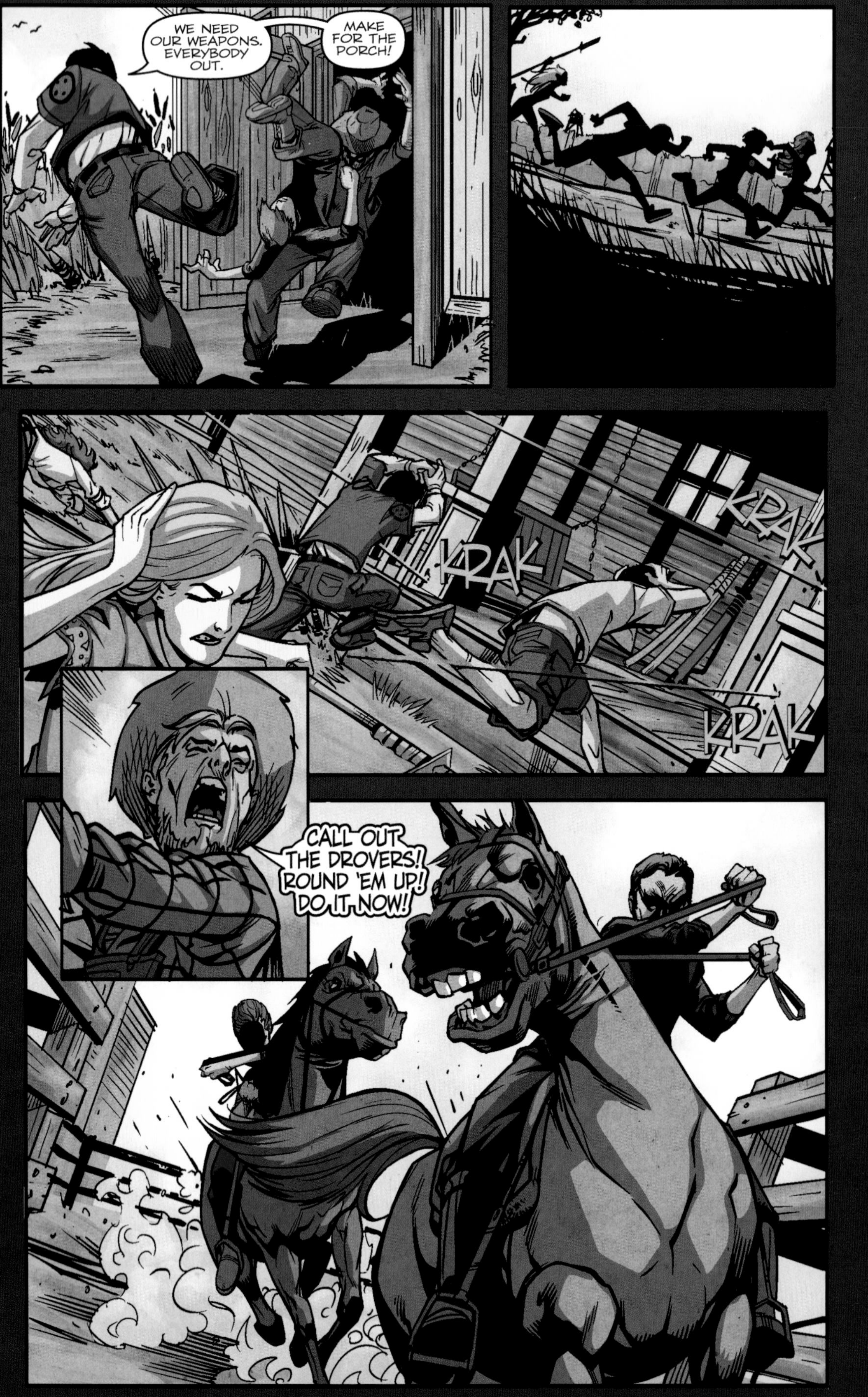
WE NEED OUR WEAPONS. EVERYBODY OUT.
MAKE FOR THE PORCH!
KRAK
KRAK
KRAK
CALL OUT THE DROVERS! ROUND 'EM UP! DO IT NOW!

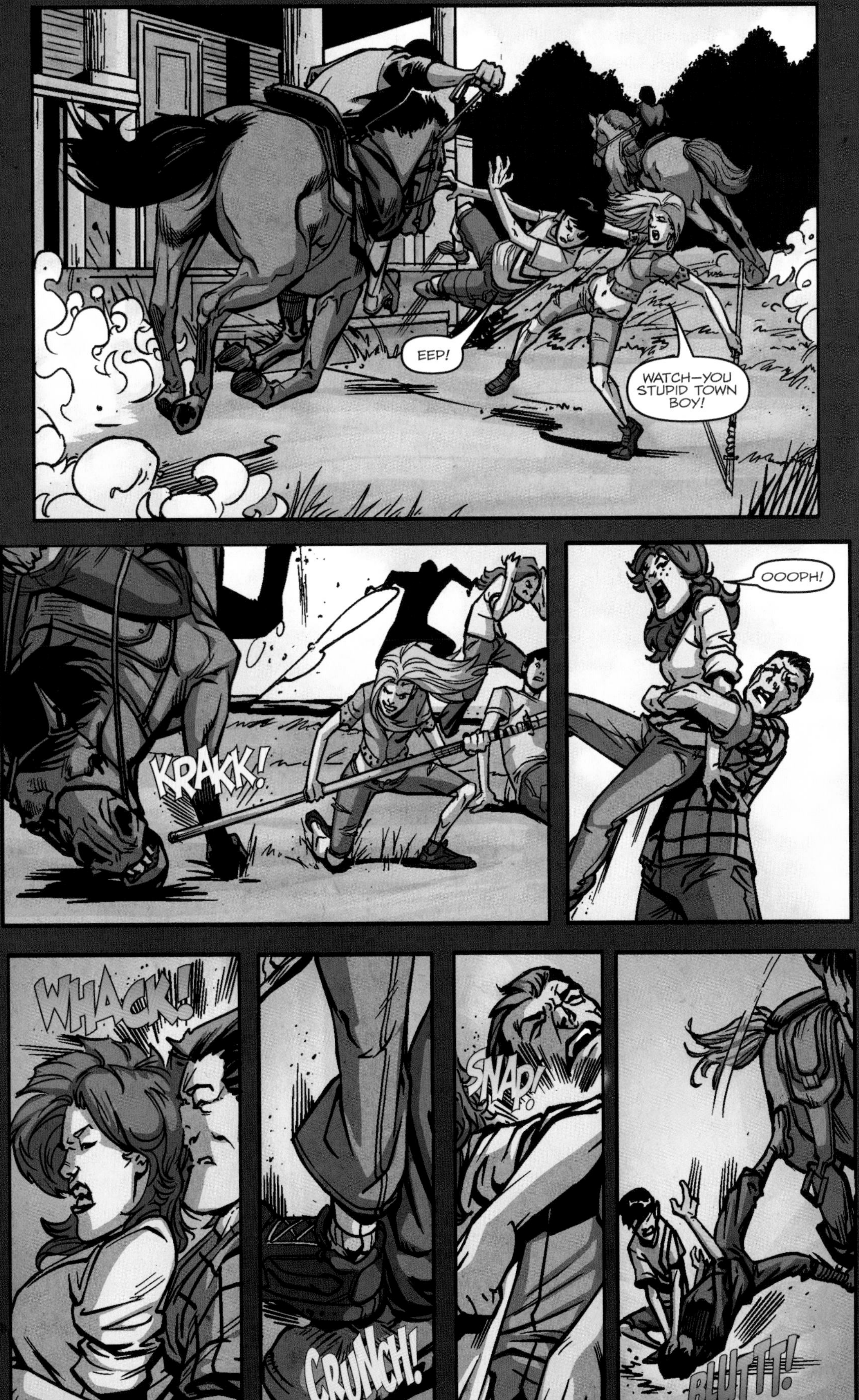
EEP!
WATCH—YOU STUPID TOWN BOY!
KRAKK!
OOOPH!
WHACK!
CRUNCH!
SNAP!
BLUTTT!

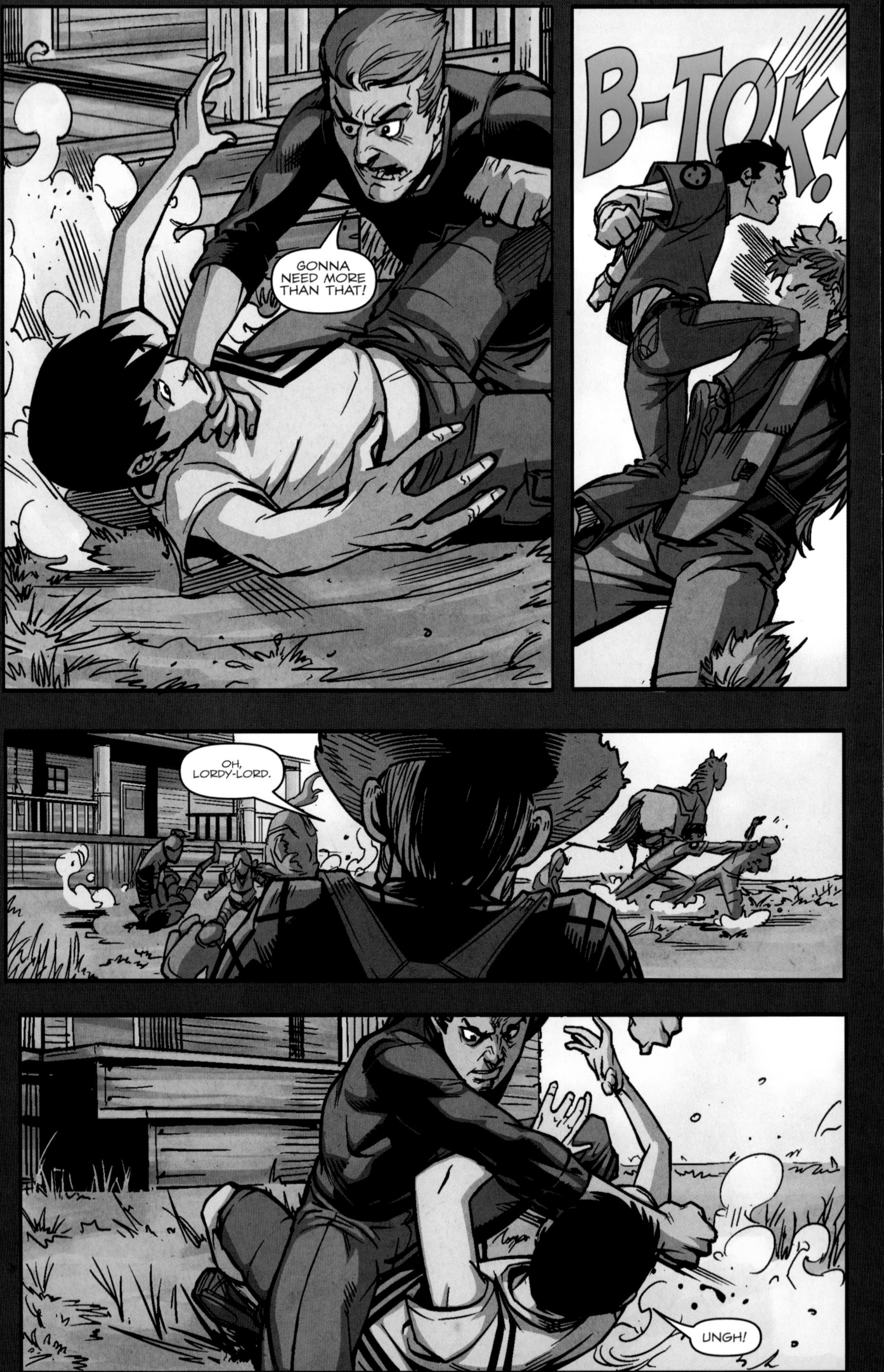
GONNA NEED MORE THAN THAT!
B-TOK!
OH, LORDY-LORD.
UNGH!

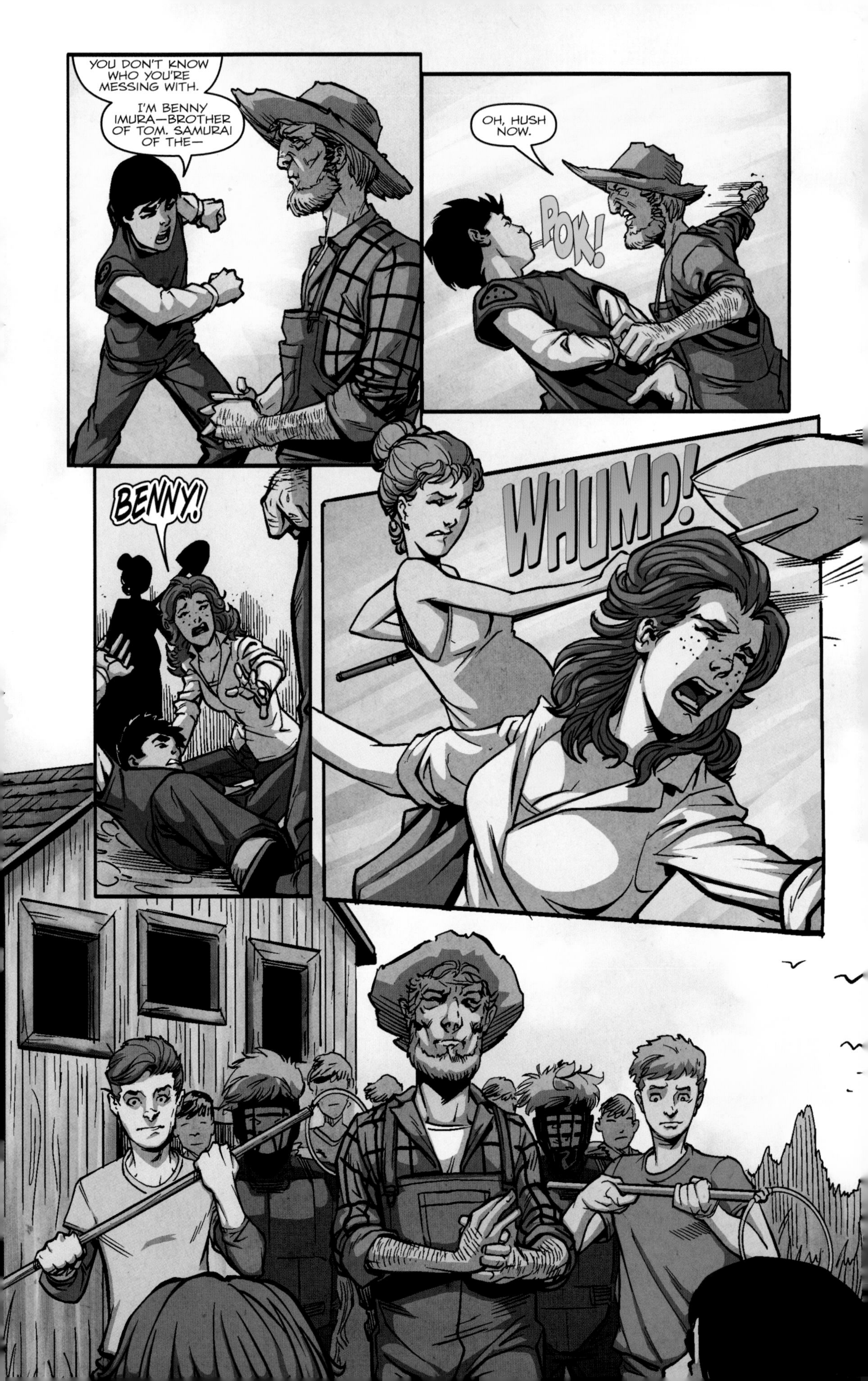
YOU DON'T KNOW WHO YOU'RE MESSING WITH.
I'M BENNY IMURA—BROTHER OF TOM. SAMURAI OF THE—
OH, HUSH NOW.
POK!
BENNY!
WHUMP!

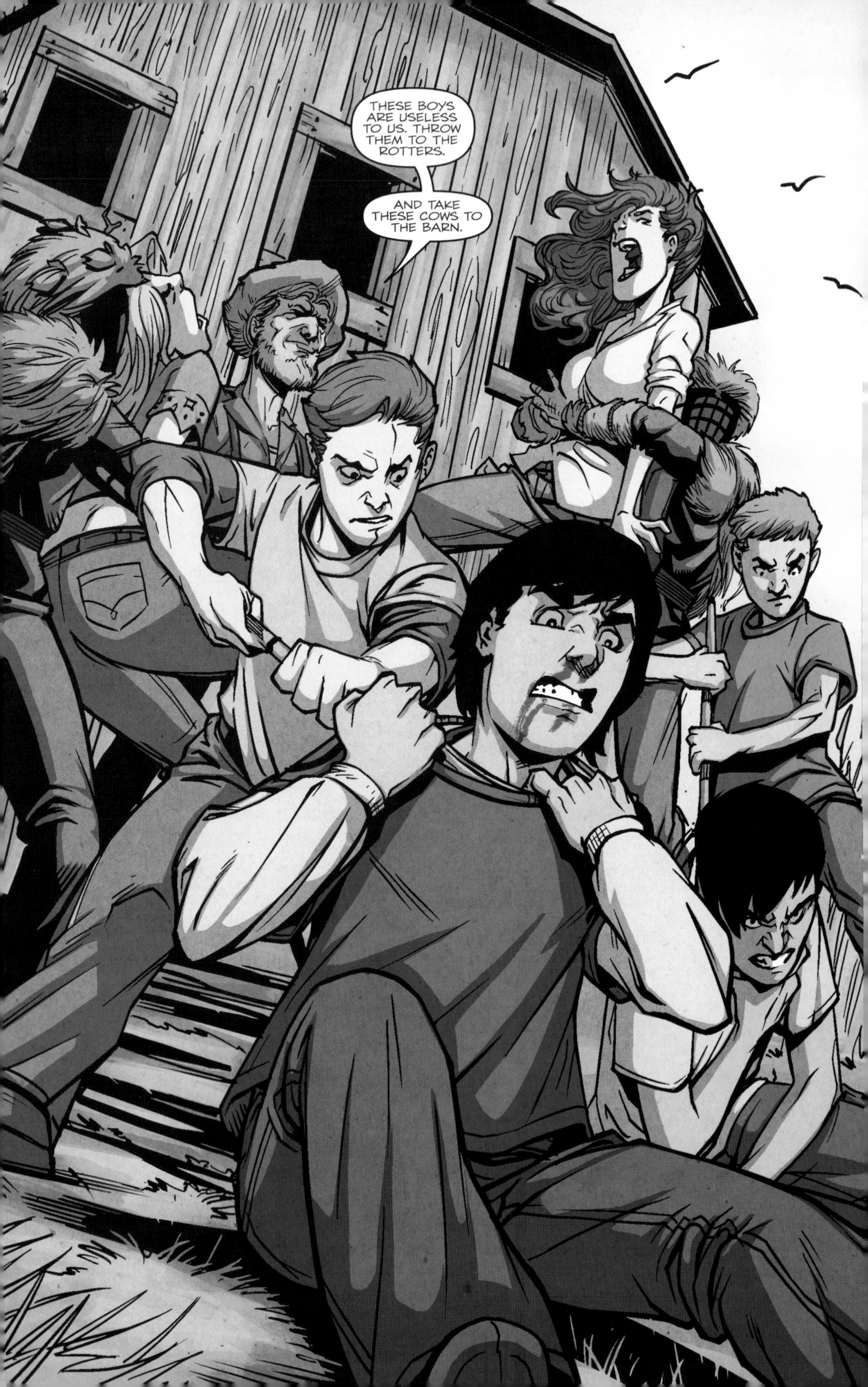
THESE BOYS ARE USELESS TO US. THROW THEM TO THE ROTTERS.
AND TAKE THESE COWS TO THE BARN.

Art by Alex Ronald

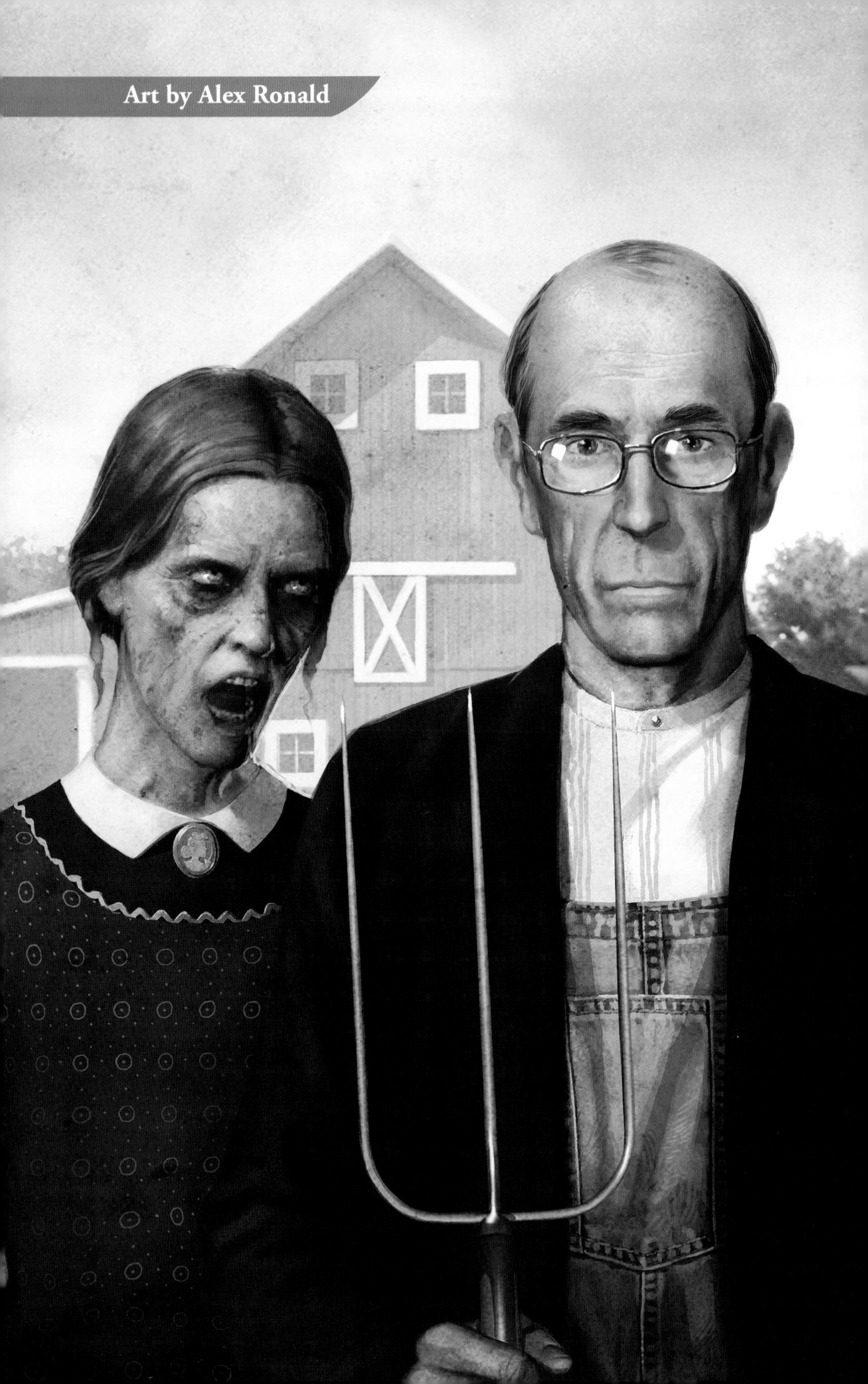

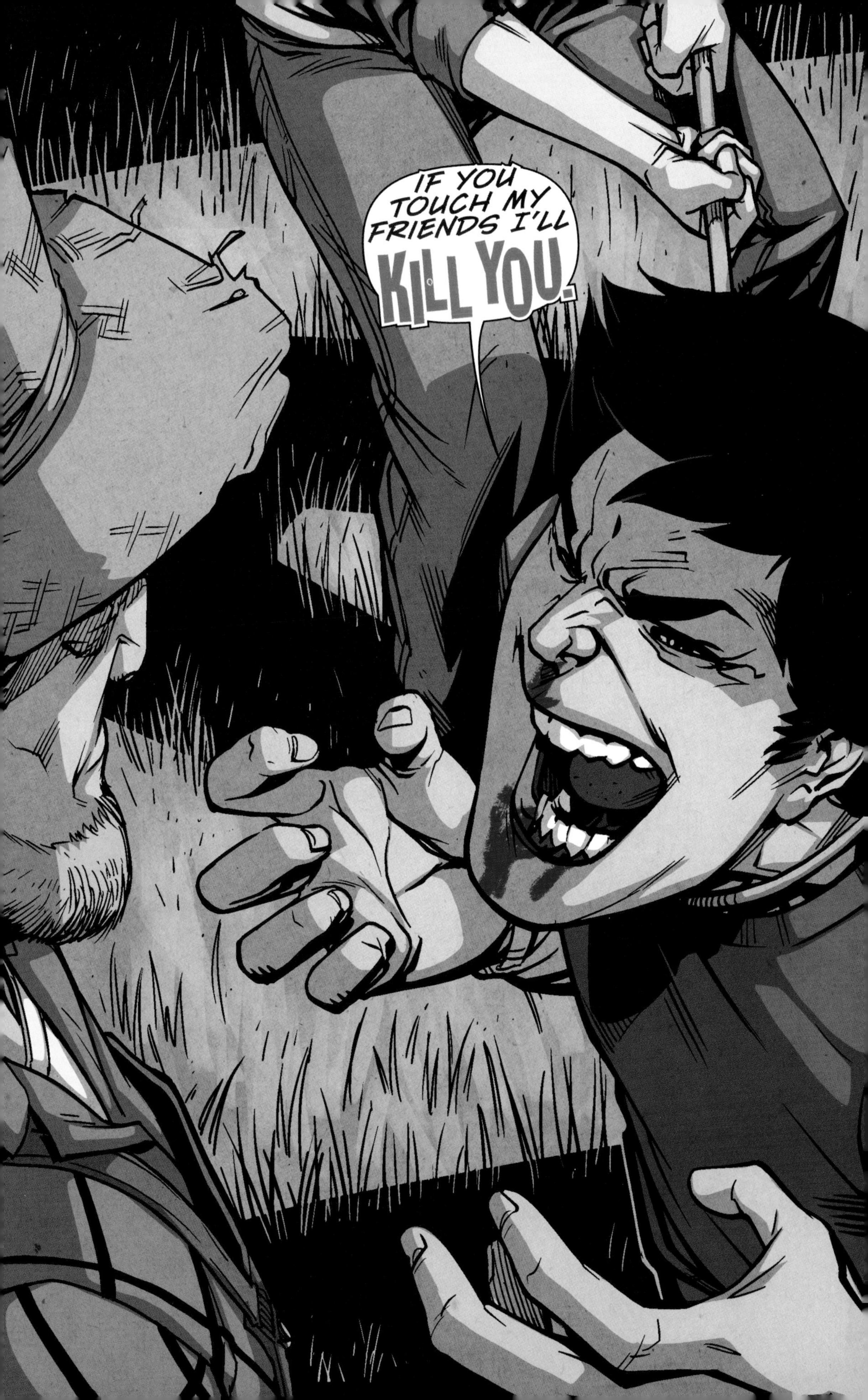
IF YOU TOUCH MY FRIENDS I'LL KILL YOU.

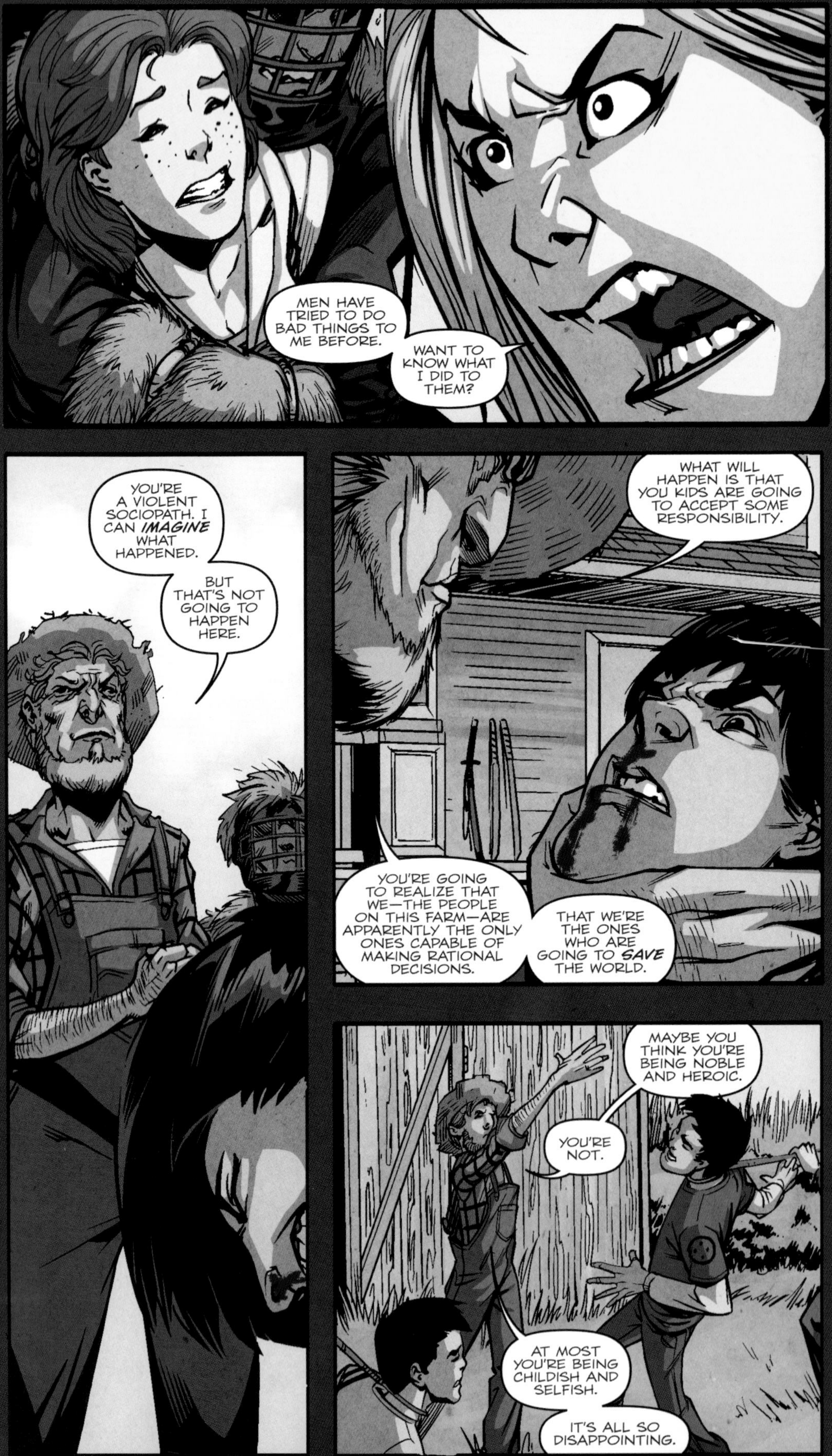
MEN HAVE TRIED TO DO BAD THINGS TO ME BEFORE.
WANT TO KNOW WHAT I DID TO THEM?
YOU'RE A VIOLENT SOCIOPATH. I CAN *IMAGINE* WHAT HAPPENED.
BUT THAT'S NOT GOING TO HAPPEN HERE.
WHAT WILL HAPPEN IS THAT YOU KIDS ARE GOING TO ACCEPT SOME RESPONSIBILITY.
YOU'RE GOING TO REALIZE THAT WE—THE PEOPLE ON THIS FARM—ARE APPARENTLY THE ONLY ONES CAPABLE OF MAKING RATIONAL DECISIONS.
THAT WE'RE THE ONES WHO ARE GOING TO *SAVE* THE WORLD.
MAYBE YOU THINK YOU'RE BEING NOBLE AND HEROIC.
YOU'RE NOT.
AT MOST YOU'RE BEING CHILDISH AND SELFISH.
IT'S ALL SO DISAPPOINTING.

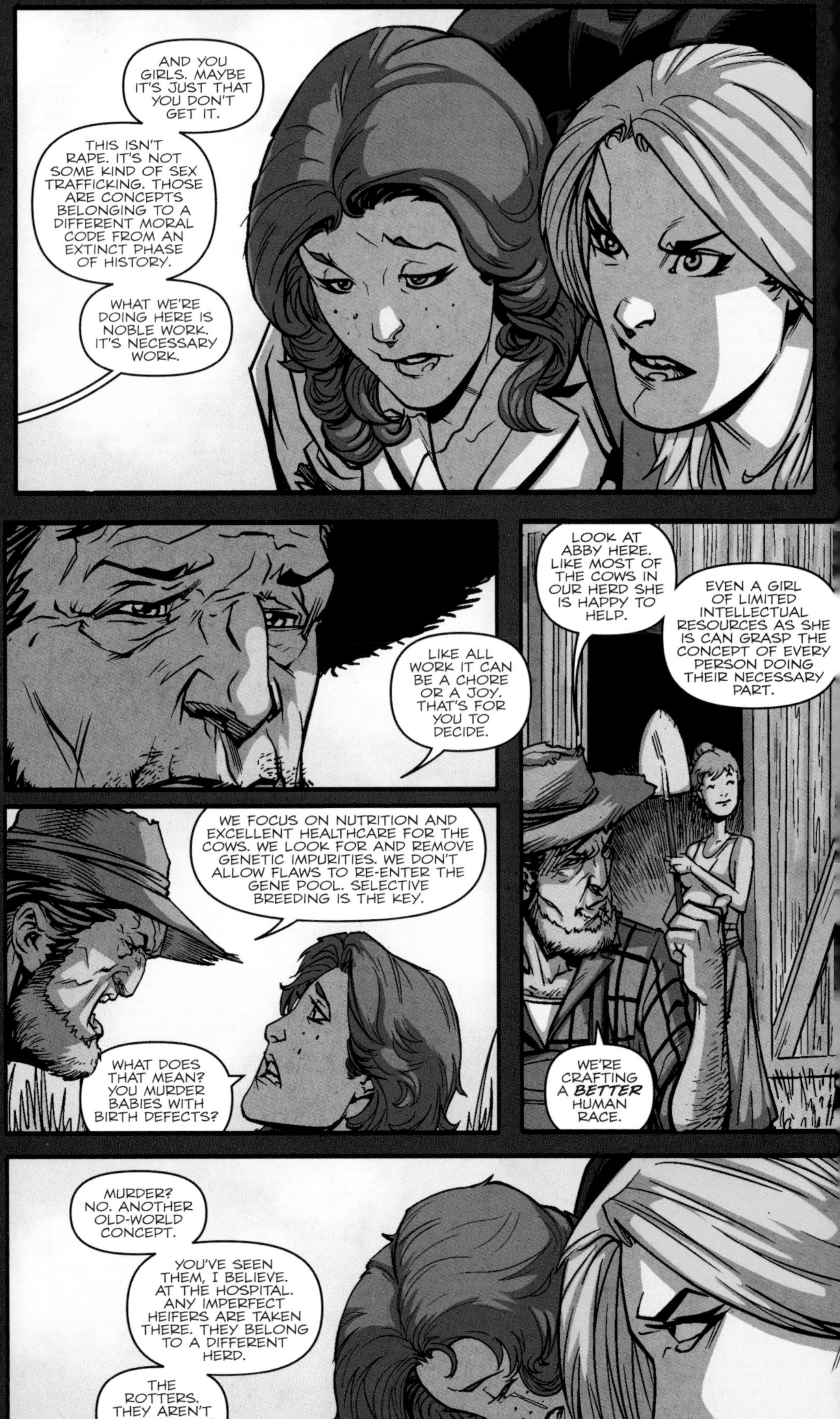
AND YOU GIRLS. MAYBE IT'S JUST THAT YOU DON'T GET IT.
THIS ISN'T RAPE. IT'S NOT SOME KIND OF SEX TRAFFICKING. THOSE ARE CONCEPTS BELONGING TO A DIFFERENT MORAL CODE FROM AN EXTINCT PHASE OF HISTORY.
WHAT WE'RE DOING HERE IS NOBLE WORK. IT'S NECESSARY WORK.
LIKE ALL WORK IT CAN BE A CHORE OR A JOY. THAT'S FOR YOU TO DECIDE.
LOOK AT ABBY HERE. LIKE MOST OF THE COWS IN OUR HERD SHE IS HAPPY TO HELP.
EVEN A GIRL OF LIMITED INTELLECTUAL RESOURCES AS SHE IS CAN GRASP THE CONCEPT OF EVERY PERSON DOING THEIR NECESSARY PART.
WE'RE CRAFTING A *BETTER* HUMAN RACE.
WE FOCUS ON NUTRITION AND EXCELLENT HEALTHCARE FOR THE COWS. WE LOOK FOR AND REMOVE GENETIC IMPURITIES. WE DON'T ALLOW FLAWS TO RE-ENTER THE GENE POOL. SELECTIVE BREEDING IS THE KEY.
WHAT DOES THAT MEAN? YOU MURDER BABIES WITH BIRTH DEFECTS?
MURDER? NO. ANOTHER OLD-WORLD CONCEPT.
YOU'VE SEEN THEM, I BELIEVE. AT THE HOSPITAL. ANY IMPERFECT HEIFERS ARE TAKEN THERE. THEY BELONG TO A DIFFERENT HERD.
THE ROTTERS. THEY AREN'T ANY PART OF OUR FUTURE.

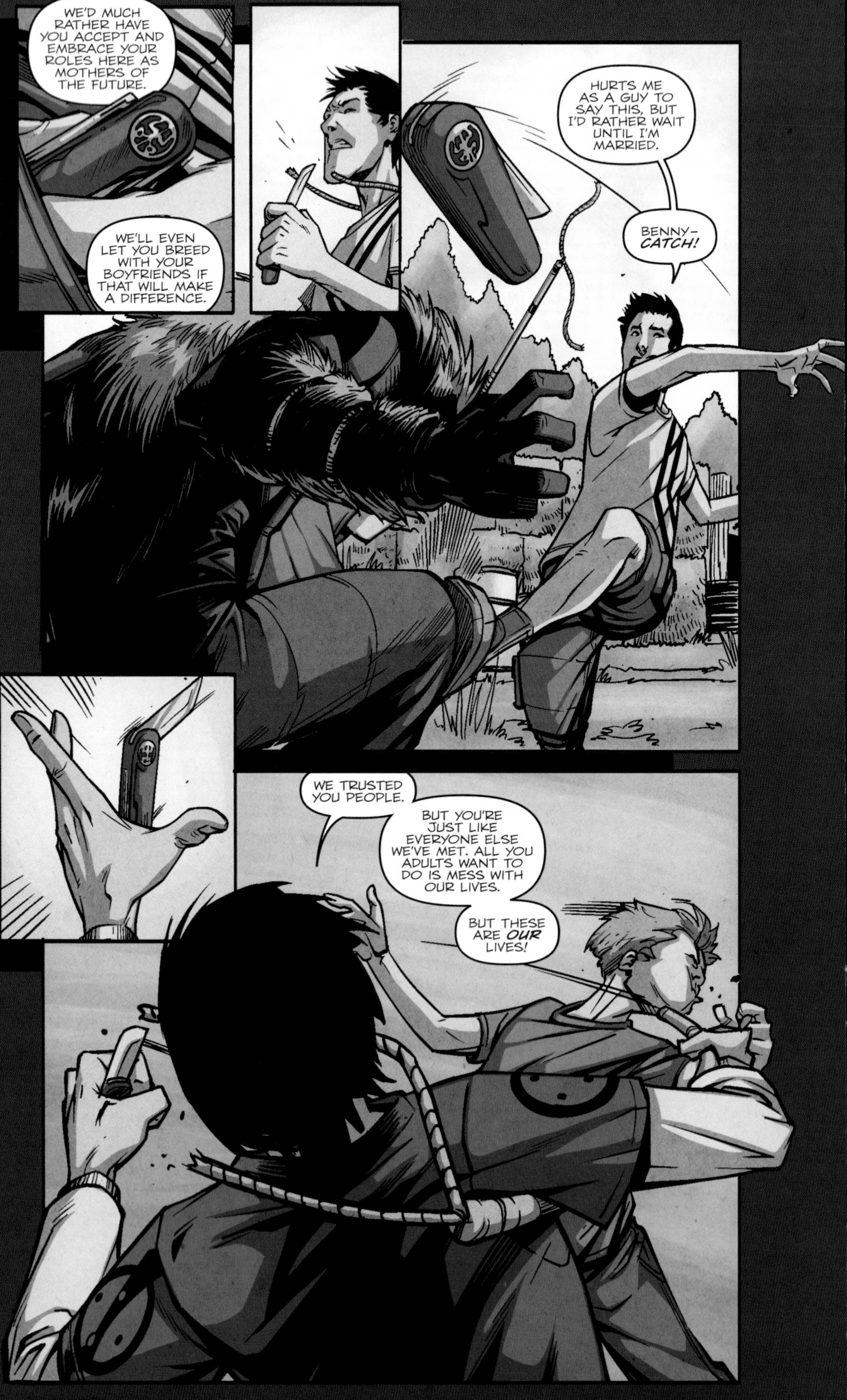

WE'D MUCH RATHER HAVE YOU ACCEPT AND EMBRACE YOUR ROLES HERE AS MOTHERS OF THE FUTURE.
WE'LL EVEN LET YOU BREED WITH YOUR BOYFRIENDS IF THAT WILL MAKE A DIFFERENCE.
HURTS ME AS A GUY TO SAY THIS, BUT I'D RATHER WAIT UNTIL I'M MARRIED.
BENNY— *CATCH!*
WE TRUSTED YOU PEOPLE.
BUT YOU'RE JUST LIKE EVERYONE ELSE WE'VE MET. ALL YOU ADULTS WANT TO DO IS MESS WITH OUR LIVES.
BUT THESE ARE ***OUR*** LIVES!

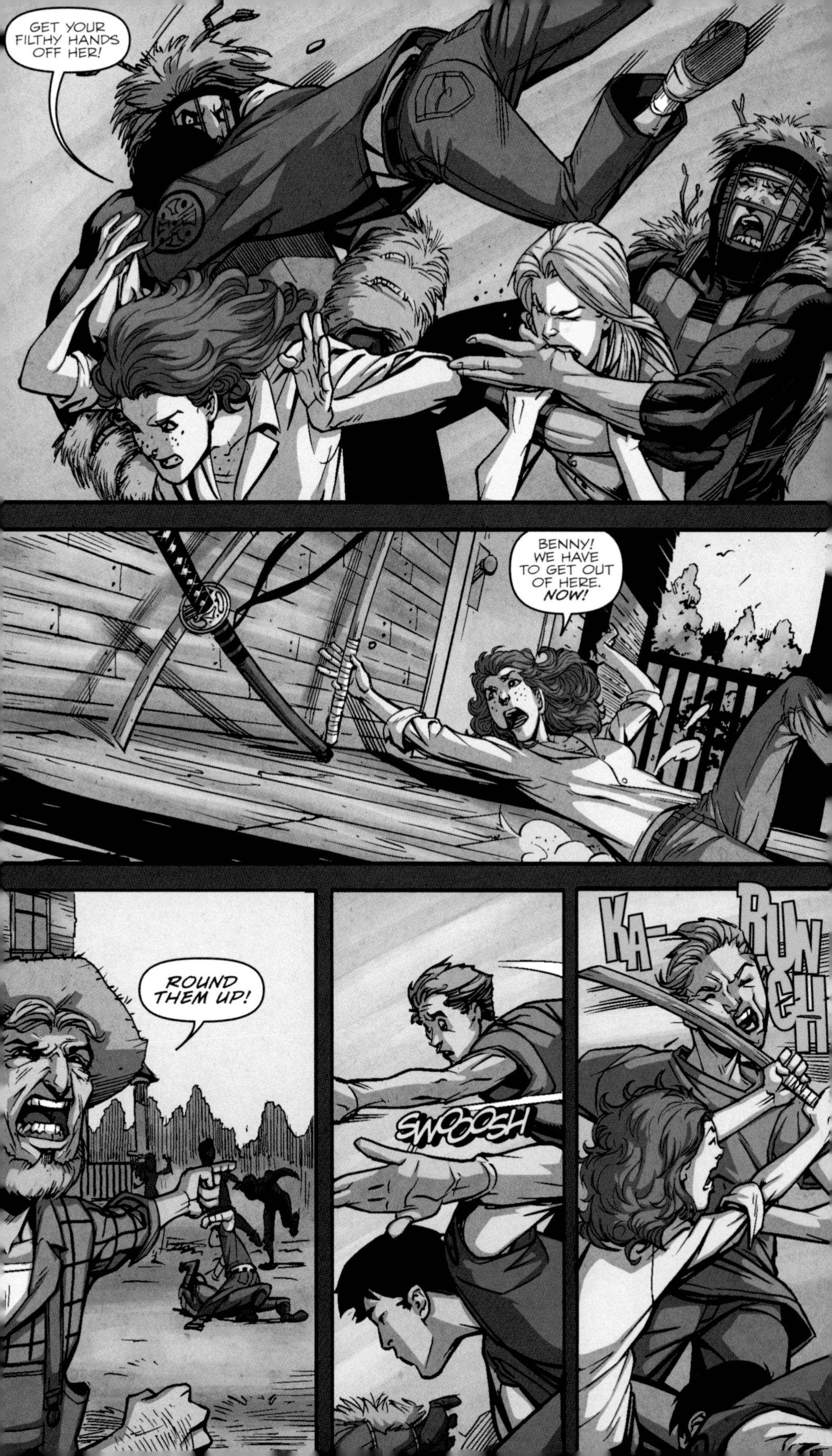
GET YOUR FILTHY HANDS OFF HER!
BENNY! WE HAVE TO GET OUT OF HERE. NOW!
ROUND THEM UP!
SWOOOSH
KA-RUNCH

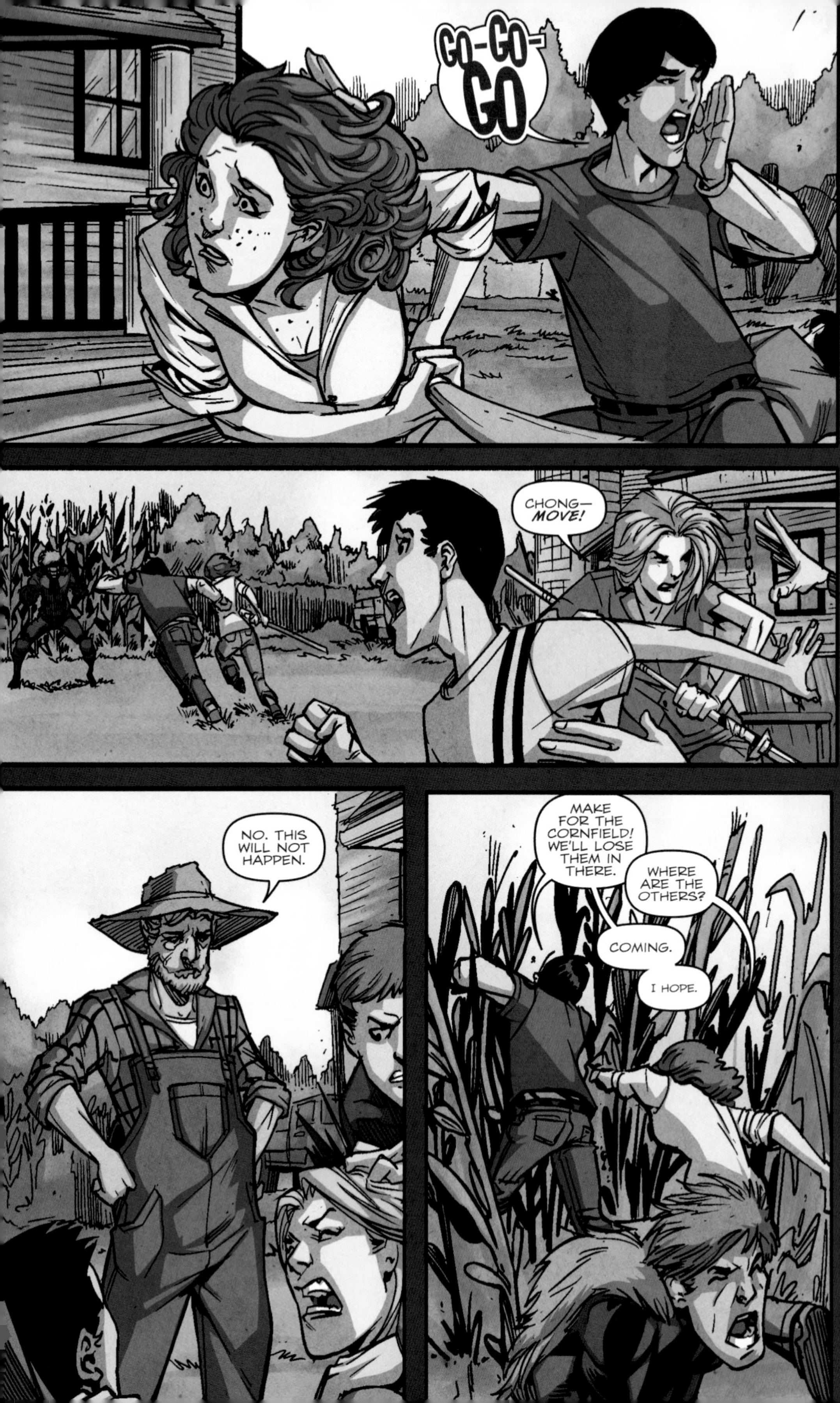
GO-GO-GO
CHONG— MOVE!
NO. THIS WILL NOT HAPPEN.
MAKE FOR THE CORNFIELD! WE'LL LOSE THEM IN THERE.
WHERE ARE THE OTHERS?
COMING.
I HOPE.

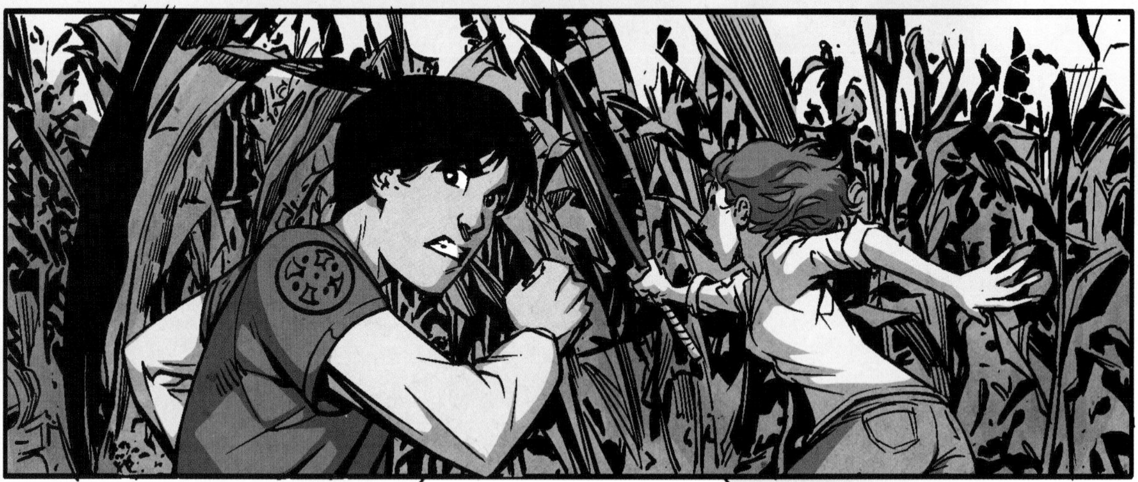

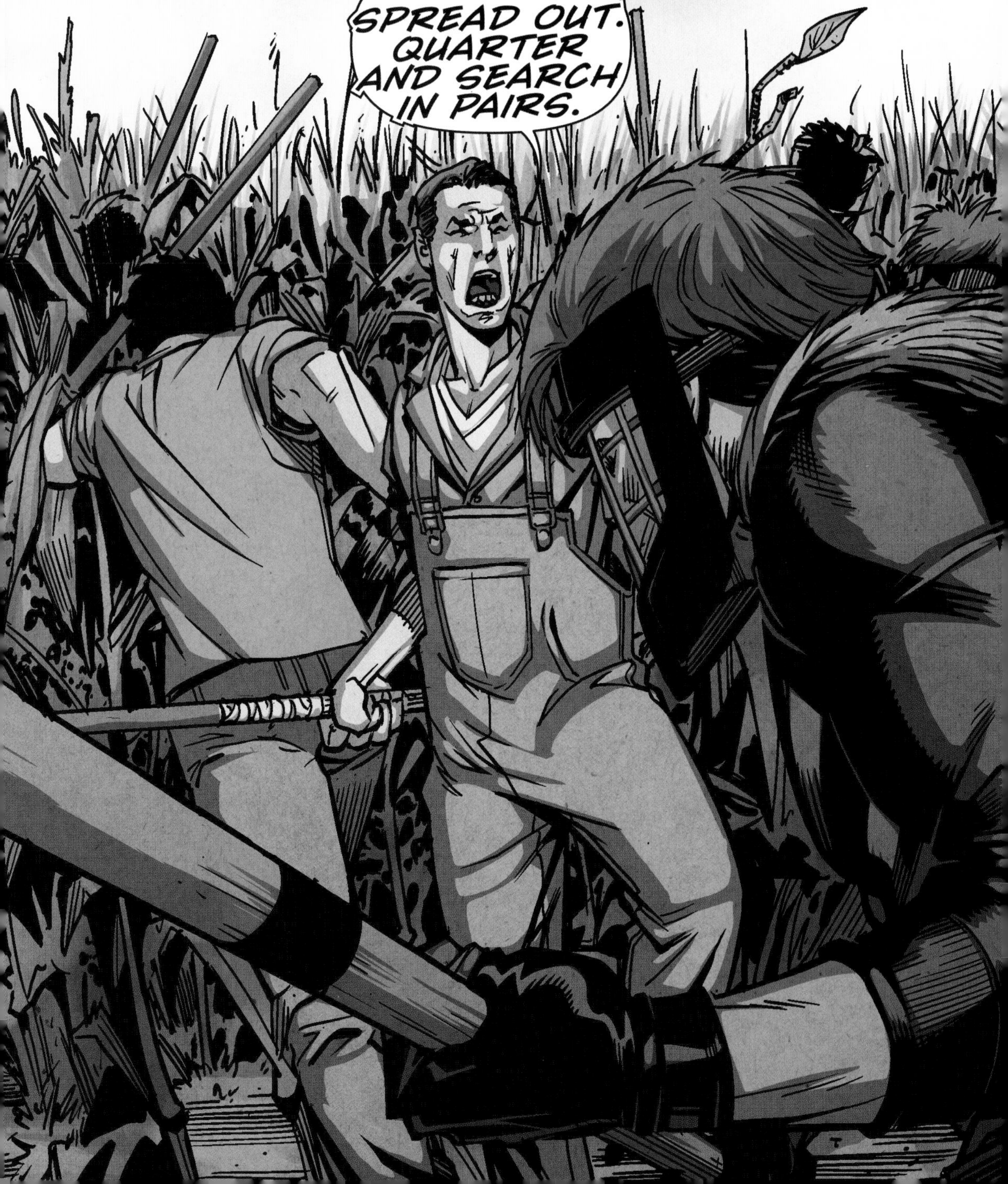
SPREAD OUT. QUARTER AND SEARCH IN PAIRS.

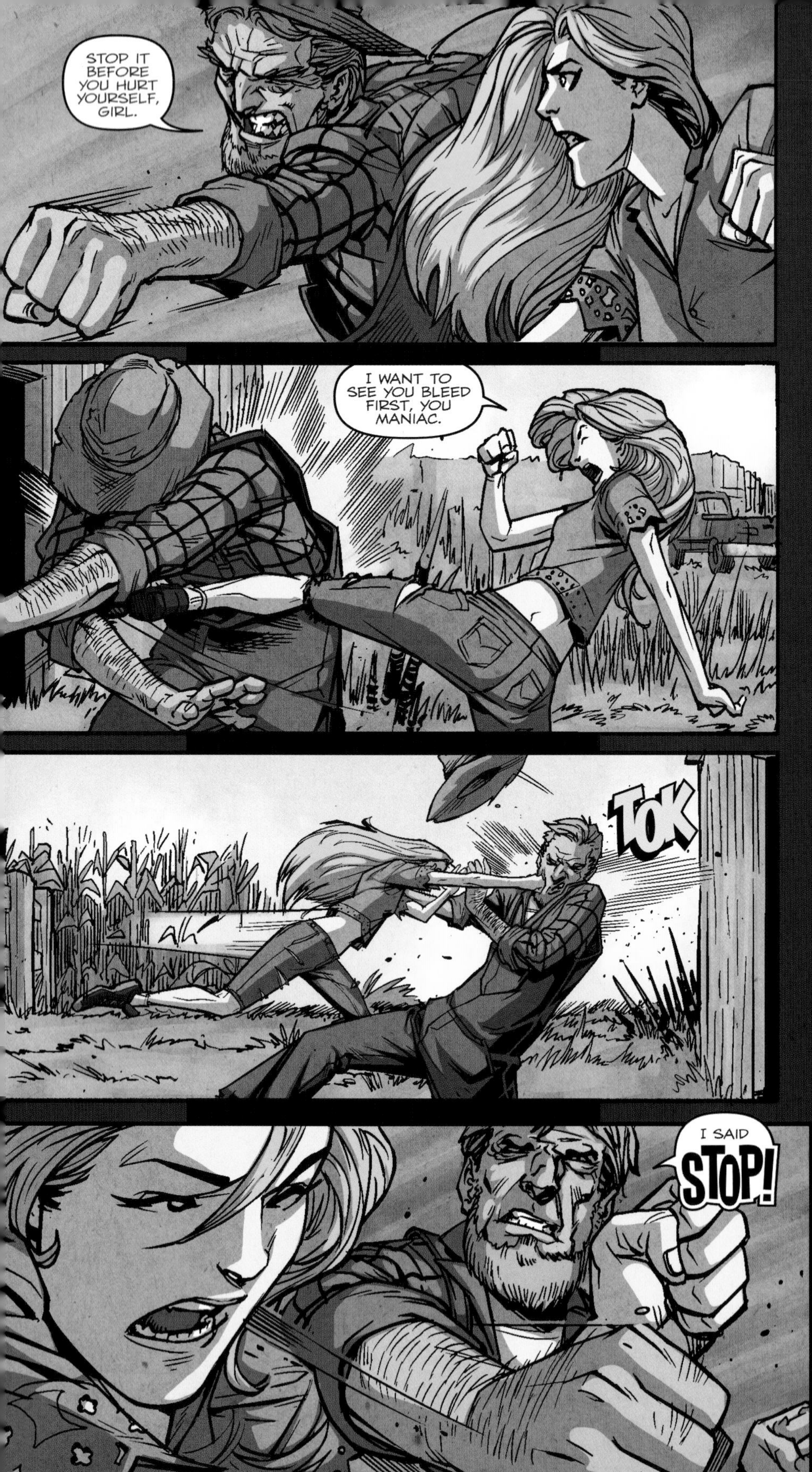
STOP IT BEFORE YOU HURT YOURSELF, GIRL.
I WANT TO SEE YOU BLEED FIRST, YOU MANIAC.
TOK
AH
I SAID STOP!

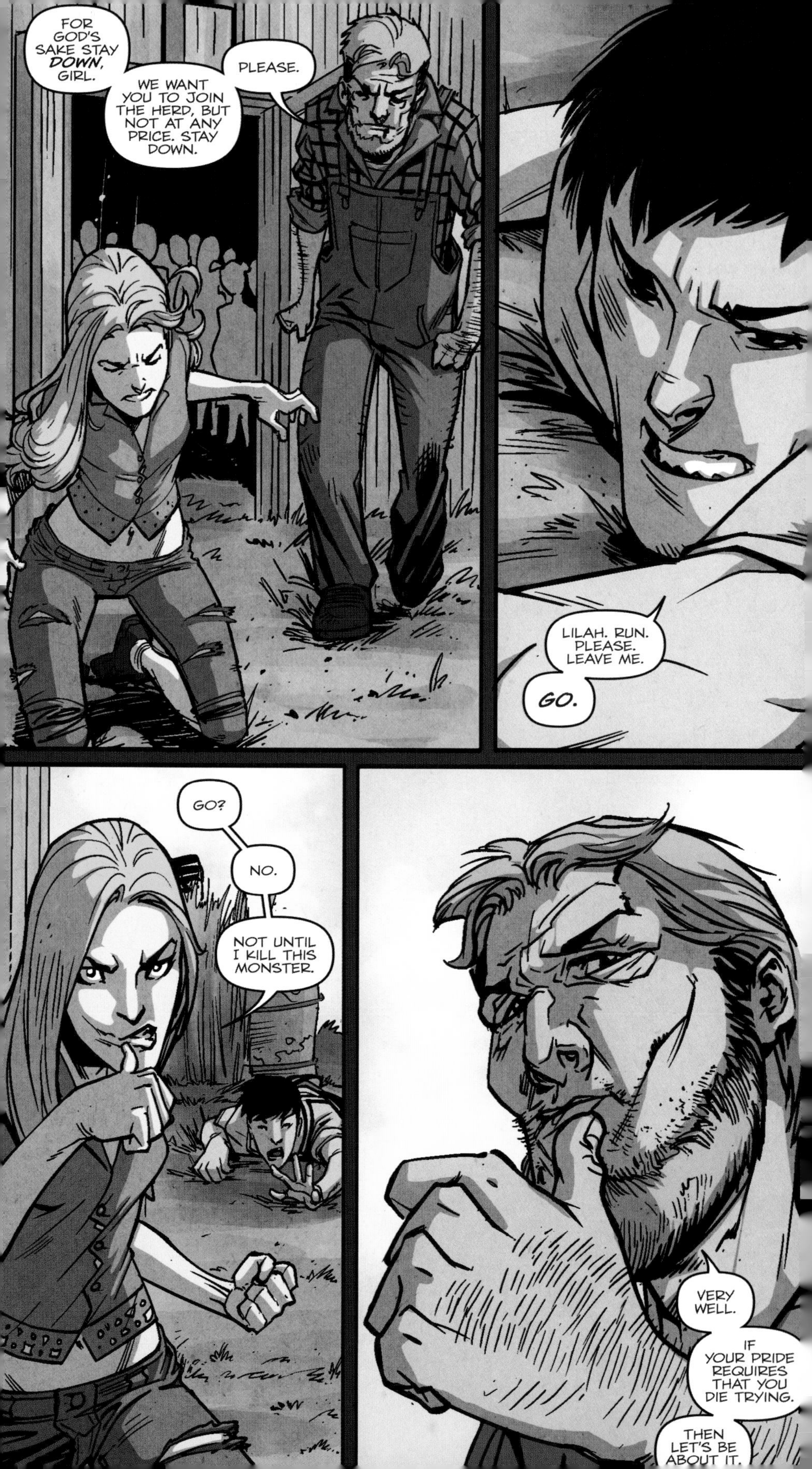
FOR GOD'S SAKE STAY DOWN, GIRL.
WE WANT YOU TO JOIN THE HERD, BUT NOT AT ANY PRICE. STAY DOWN.
PLEASE.
LILAH. RUN. PLEASE. LEAVE ME.
GO.
GO?
NO.
NOT UNTIL I KILL THIS MONSTER.
VERY WELL.
IF YOUR PRIDE REQUIRES THAT YOU DIE TRYING.
THEN LET'S BE ABOUT IT.

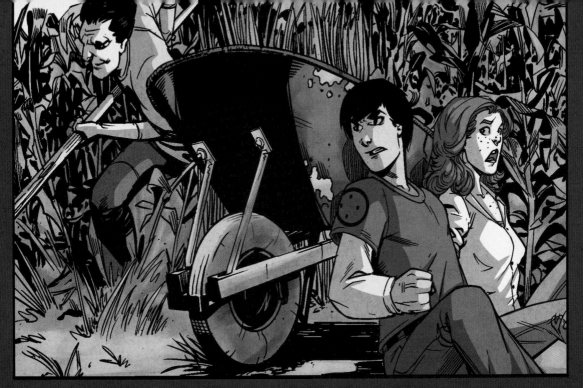

THE FENCE IS CLOSE TO HERE.

WE CAN GET THROUGH IT AND HIDE AND THEN COME BACK LATER TO HELP THE OTHERS.

WHAT IF THERE ISN'T TIME? GOD KNOWS WHAT THEY'RE DOING TO THEM IN THERE.

NOT MY SWORD BUT IT'LL DO.

SHHH— SOMEONE'S COMING

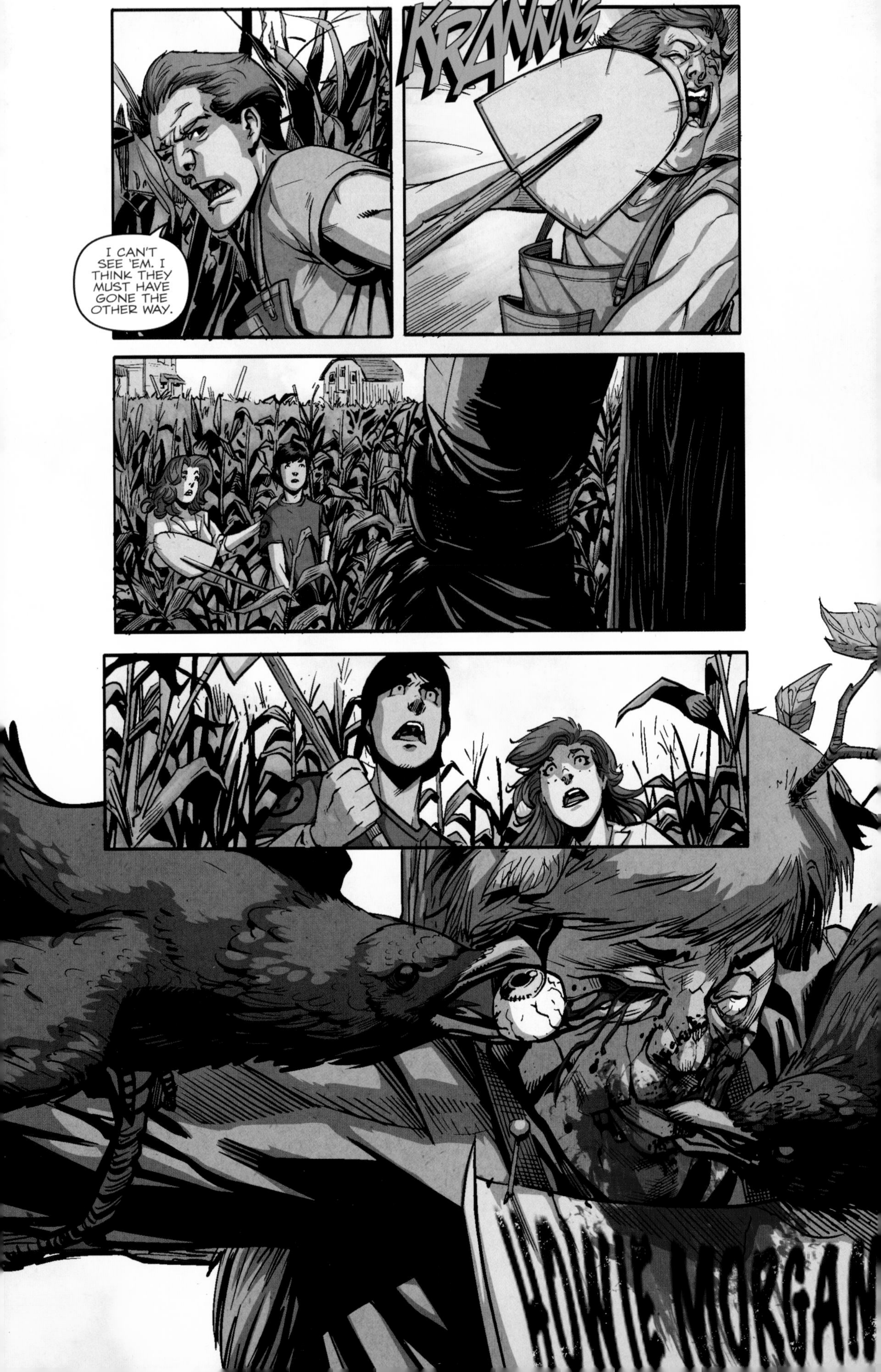
I CAN'T SEE 'EM. I THINK THEY MUST HAVE GONE THE OTHER WAY.
KRANNNG
HOWIE MORGAN

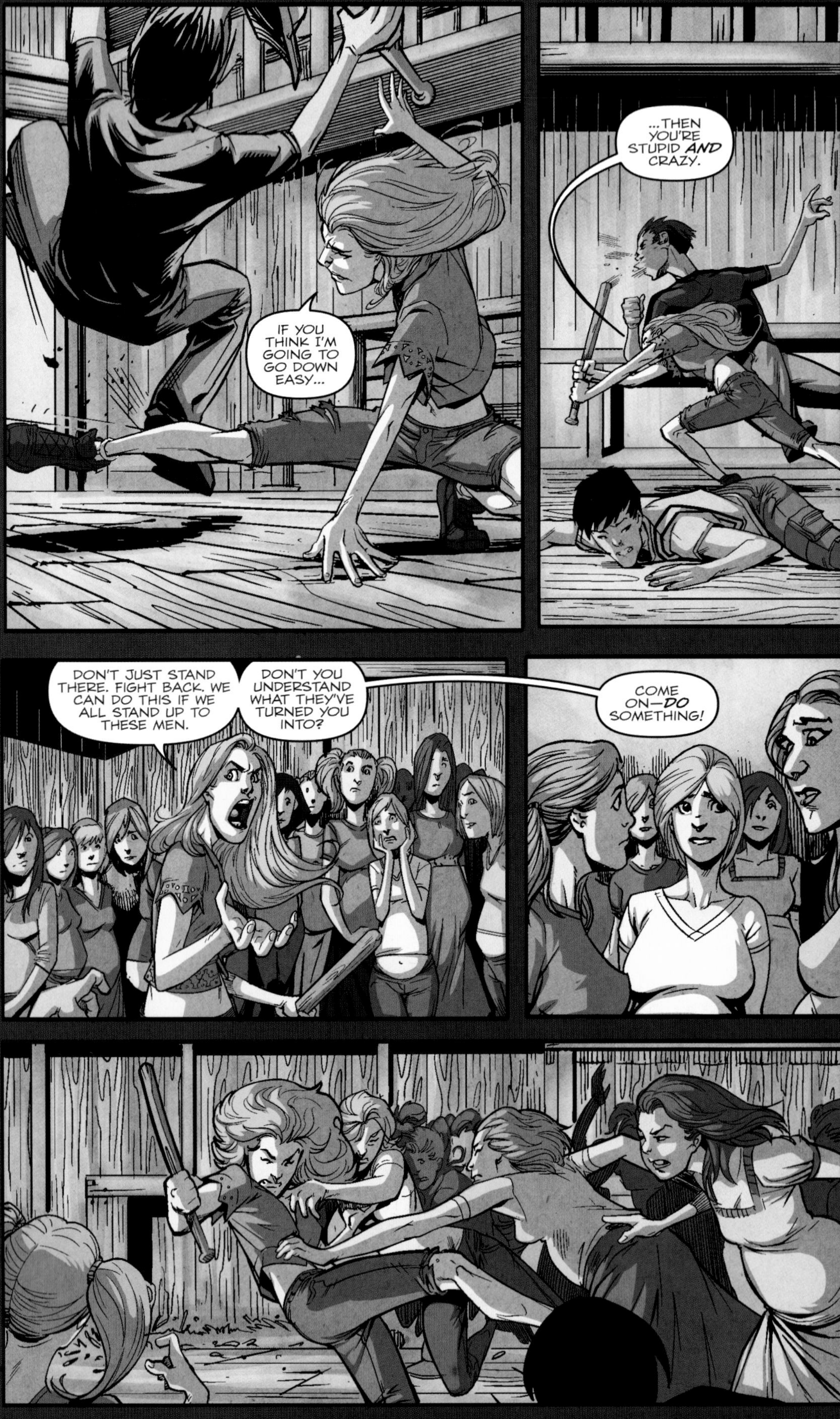
IF YOU THINK I'M GOING TO GO DOWN EASY...
...THEN YOU'RE STUPID AND CRAZY.
DON'T JUST STAND THERE. FIGHT BACK. WE CAN DO THIS IF WE ALL STAND UP TO THESE MEN.
DON'T YOU UNDERSTAND WHAT THEY'VE TURNED YOU INTO?
COME ON—DO SOMETHING!

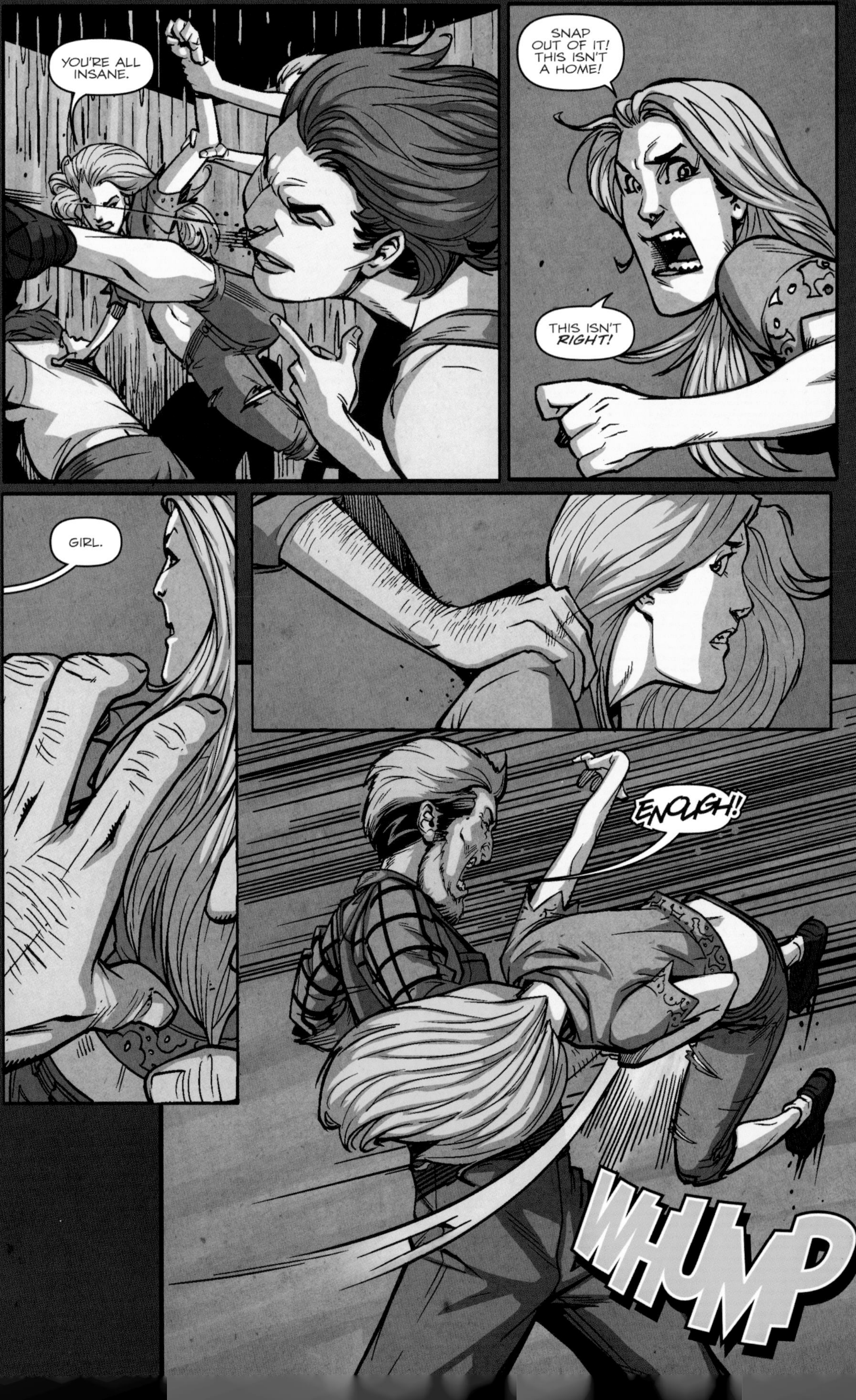
YOU'RE ALL INSANE.
SNAP OUT OF IT! THIS ISN'T A HOME!
THIS ISN'T *RIGHT!*
GIRL.
ENOUGH!
WHUMP

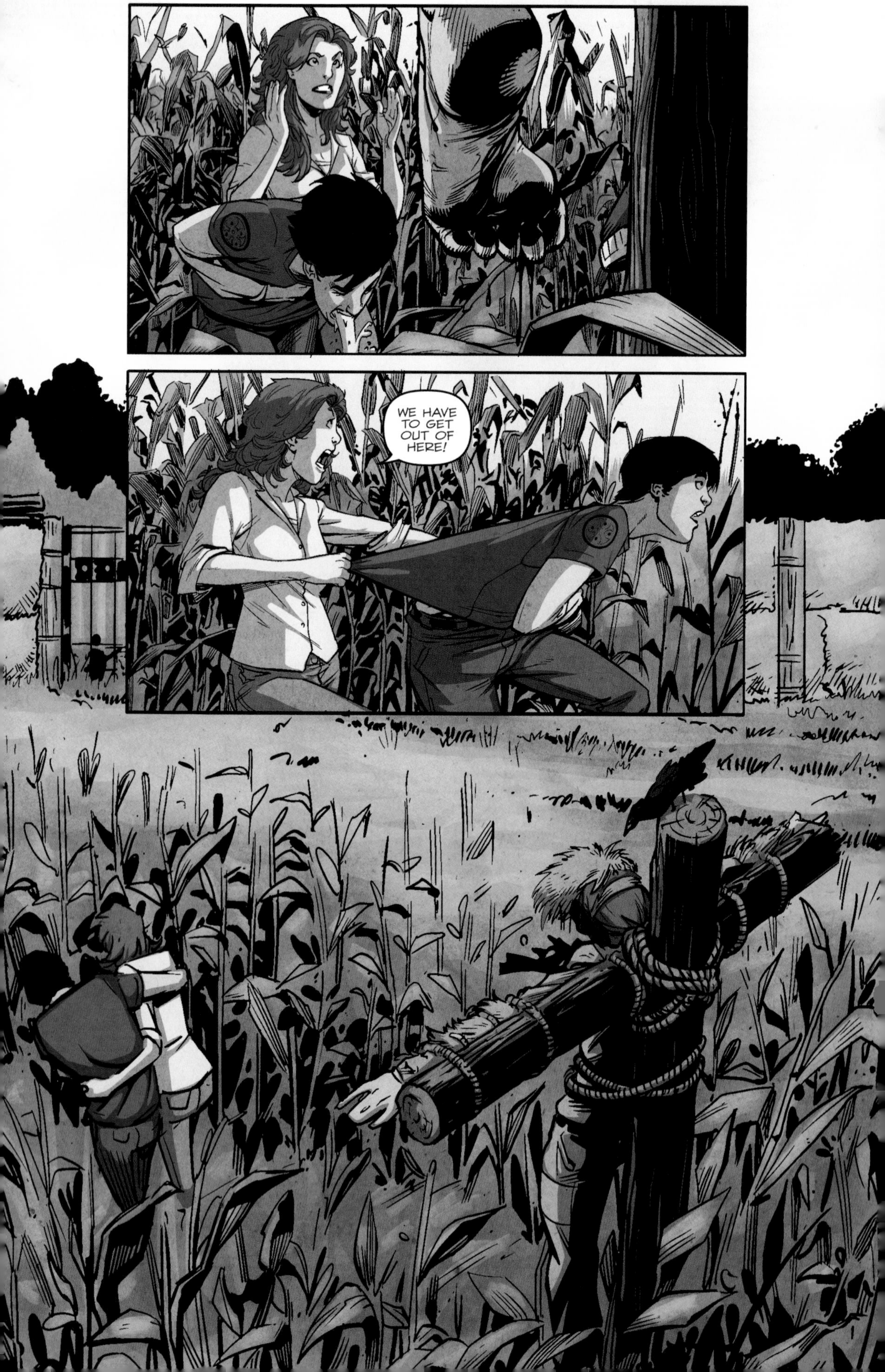
WE HAVE TO GET OUT OF HERE!

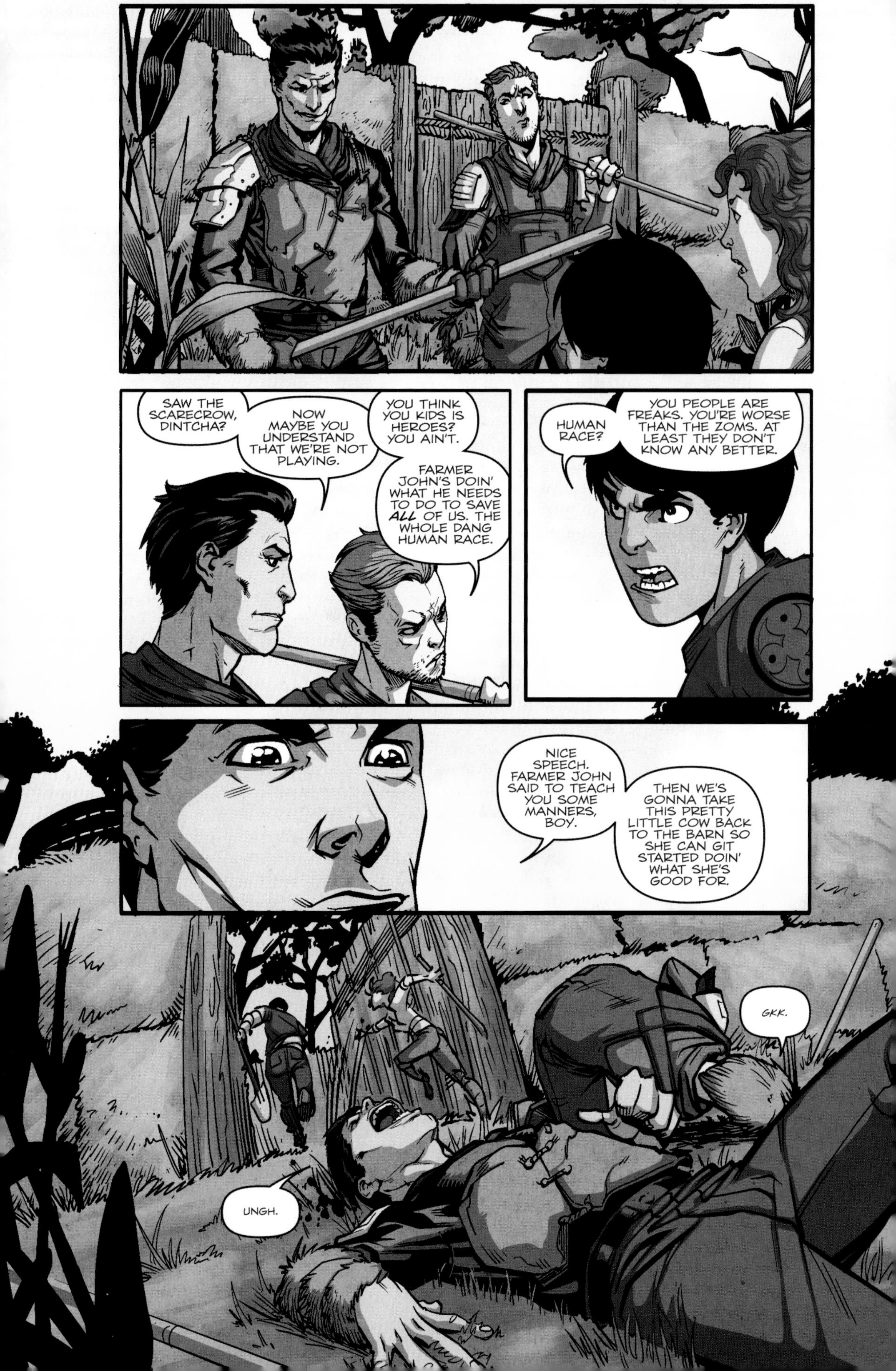
SAW THE SCARECROW, DINTCHA?
NOW MAYBE YOU UNDERSTAND THAT WE'RE NOT PLAYING.
YOU THINK YOU KIDS IS HEROES? YOU AIN'T.
FARMER JOHN'S DOIN' WHAT HE NEEDS TO DO TO SAVE ALL OF US. THE WHOLE DANG HUMAN RACE.
HUMAN RACE?
YOU PEOPLE ARE FREAKS. YOU'RE WORSE THAN THE ZOMS. AT LEAST THEY DON'T KNOW ANY BETTER.
NICE SPEECH. FARMER JOHN SAID TO TEACH YOU SOME MANNERS, BOY.
THEN WE'S GONNA TAKE THIS PRETTY LITTLE COW BACK TO THE BARN SO SHE CAN GIT STARTED DOIN' WHAT SHE'S GOOD FOR.
GKK.
UNGH.

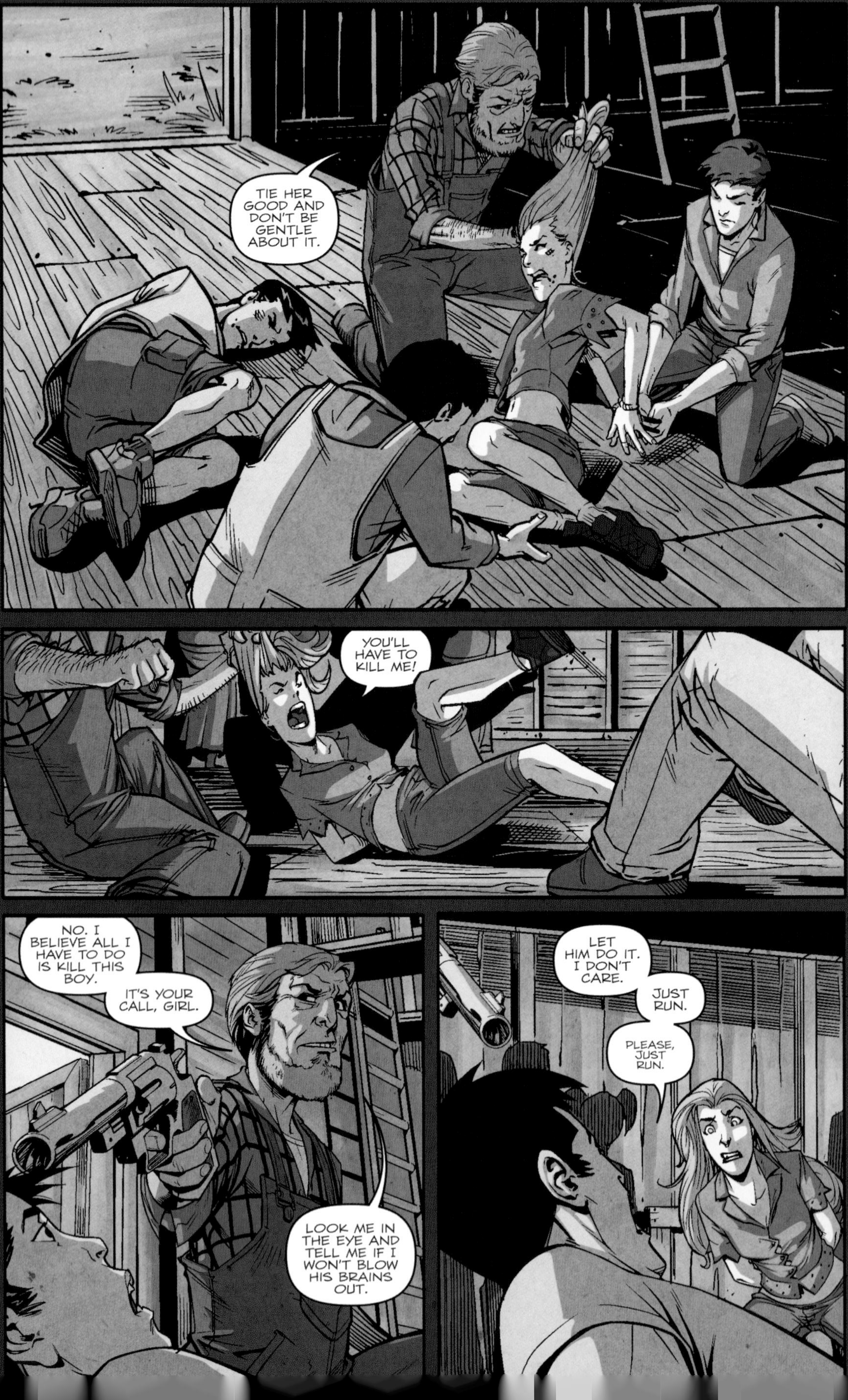
TIE HER GOOD AND DON'T BE GENTLE ABOUT IT.
YOU'LL HAVE TO KILL ME!
NO. I BELIEVE ALL I HAVE TO DO IS KILL THIS BOY.
IT'S YOUR CALL, GIRL.
LOOK ME IN THE EYE AND TELL ME IF I WON'T BLOW HIS BRAINS OUT.
LET HIM DO IT. I DON'T CARE.
JUST RUN.
PLEASE, JUST RUN.

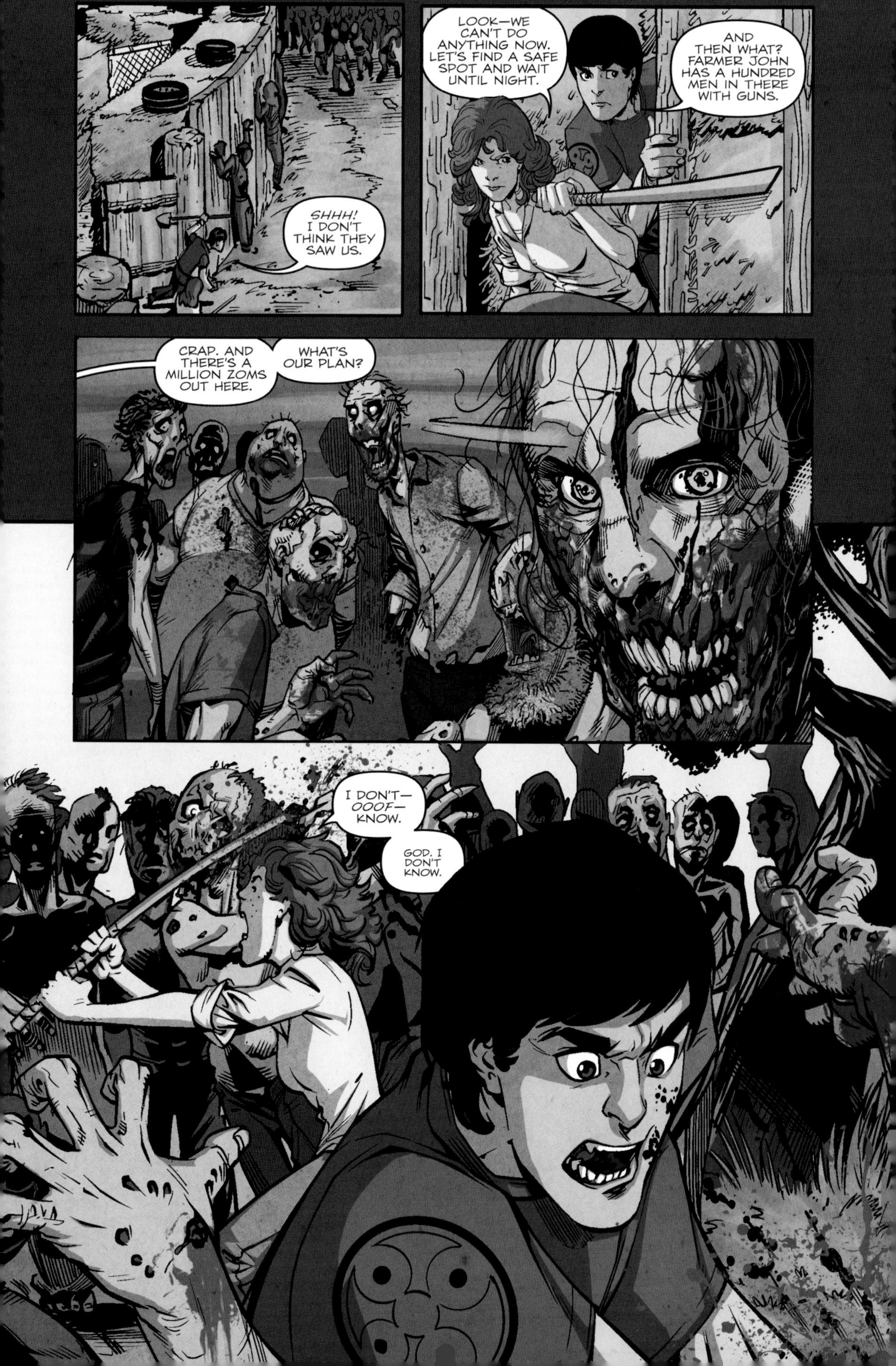
SHHH! I DON'T THINK THEY SAW US.
LOOK—WE CAN'T DO ANYTHING NOW. LET'S FIND A SAFE SPOT AND WAIT UNTIL NIGHT.
AND THEN WHAT? FARMER JOHN HAS A HUNDRED MEN IN THERE WITH GUNS.
CRAP. AND THERE'S A MILLION ZOMS OUT HERE.
WHAT'S OUR PLAN?
I DON'T— OOOF— KNOW.
GOD. I DON'T KNOW.

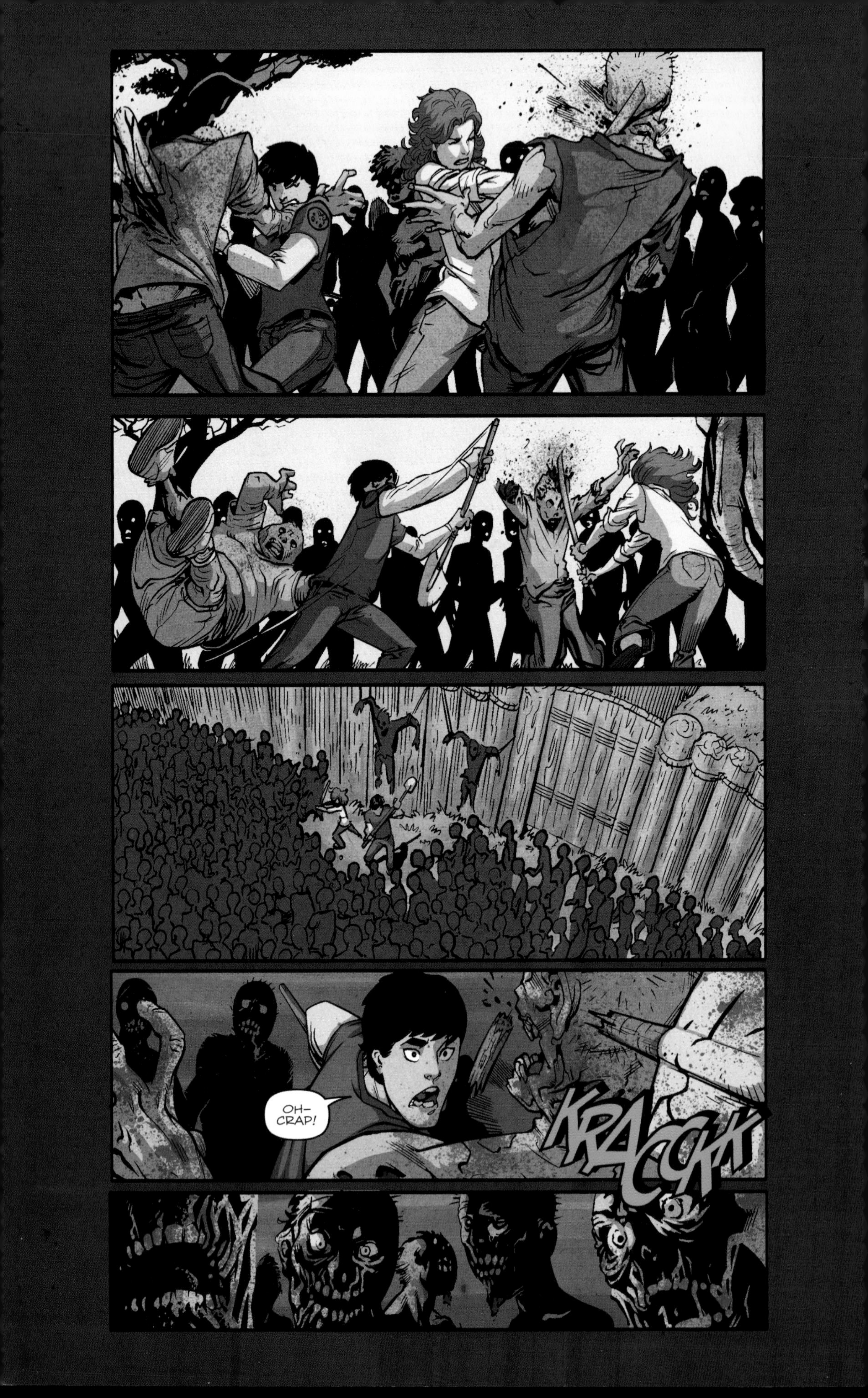
OH-CRAP!
KRACGKK

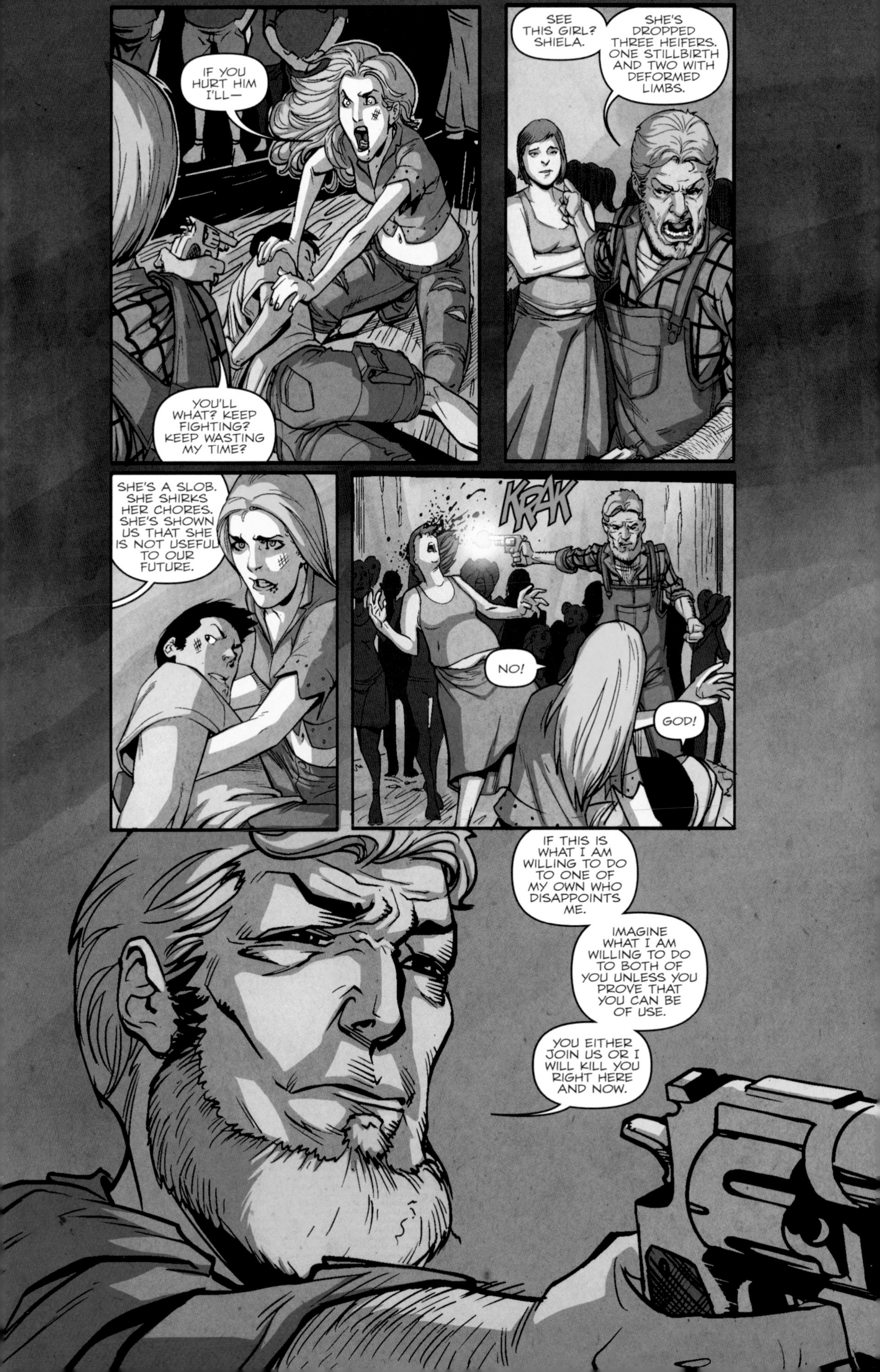
IF YOU HURT HIM I'LL—
YOU'LL WHAT? KEEP FIGHTING? KEEP WASTING MY TIME?
SEE THIS GIRL? SHIELA.
SHE'S DROPPED THREE HEIFERS. ONE STILLBIRTH AND TWO WITH DEFORMED LIMBS.
SHE'S A SLOB. SHE SHIRKS HER CHORES. SHE'S SHOWN US THAT SHE IS NOT USEFUL TO OUR FUTURE.
KRAK
NO!
GOD!
IF THIS IS WHAT I AM WILLING TO DO TO ONE OF MY OWN WHO DISAPPOINTS ME.
IMAGINE WHAT I AM WILLING TO DO TO BOTH OF YOU UNLESS YOU PROVE THAT YOU CAN BE OF USE.
YOU EITHER JOIN US OR I WILL KILL YOU RIGHT HERE AND NOW.

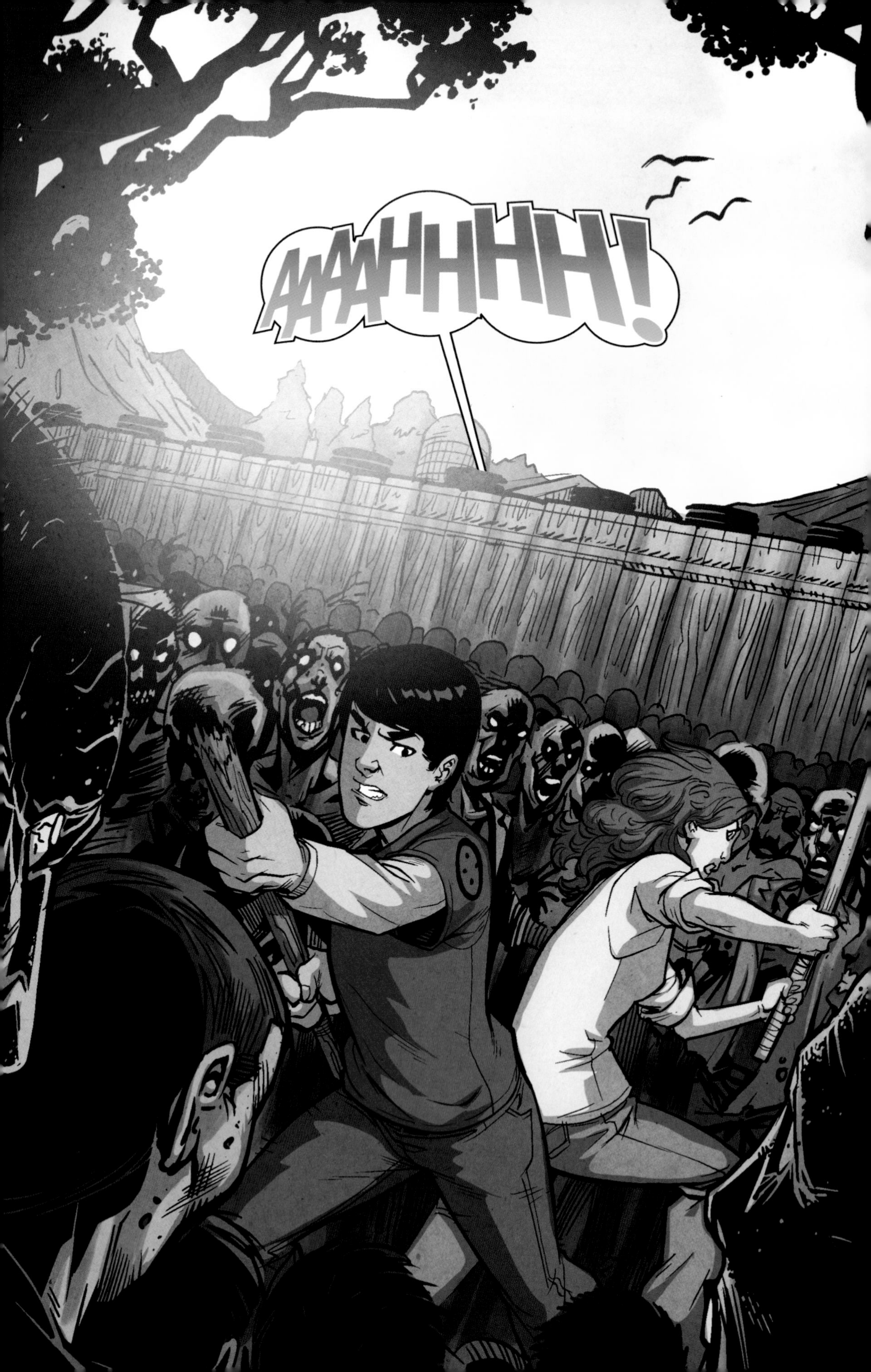
AAAAHHHHH!

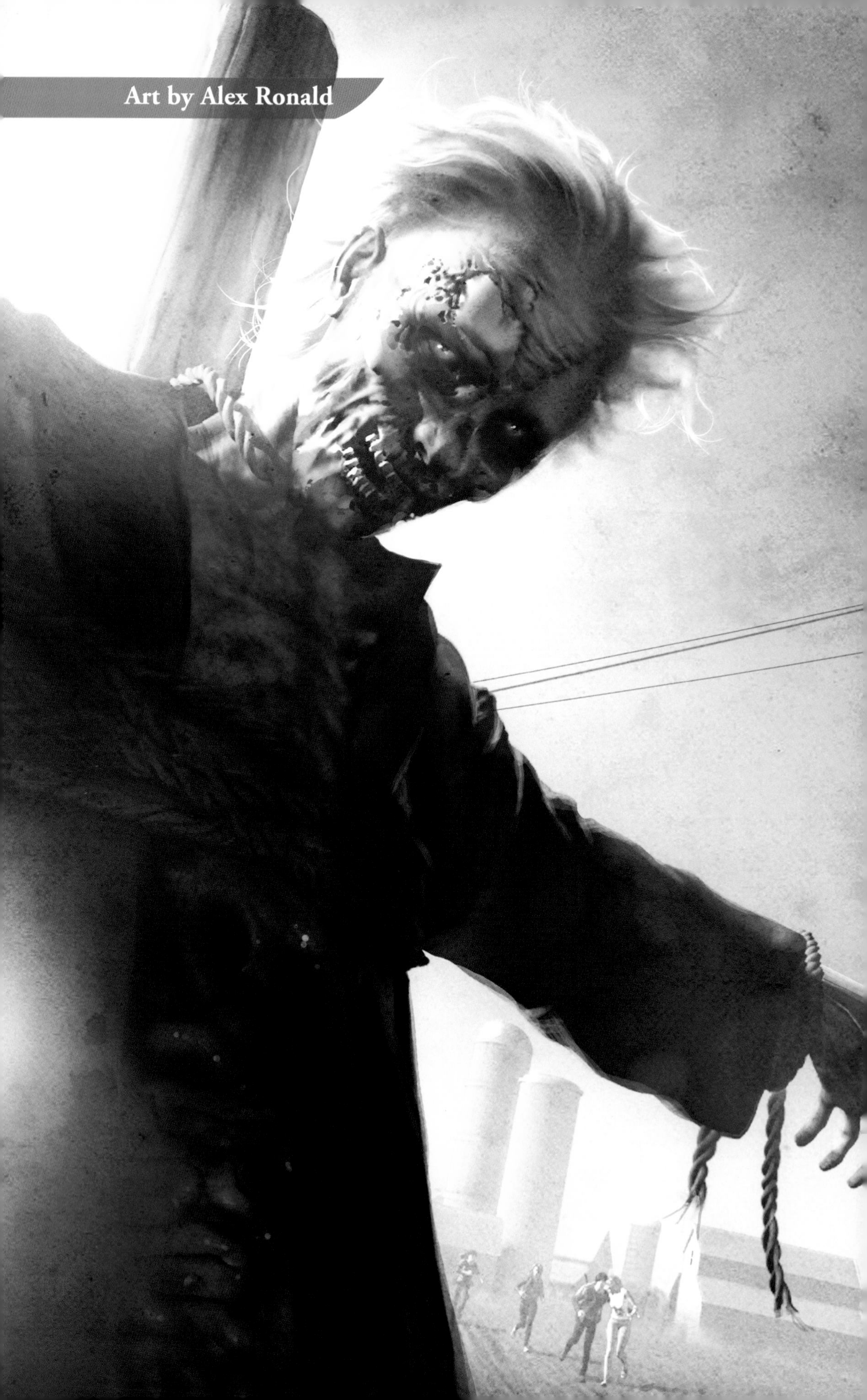
Art by Alex Ronald

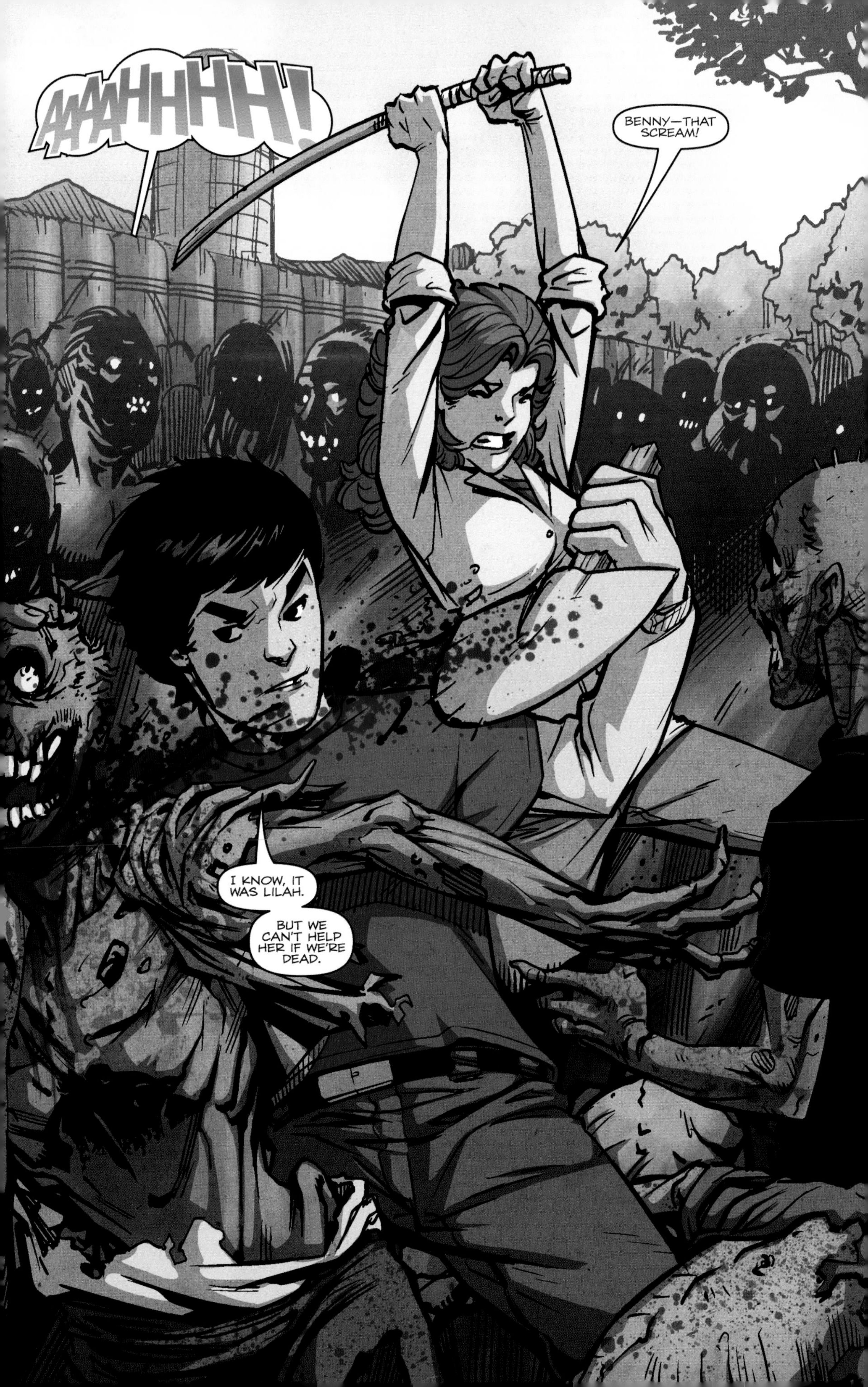
AAAAHHHHH!
BENNY—THAT SCREAM!
I KNOW, IT WAS LILAH.
BUT WE CAN'T HELP HER IF WE'RE DEAD.

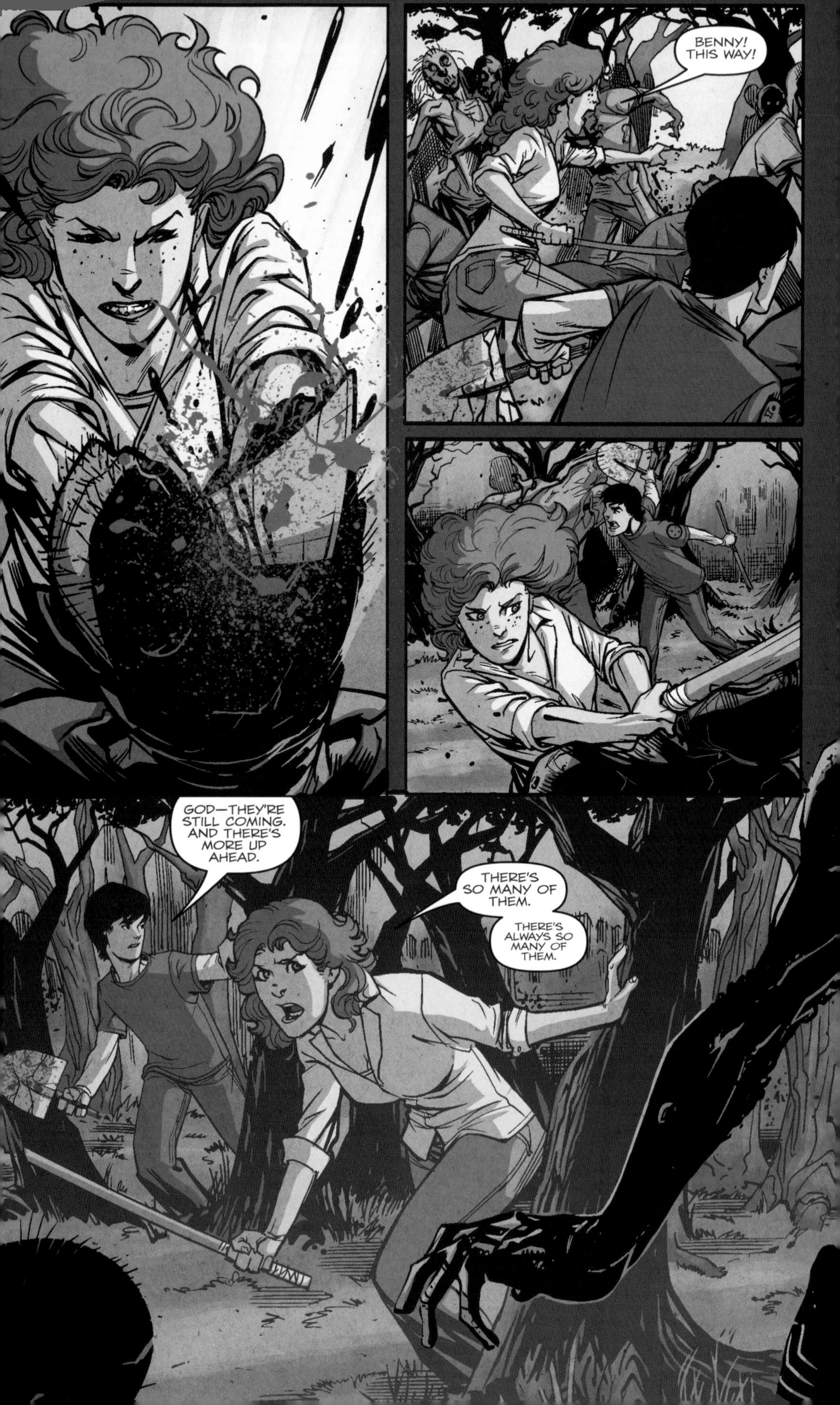
BENNY! THIS WAY!
GOD—THEY'RE STILL COMING. AND THERE'S MORE UP AHEAD.
THERE'S SO MANY OF THEM.
THERE'S ALWAYS SO MANY OF THEM.

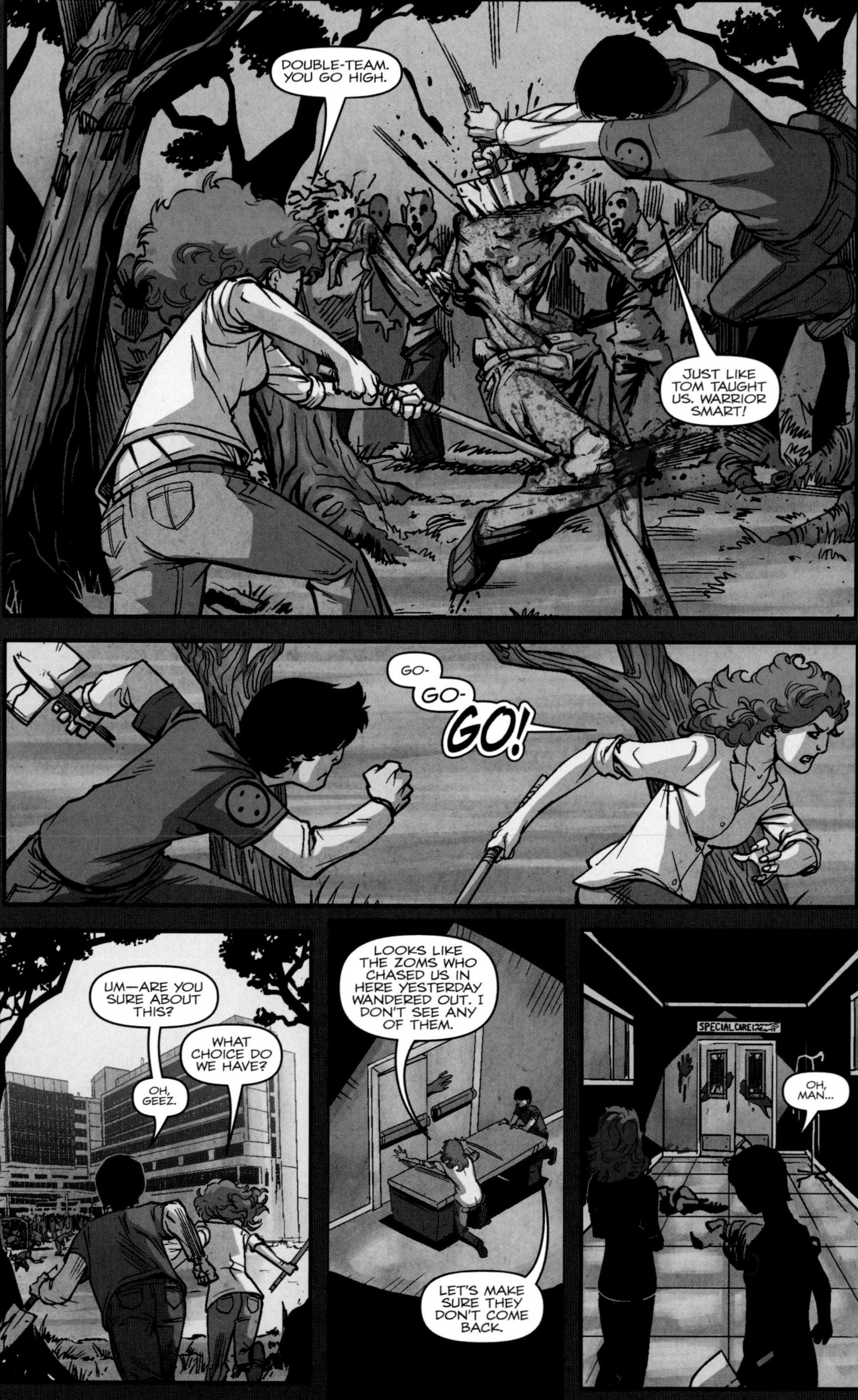
DOUBLE-TEAM. YOU GO HIGH.
JUST LIKE TOM TAUGHT US. WARRIOR SMART!
GO-
GO-
GO!
UM—ARE YOU SURE ABOUT THIS?
WHAT CHOICE DO WE HAVE?
OH, GEEZ.
LOOKS LIKE THE ZOMS WHO CHASED US IN HERE YESTERDAY WANDERED OUT. I DON'T SEE ANY OF THEM.
LET'S MAKE SURE THEY DON'T COME BACK.
SPECIAL CARE
OH, MAN...

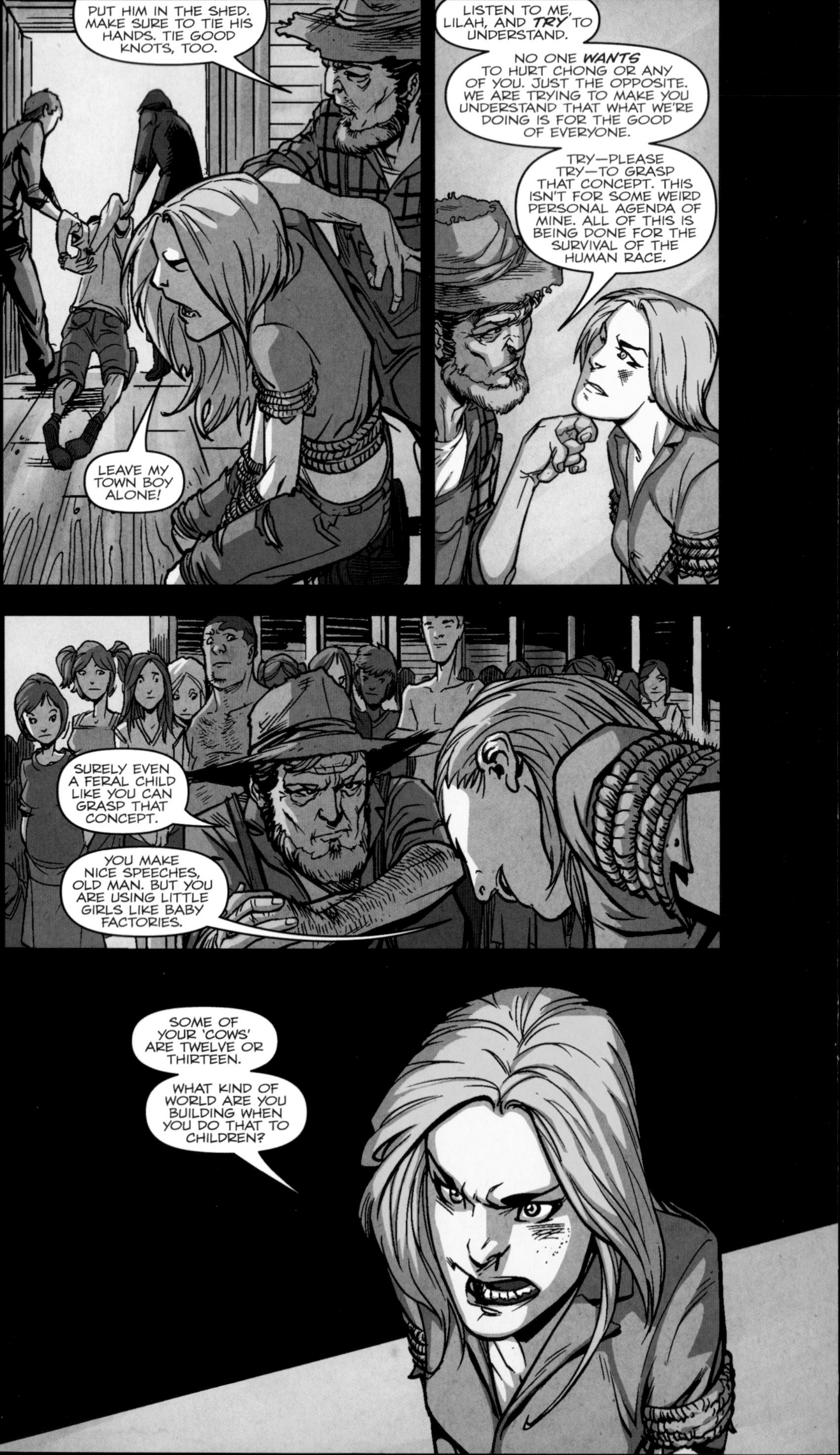

PUT HIM IN THE SHED. MAKE SURE TO TIE HIS HANDS. TIE GOOD KNOTS, TOO.
LEAVE MY TOWN BOY ALONE!
LISTEN TO ME, LILAH, AND *TRY* TO UNDERSTAND.
NO ONE *WANTS* TO HURT CHONG OR ANY OF YOU. JUST THE OPPOSITE. WE ARE TRYING TO MAKE YOU UNDERSTAND THAT WHAT WE'RE DOING IS FOR THE GOOD OF EVERYONE.
TRY—PLEASE TRY—TO GRASP THAT CONCEPT. THIS ISN'T FOR SOME WEIRD PERSONAL AGENDA OF MINE. ALL OF THIS IS BEING DONE FOR THE SURVIVAL OF THE HUMAN RACE.
SURELY EVEN A FERAL CHILD LIKE YOU CAN GRASP THAT CONCEPT.
YOU MAKE NICE SPEECHES, OLD MAN. BUT YOU ARE USING LITTLE GIRLS LIKE BABY FACTORIES.
SOME OF YOUR 'COWS' ARE TWELVE OR THIRTEEN.
WHAT KIND OF WORLD ARE YOU BUILDING WHEN YOU DO THAT TO CHILDREN?

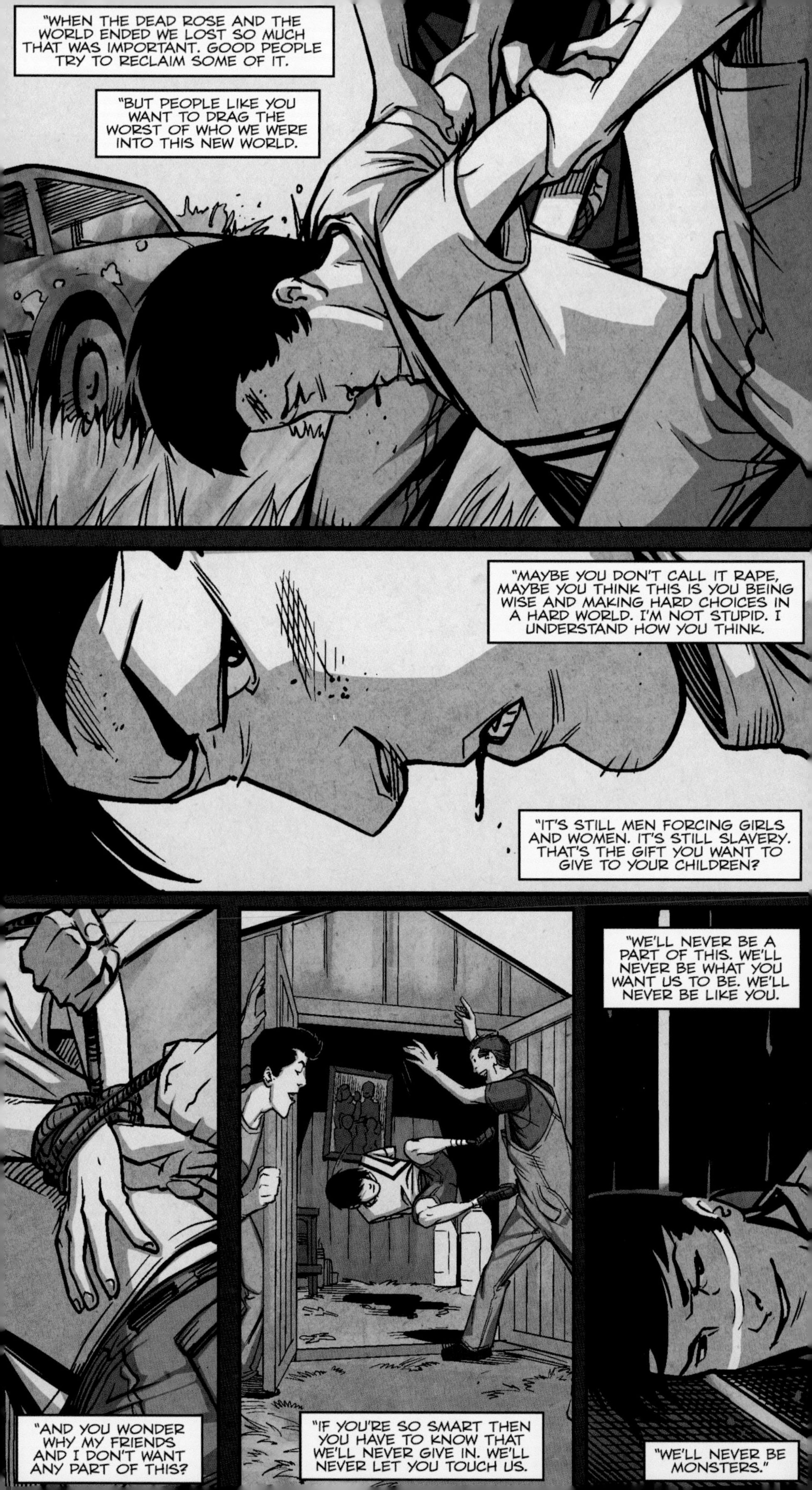
"WHEN THE DEAD ROSE AND THE WORLD ENDED WE LOST SO MUCH THAT WAS IMPORTANT. GOOD PEOPLE TRY TO RECLAIM SOME OF IT.
"BUT PEOPLE LIKE YOU WANT TO DRAG THE WORST OF WHO WE WERE INTO THIS NEW WORLD.
"MAYBE YOU DON'T CALL IT RAPE, MAYBE YOU THINK THIS IS YOU BEING WISE AND MAKING HARD CHOICES IN A HARD WORLD. I'M NOT STUPID. I UNDERSTAND HOW YOU THINK.
"IT'S STILL MEN FORCING GIRLS AND WOMEN. IT'S STILL SLAVERY. THAT'S THE GIFT YOU WANT TO GIVE TO YOUR CHILDREN?
"AND YOU WONDER WHY MY FRIENDS AND I DON'T WANT ANY PART OF THIS?
"IF YOU'RE SO SMART THEN YOU HAVE TO KNOW THAT WE'LL NEVER GIVE IN. WE'LL NEVER LET YOU TOUCH US.
"WE'LL NEVER BE A PART OF THIS. WE'LL NEVER BE WHAT YOU WANT US TO BE. WE'LL NEVER BE LIKE YOU.
"WE'LL NEVER BE MONSTERS."

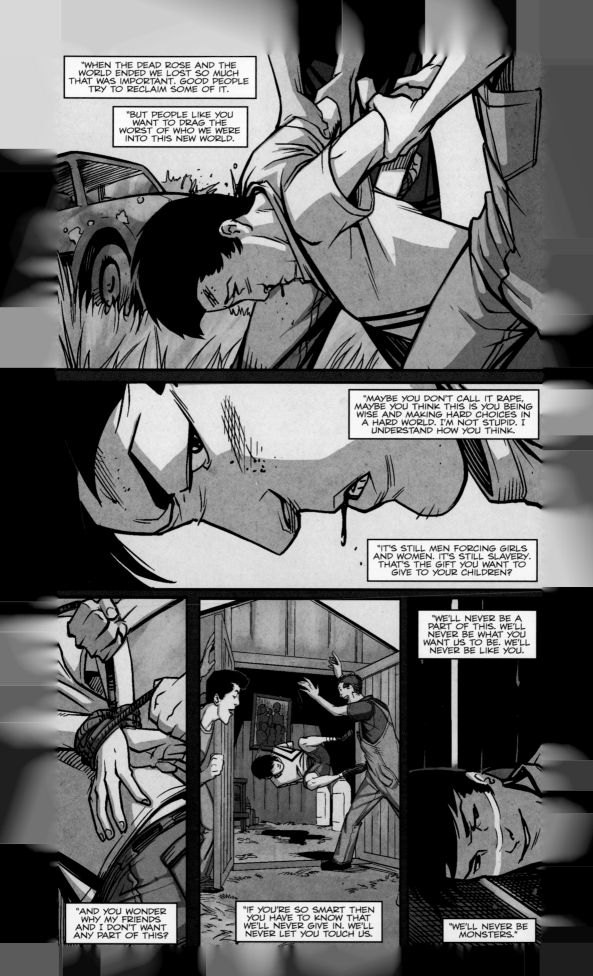

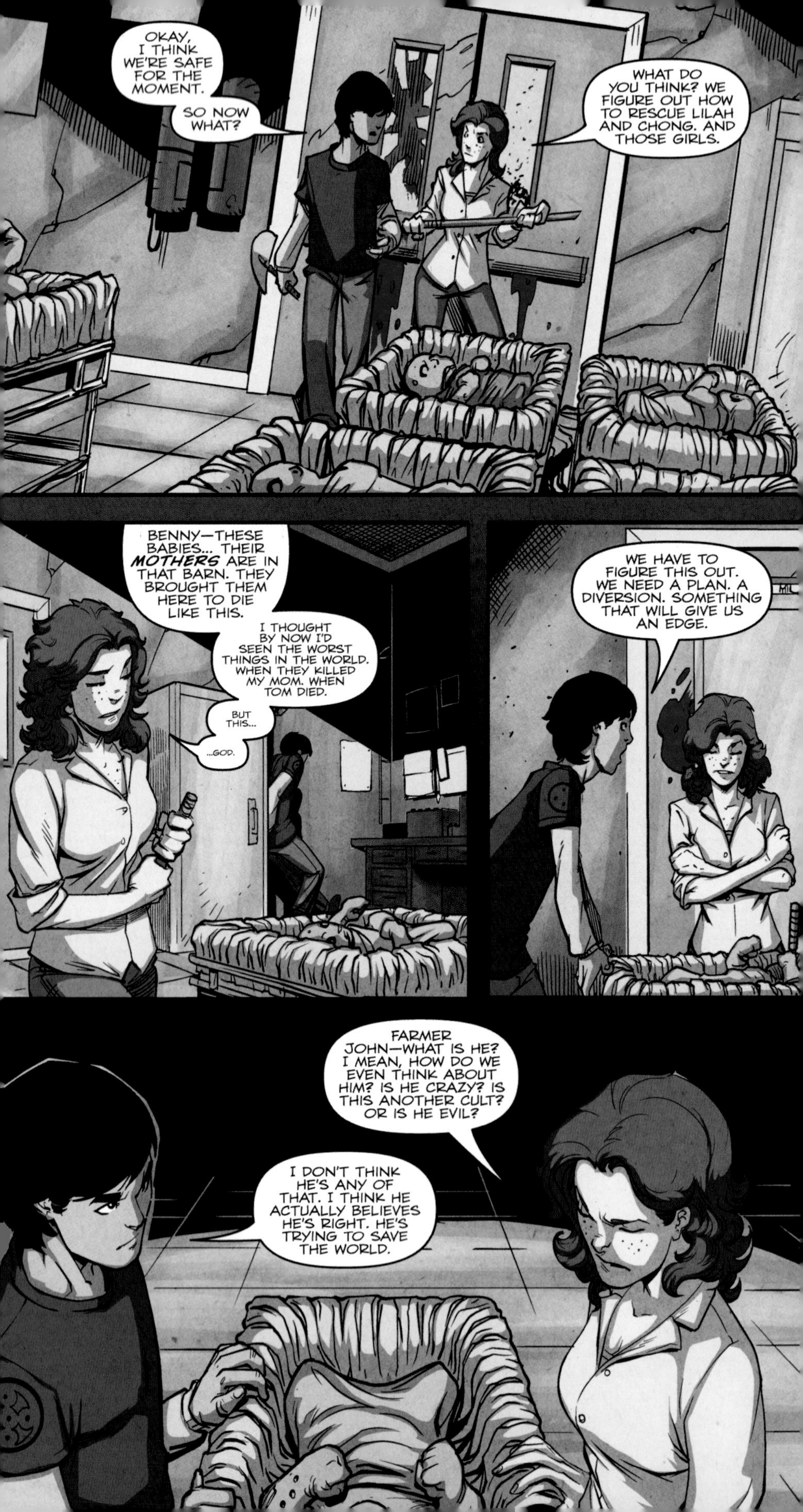
OKAY, I THINK WE'RE SAFE FOR THE MOMENT.
SO NOW WHAT?
WHAT DO YOU THINK? WE FIGURE OUT HOW TO RESCUE LILAH AND CHONG. AND THOSE GIRLS.
BENNY—THESE BABIES... THEIR *MOTHERS* ARE IN THAT BARN. THEY BROUGHT THEM HERE TO DIE LIKE THIS.
I THOUGHT BY NOW I'D SEEN THE WORST THINGS IN THE WORLD. WHEN THEY KILLED MY MOM. WHEN TOM DIED.
BUT THIS...
...GOD.
WE HAVE TO FIGURE THIS OUT. WE NEED A PLAN. A DIVERSION. SOMETHING THAT WILL GIVE US AN EDGE.
FARMER JOHN—WHAT IS HE? I MEAN, HOW DO WE EVEN THINK ABOUT HIM? IS HE CRAZY? IS THIS ANOTHER CULT? OR IS HE EVIL?
I DON'T THINK HE'S ANY OF THAT. I THINK HE ACTUALLY BELIEVES HE'S RIGHT. HE'S TRYING TO SAVE THE WORLD.

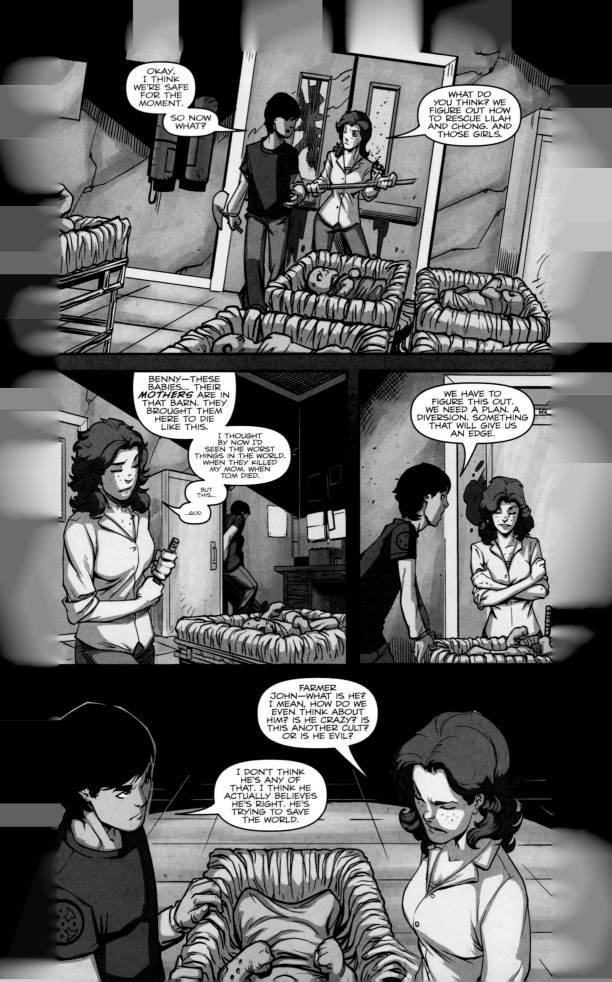

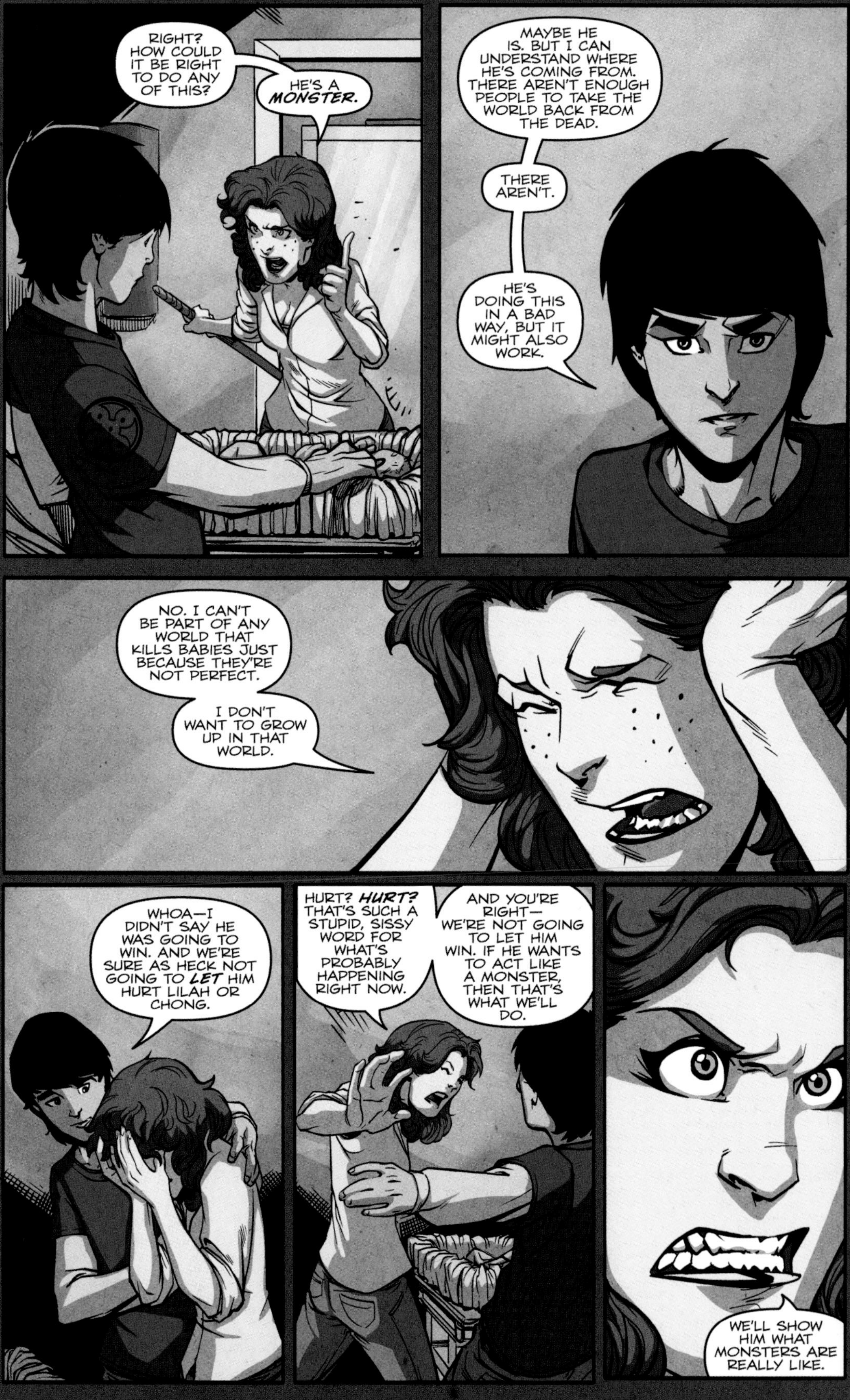
RIGHT? HOW COULD IT BE RIGHT TO DO ANY OF THIS?
HE'S A *MONSTER.*
MAYBE HE IS. BUT I CAN UNDERSTAND WHERE HE'S COMING FROM. THERE AREN'T ENOUGH PEOPLE TO TAKE THE WORLD BACK FROM THE DEAD.
THERE AREN'T.
HE'S DOING THIS IN A BAD WAY, BUT IT MIGHT ALSO WORK.
NO. I CAN'T BE PART OF ANY WORLD THAT KILLS BABIES JUST BECAUSE THEY'RE NOT PERFECT.
I DON'T WANT TO GROW UP IN THAT WORLD.
WHOA—I DIDN'T SAY HE WAS GOING TO WIN. AND WE'RE SURE AS HECK NOT GOING TO *LET* HIM HURT LILAH OR CHONG.
HURT? *HURT?* THAT'S SUCH A STUPID, SISSY WORD FOR WHAT'S PROBABLY HAPPENING RIGHT NOW.
AND YOU'RE RIGHT— WE'RE NOT GOING TO LET HIM WIN. IF HE WANTS TO ACT LIKE A MONSTER, THEN THAT'S WHAT WE'LL DO.
WE'LL SHOW HIM WHAT MONSTERS ARE REALLY LIKE.

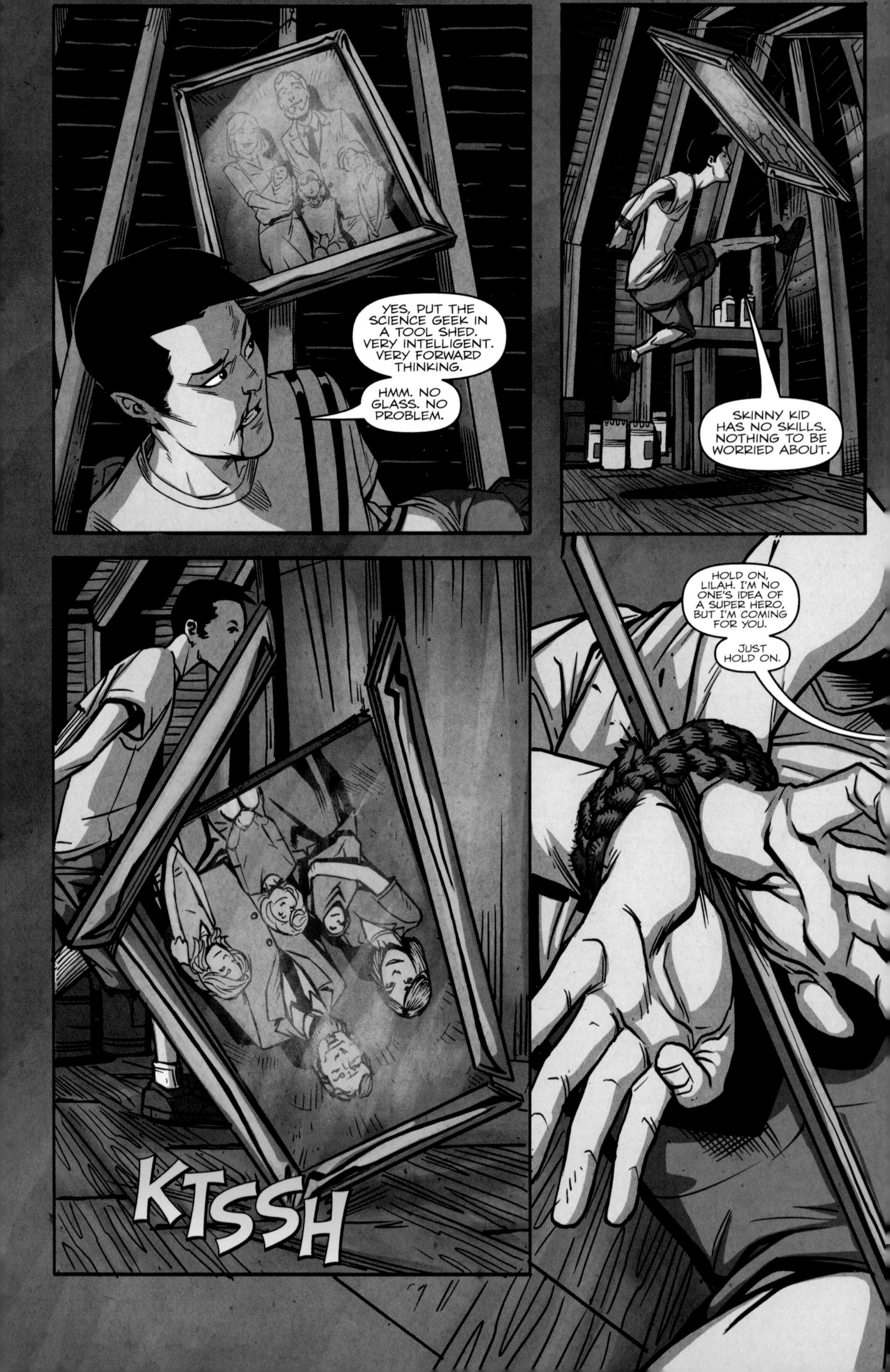
YES, PUT THE SCIENCE GEEK IN A TOOL SHED. VERY INTELLIGENT. VERY FORWARD THINKING.
HMM. NO GLASS. NO PROBLEM.
SKINNY KID HAS NO SKILLS. NOTHING TO BE WORRIED ABOUT.
KTSSH
HOLD ON, LILAH. I'M NO ONE'S IDEA OF A SUPER HERO, BUT I'M COMING FOR YOU.
JUST HOLD ON.

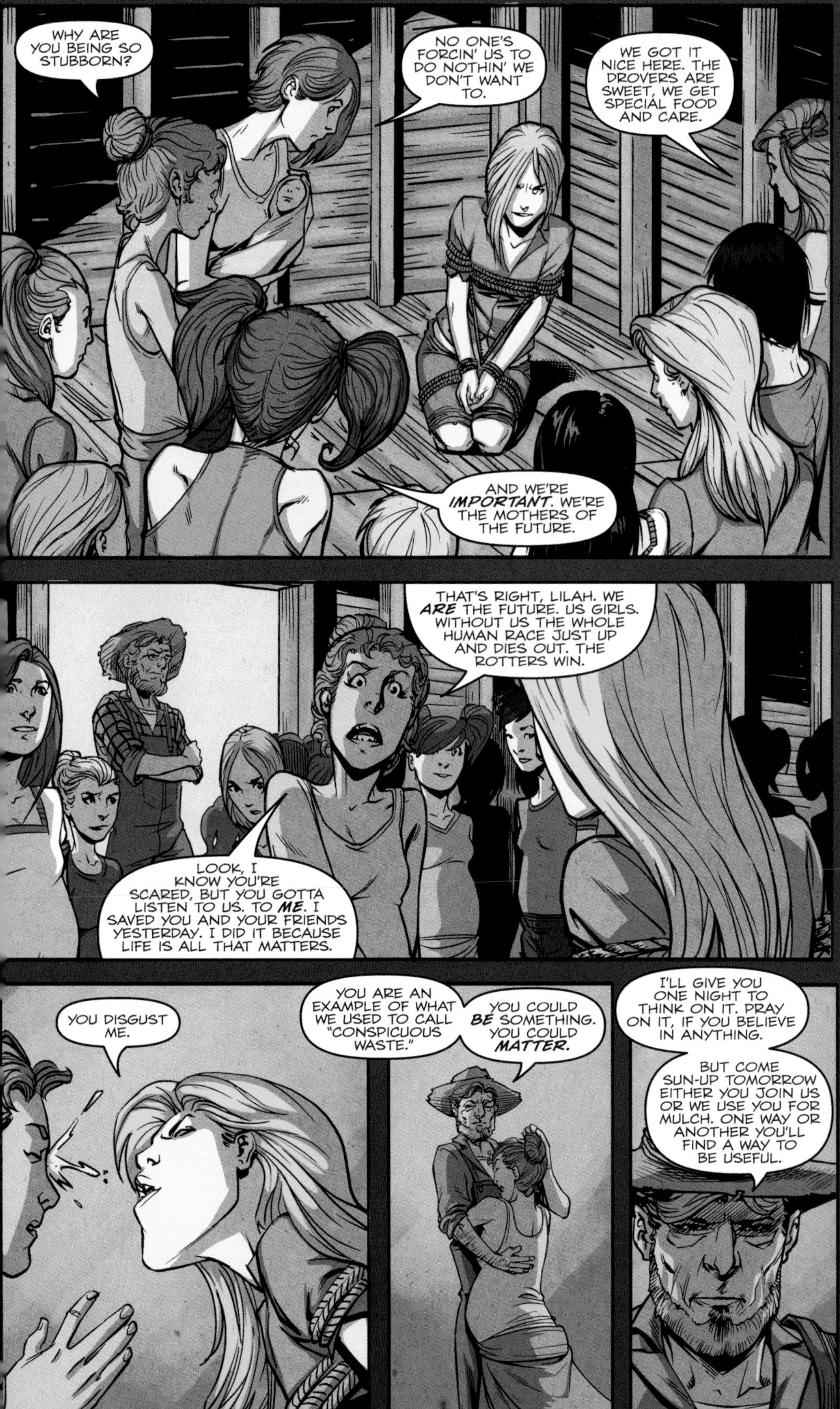
WHY ARE YOU BEING SO STUBBORN?
NO ONE'S FORCIN' US TO DO NOTHIN' WE DON'T WANT TO.
WE GOT IT NICE HERE. THE DROVERS ARE SWEET, WE GET SPECIAL FOOD AND CARE.
AND WE'RE *IMPORTANT*. WE'RE THE MOTHERS OF THE FUTURE.
THAT'S RIGHT, LILAH. WE *ARE* THE FUTURE. US GIRLS. WITHOUT US THE WHOLE HUMAN RACE JUST UP AND DIES OUT. THE ROTTERS WIN.
LOOK, I KNOW YOU'RE SCARED, BUT YOU GOTTA LISTEN TO US. TO *ME*. I SAVED YOU AND YOUR FRIENDS YESTERDAY. I DID IT BECAUSE LIFE IS ALL THAT MATTERS.
YOU DISGUST ME.
YOU ARE AN EXAMPLE OF WHAT WE USED TO CALL "CONSPICUOUS WASTE."
YOU COULD *BE* SOMETHING. YOU COULD *MATTER.*
I'LL GIVE YOU ONE NIGHT TO THINK ON IT. PRAY ON IT, IF YOU BELIEVE IN ANYTHING.
BUT COME SUN-UP TOMORROW EITHER YOU JOIN US OR WE USE YOU FOR MULCH. ONE WAY OR ANOTHER YOU'LL FIND A WAY TO BE USEFUL.

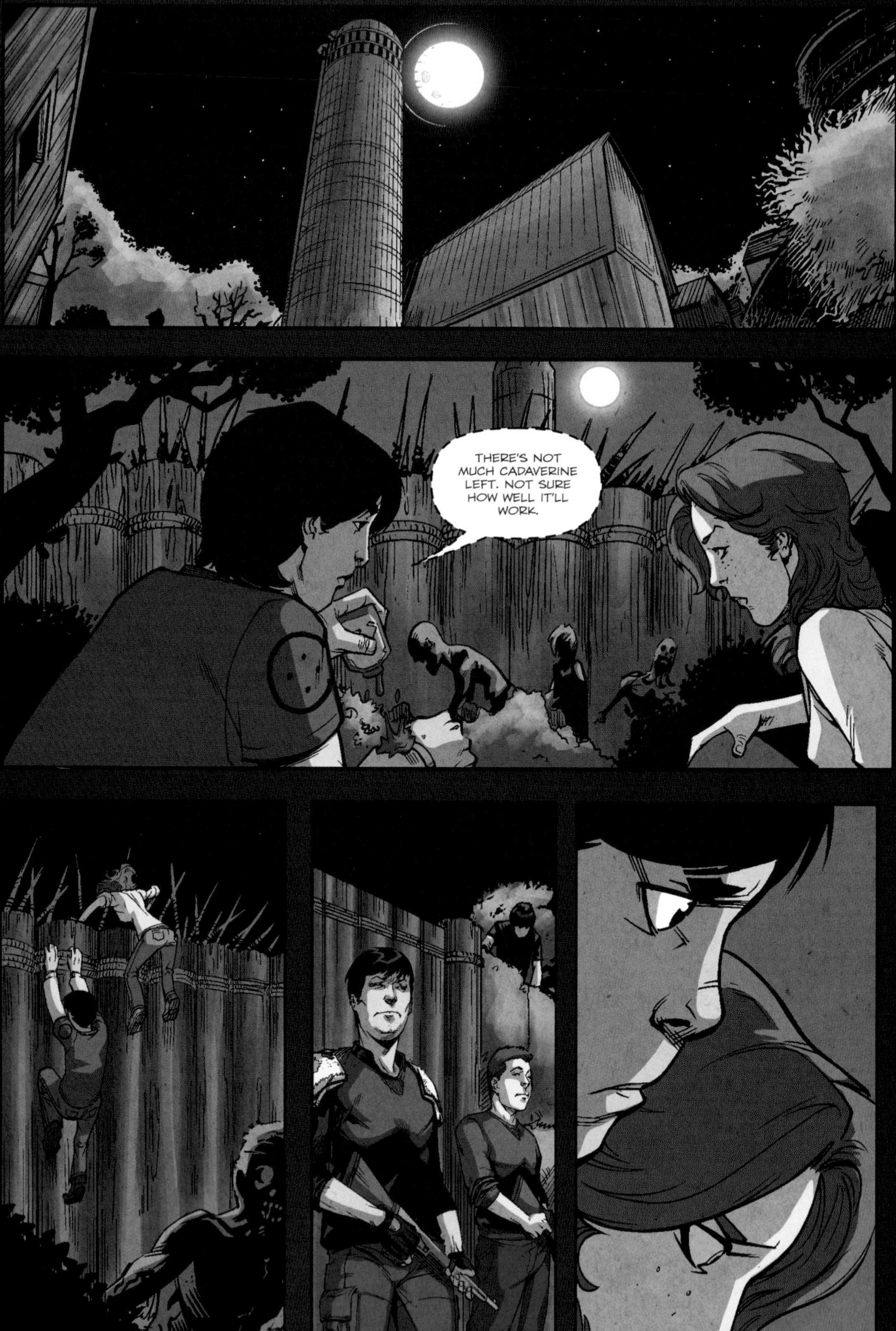
THERE'S NOT MUCH CADAVERINE LEFT. NOT SURE HOW WELL IT'LL WORK.

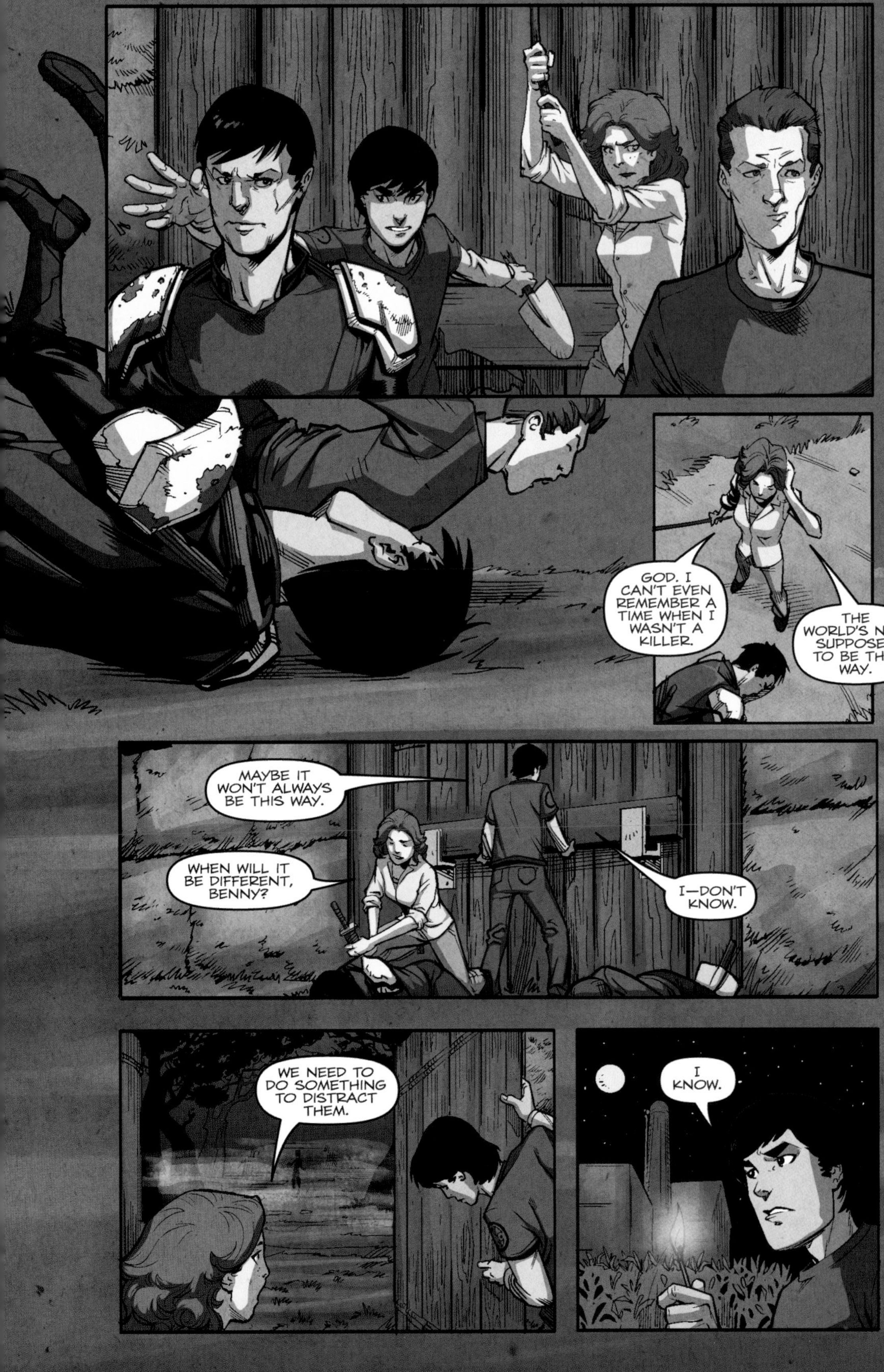
GOD. I CAN'T EVEN REMEMBER A TIME WHEN I WASN'T A KILLER.
THE WORLD'S NOT SUPPOSED TO BE THIS WAY.
MAYBE IT WON'T ALWAYS BE THIS WAY.
WHEN WILL IT BE DIFFERENT, BENNY?
I—DON'T KNOW.
WE NEED TO DO SOMETHING TO DISTRACT THEM.
I KNOW.

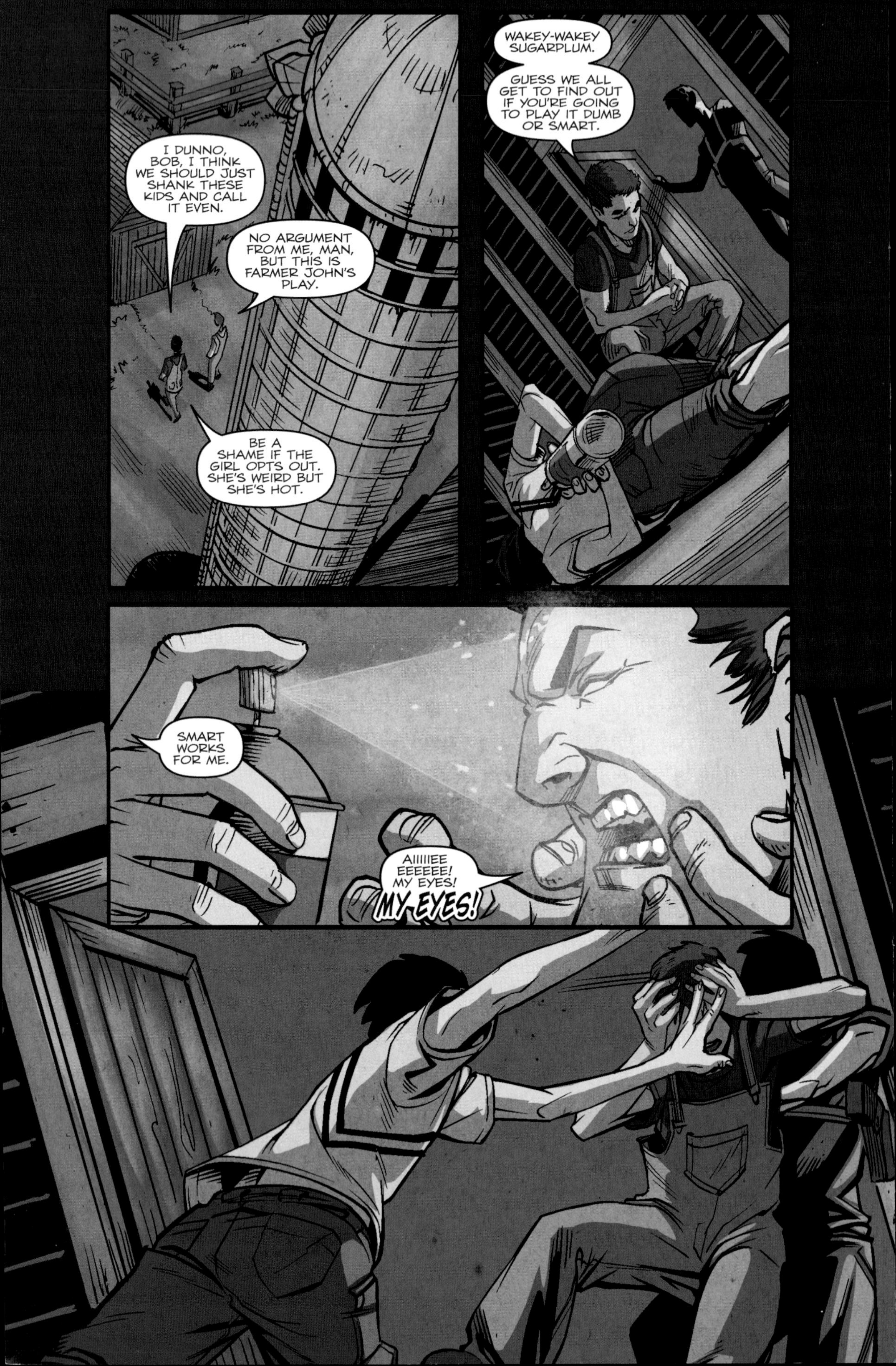
I DUNNO, BOB, I THINK WE SHOULD JUST SHANK THESE KIDS AND CALL IT EVEN.
NO ARGUMENT FROM ME, MAN, BUT THIS IS FARMER JOHN'S PLAY.
BE A SHAME IF THE GIRL OPTS OUT. SHE'S WEIRD BUT SHE'S HOT.
WAKEY-WAKEY SUGARPLUM.
GUESS WE ALL GET TO FIND OUT IF YOU'RE GOING TO PLAY IT DUMB OR SMART.
SMART WORKS FOR ME.
AIIIIIEE EEEEEE! MY EYES!
MY EYES!

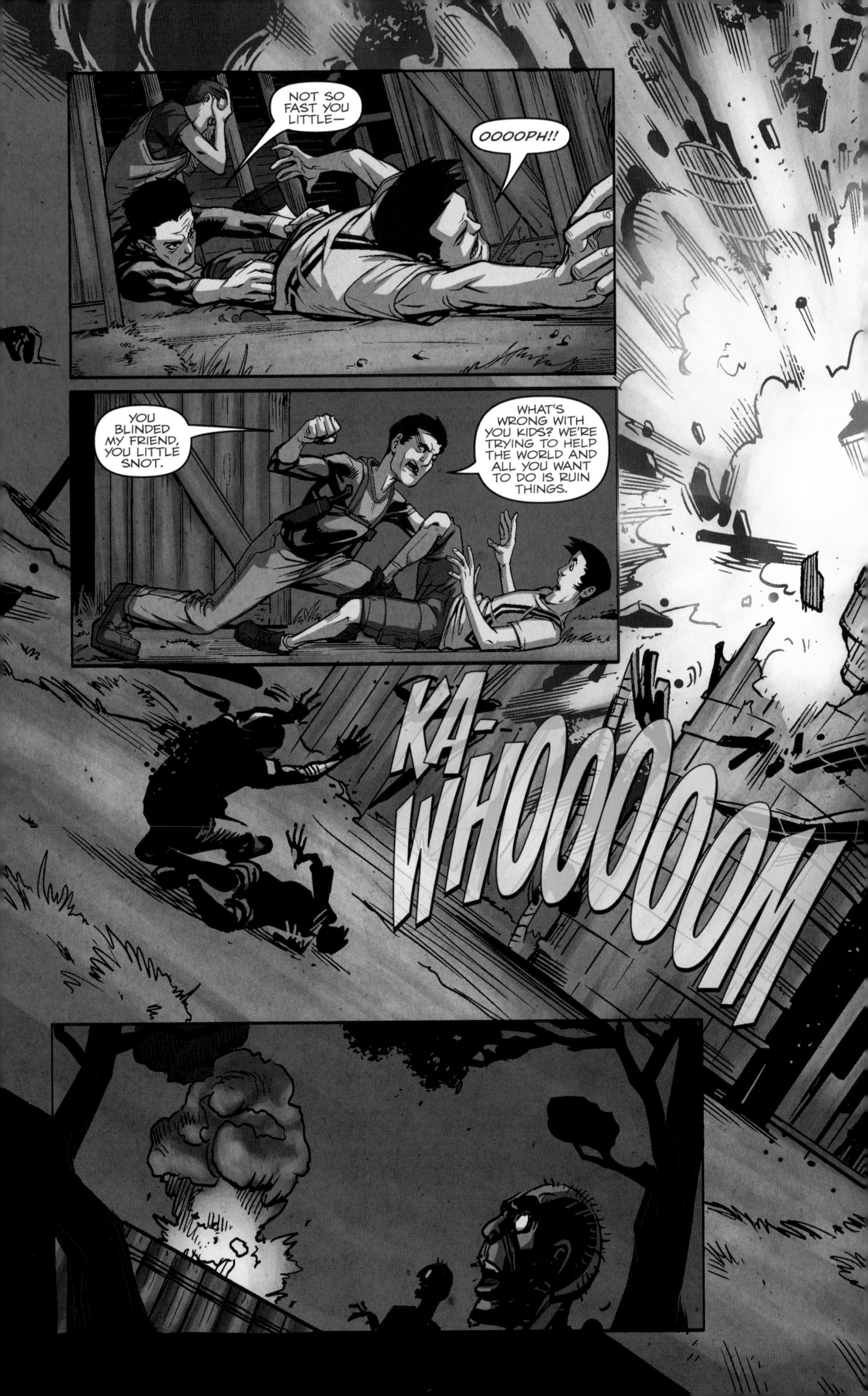
NOT SO FAST YOU LITTLE—
OOOOPH!!
YOU BLINDED MY FRIEND, YOU LITTLE SNOT.
WHAT'S WRONG WITH YOU KIDS? WE'RE TRYING TO HELP THE WORLD AND ALL YOU WANT TO DO IS RUIN THINGS.
KA-WHOOOOOM

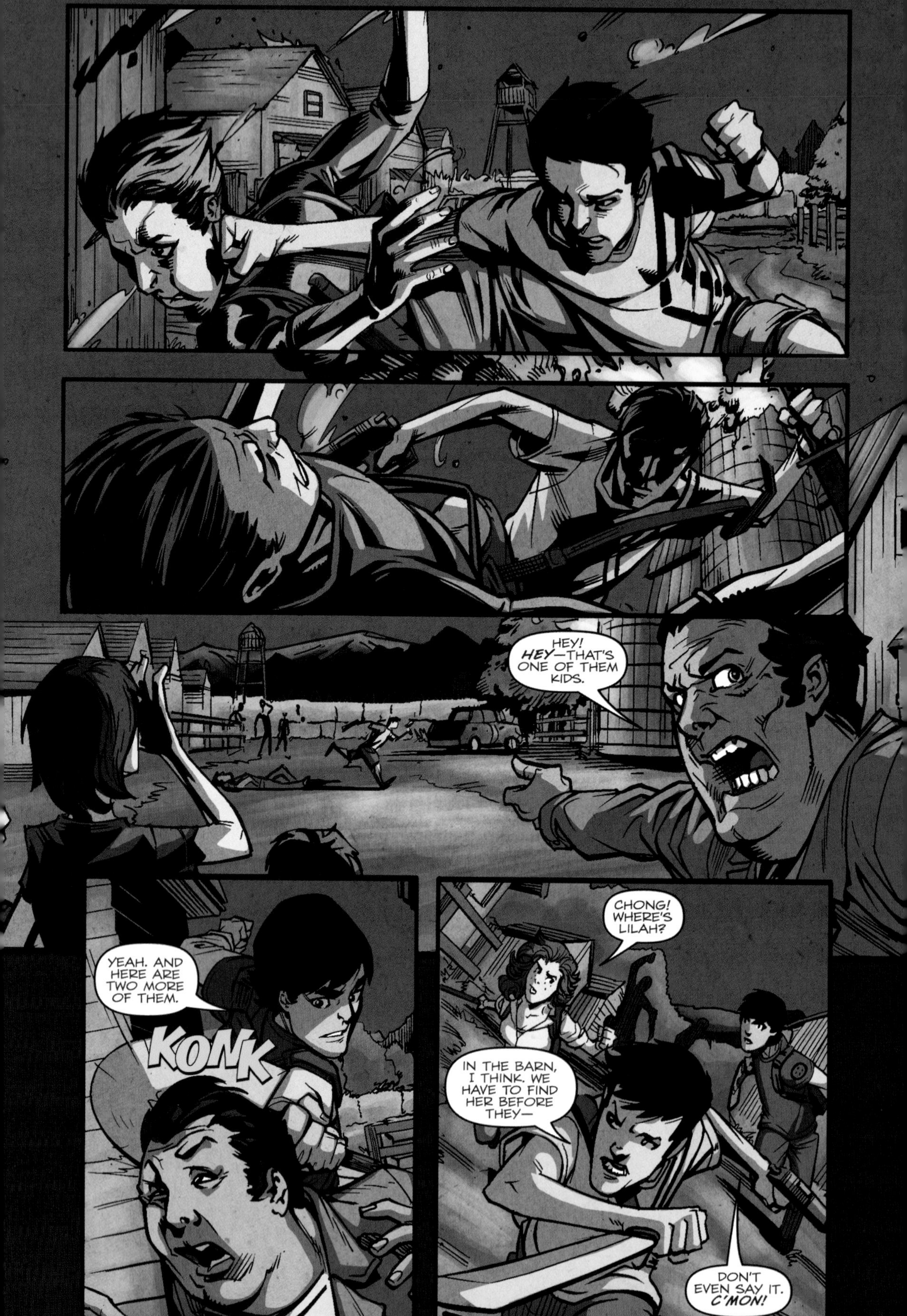
HEY! HEY—THAT'S ONE OF THEM KIDS.
YEAH. AND HERE ARE TWO MORE OF THEM.
KONK
CHONG! WHERE'S LILAH?
IN THE BARN, I THINK. WE HAVE TO FIND HER BEFORE THEY—
DON'T EVEN SAY IT. C'MON!

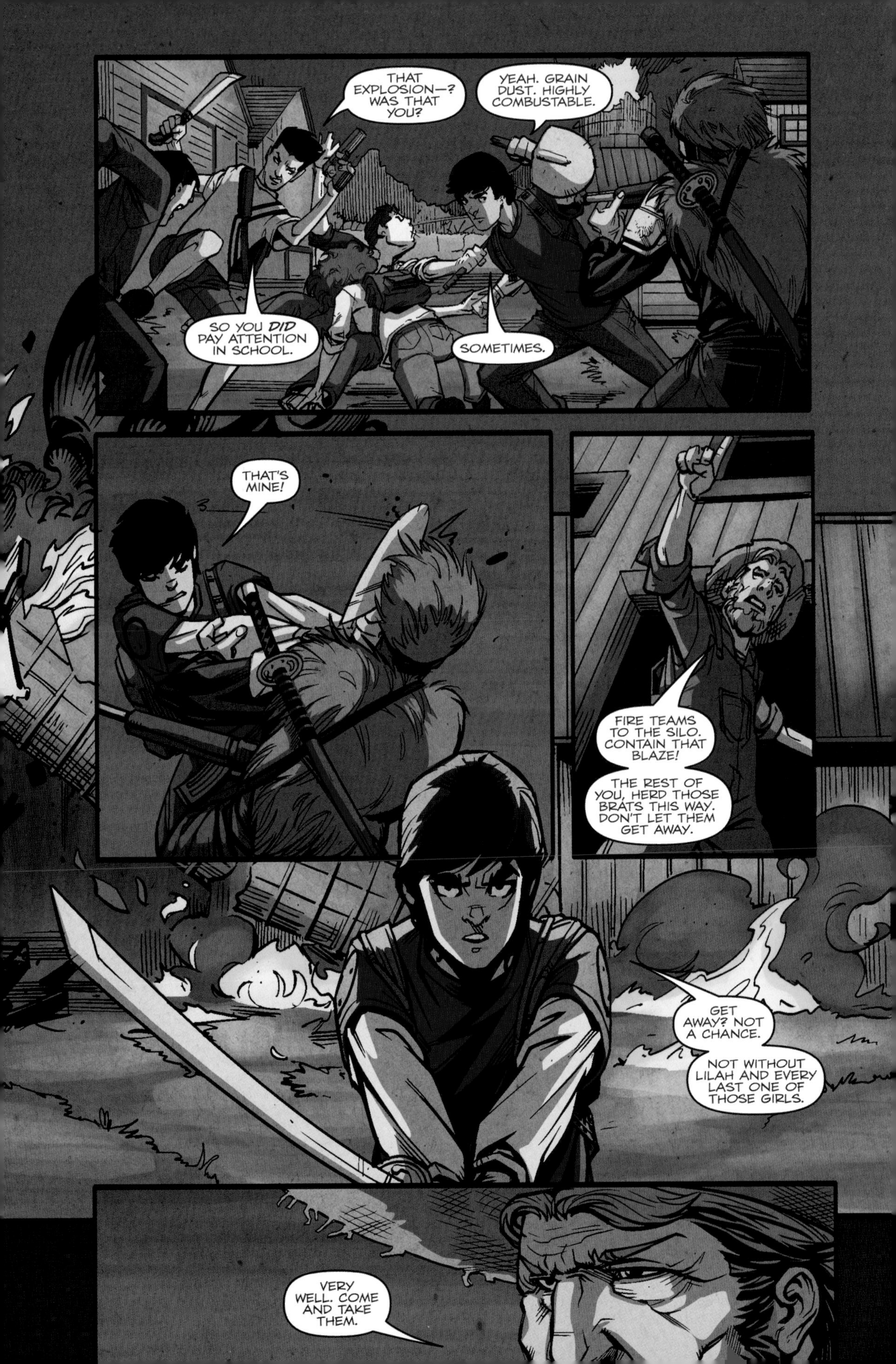
THAT EXPLOSION—? WAS THAT YOU?
YEAH. GRAIN DUST. HIGHLY COMBUSTABLE.
SO YOU *DID* PAY ATTENTION IN SCHOOL.
SOMETIMES.
THAT'S MINE!
FIRE TEAMS TO THE SILO. CONTAIN THAT BLAZE!
THE REST OF YOU, HERD THOSE BRATS THIS WAY. DON'T LET THEM GET AWAY.
GET AWAY? NOT A CHANCE.
NOT WITHOUT LILAH AND EVERY LAST ONE OF THOSE GIRLS.
VERY WELL. COME AND TAKE THEM.

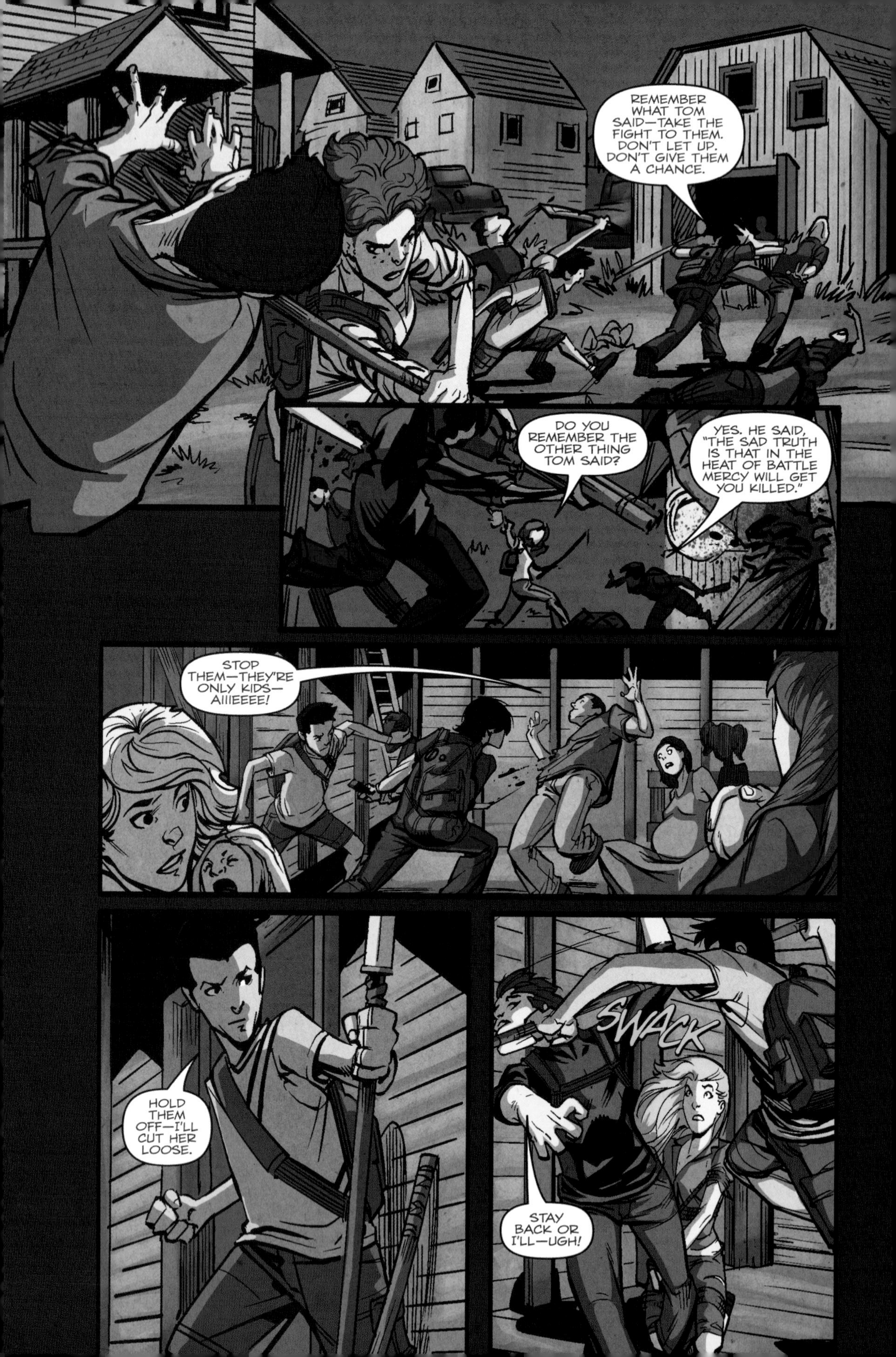

REMEMBER WHAT TOM SAID—TAKE THE FIGHT TO THEM. DON'T LET UP. DON'T GIVE THEM A CHANCE.
DO YOU REMEMBER THE OTHER THING TOM SAID?
YES. HE SAID, "THE SAD TRUTH IS THAT IN THE HEAT OF BATTLE MERCY WILL GET YOU KILLED."
STOP THEM—THEY'RE ONLY KIDS— AIIIEEEE!
HOLD THEM OFF—I'LL CUT HER LOOSE.
SWACK
STAY BACK OR I'LL—UGH!

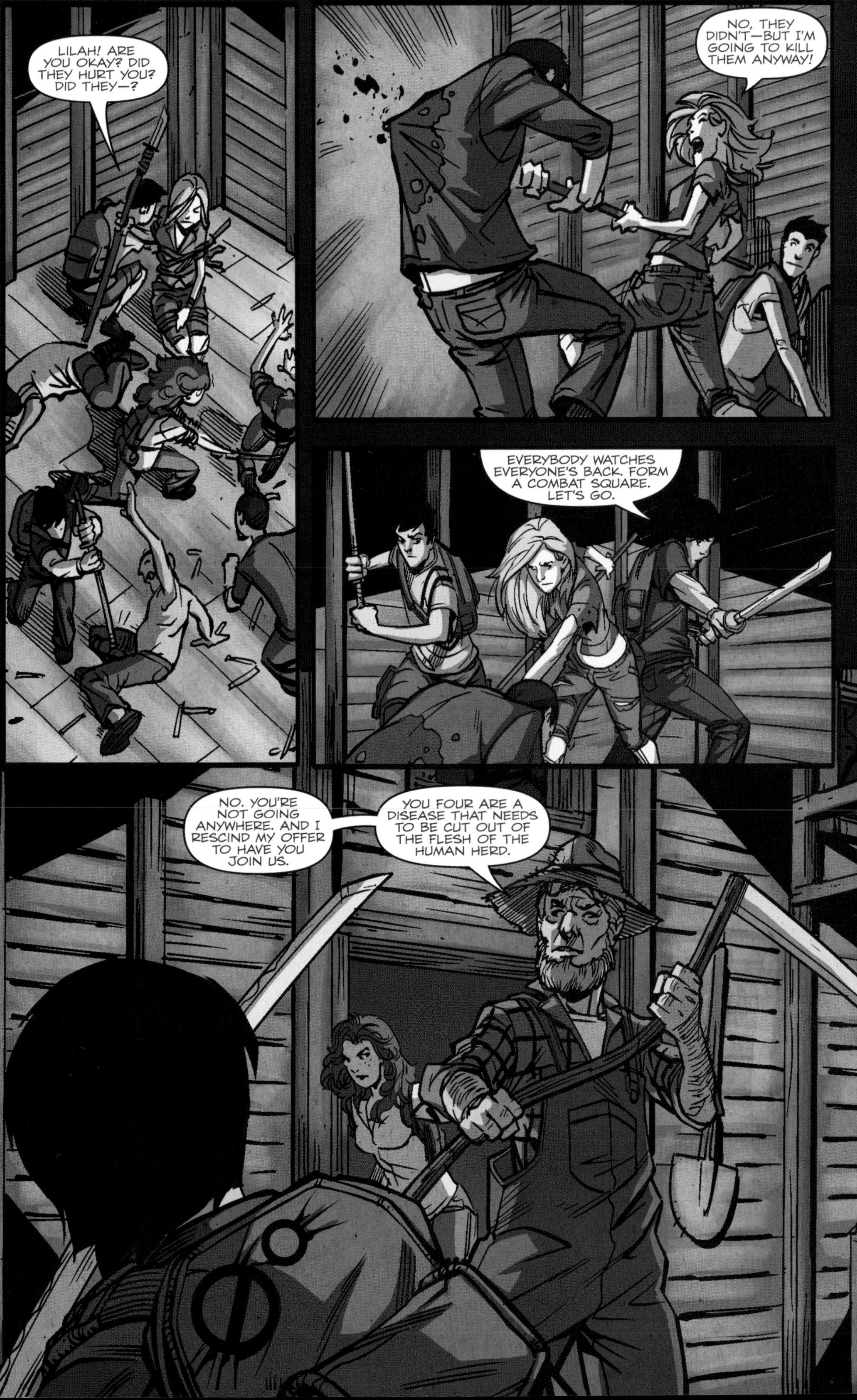
LILAH! ARE YOU OKAY? DID THEY HURT YOU? DID THEY—?
NO, THEY DIDN'T—BUT I'M GOING TO KILL THEM ANYWAY!
EVERYBODY WATCHES EVERYONE'S BACK. FORM A COMBAT SQUARE. LET'S GO.
NO. YOU'RE NOT GOING ANYWHERE. AND I RESCIND MY OFFER TO HAVE YOU JOIN US.
YOU FOUR ARE A DISEASE THAT NEEDS TO BE CUT OUT OF THE FLESH OF THE HUMAN HERD.

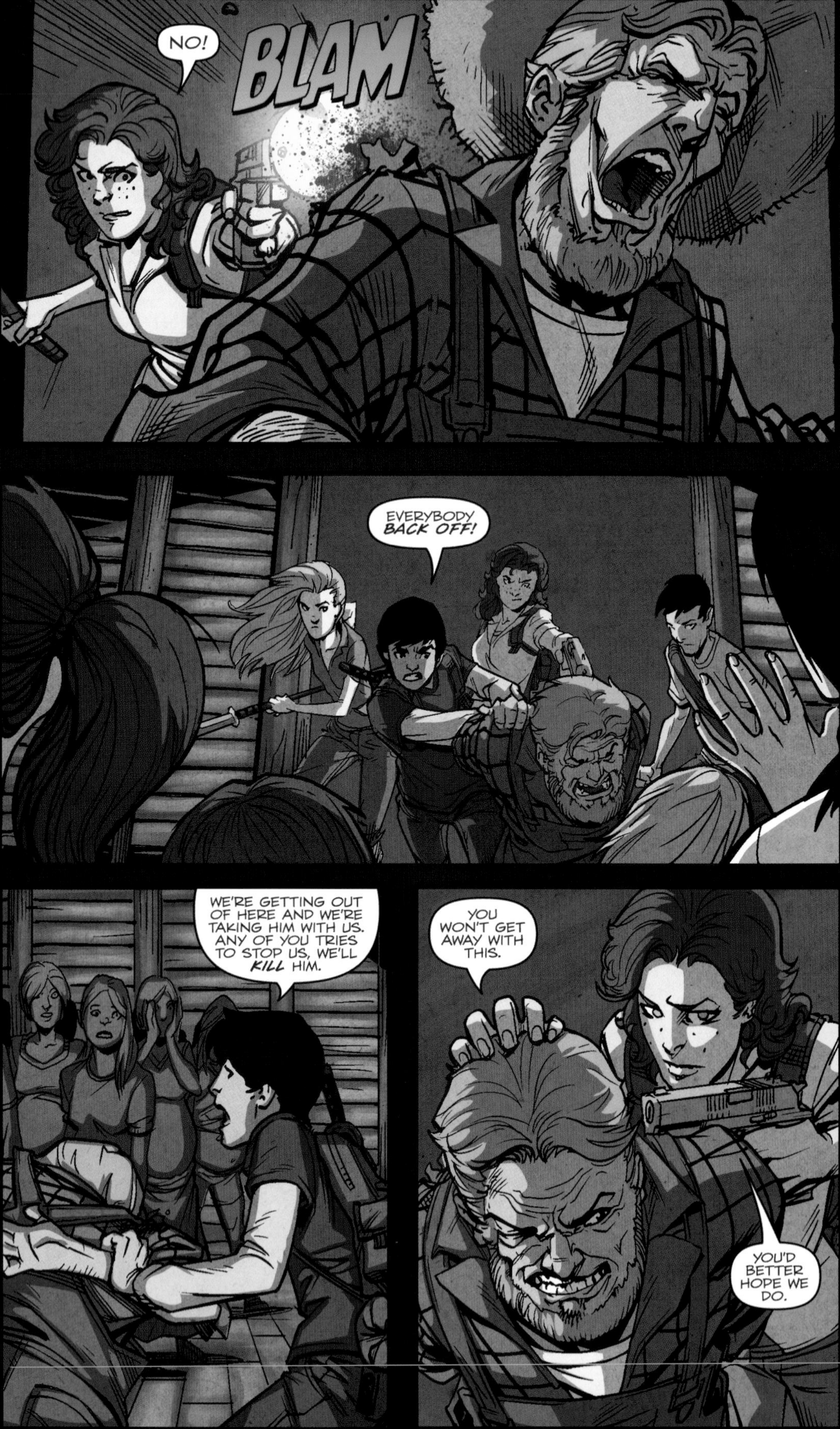
NO!
BLAM
EVERYBODY BACK OFF!
WE'RE GETTING OUT OF HERE AND WE'RE TAKING HIM WITH US. ANY OF YOU TRIES TO STOP US, WE'LL KILL HIM.
YOU WON'T GET AWAY WITH THIS.
YOU'D BETTER HOPE WE DO.

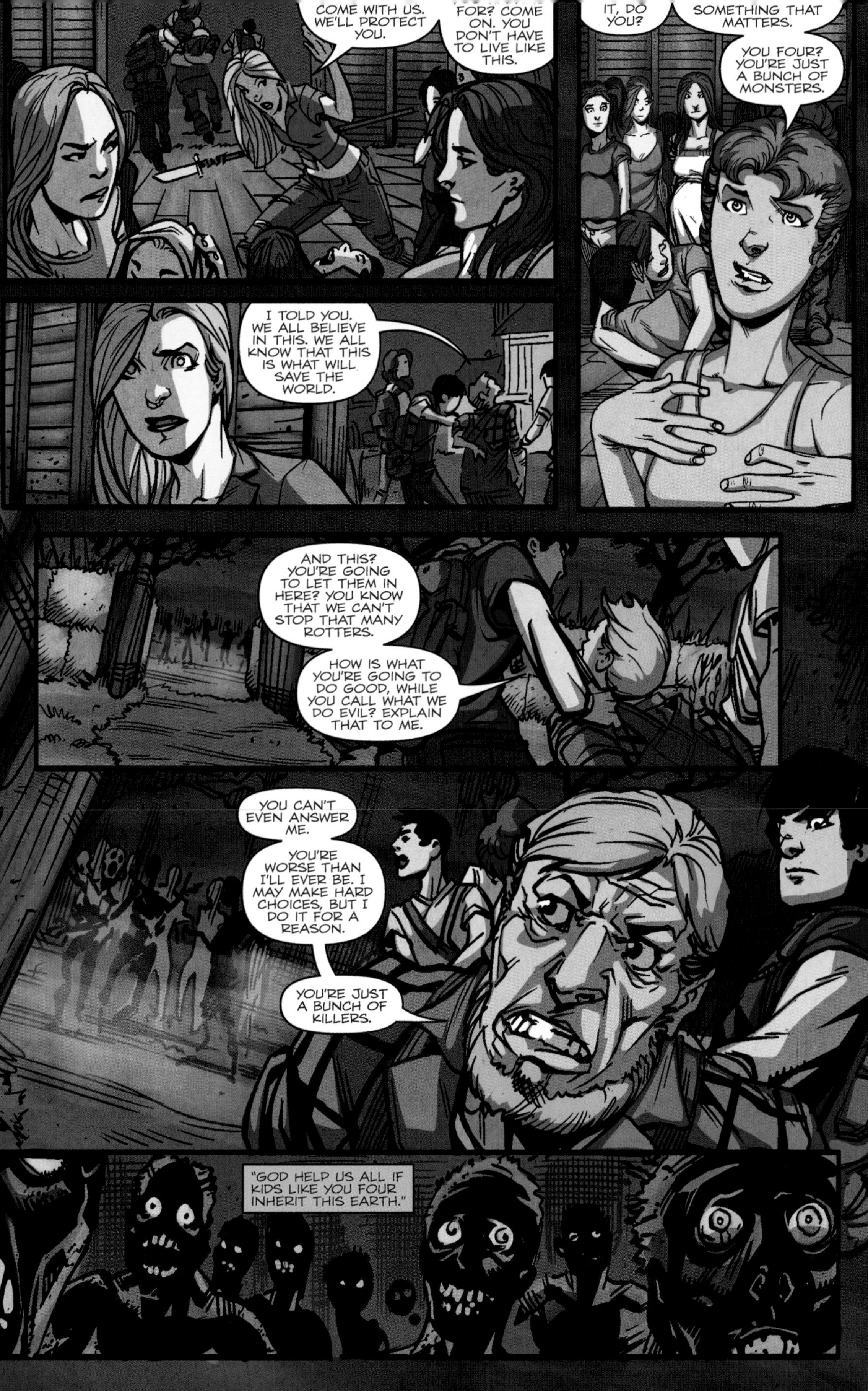
COME WITH US. WE'LL PROTECT YOU.
FOR? COME ON. YOU DON'T HAVE TO LIVE LIKE THIS.
IT, DO YOU?
SOMETHING THAT MATTERS.
YOU FOUR? YOU'RE JUST A BUNCH OF MONSTERS.
I TOLD YOU. WE ALL BELIEVE IN THIS. WE ALL KNOW THAT THIS IS WHAT WILL SAVE THE WORLD.
AND THIS? YOU'RE GOING TO LET THEM IN HERE? YOU KNOW THAT WE CAN'T STOP THAT MANY ROTTERS.
HOW IS WHAT YOU'RE GOING TO DO GOOD, WHILE YOU CALL WHAT WE DO EVIL? EXPLAIN THAT TO ME.
YOU CAN'T EVEN ANSWER ME.
YOU'RE WORSE THAN I'LL EVER BE. I MAY MAKE HARD CHOICES, BUT I DO IT FOR A REASON.
YOU'RE JUST A BUNCH OF KILLERS.
"GOD HELP US ALL IF KIDS LIKE YOU FOUR INHERIT THIS EARTH."

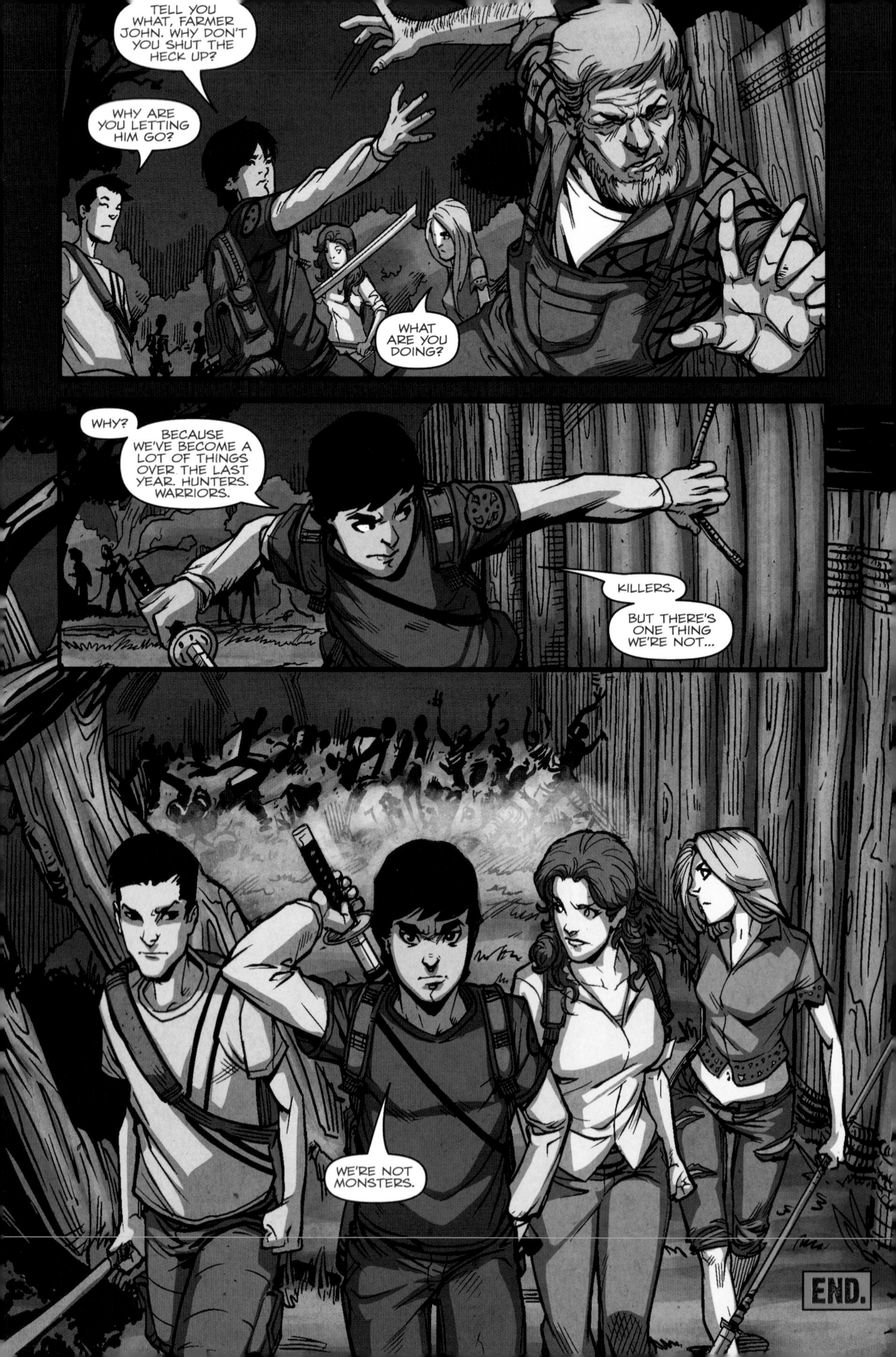
TELL YOU WHAT, FARMER JOHN. WHY DON'T YOU SHUT THE HECK UP?
WHY ARE YOU LETTING HIM GO?
WHAT ARE YOU DOING?
WHY?
BECAUSE WE'VE BECOME A LOT OF THINGS OVER THE LAST YEAR. HUNTERS. WARRIORS.
KILLERS.
BUT THERE'S ONE THING WE'RE NOT...
WE'RE NOT MONSTERS.
END.

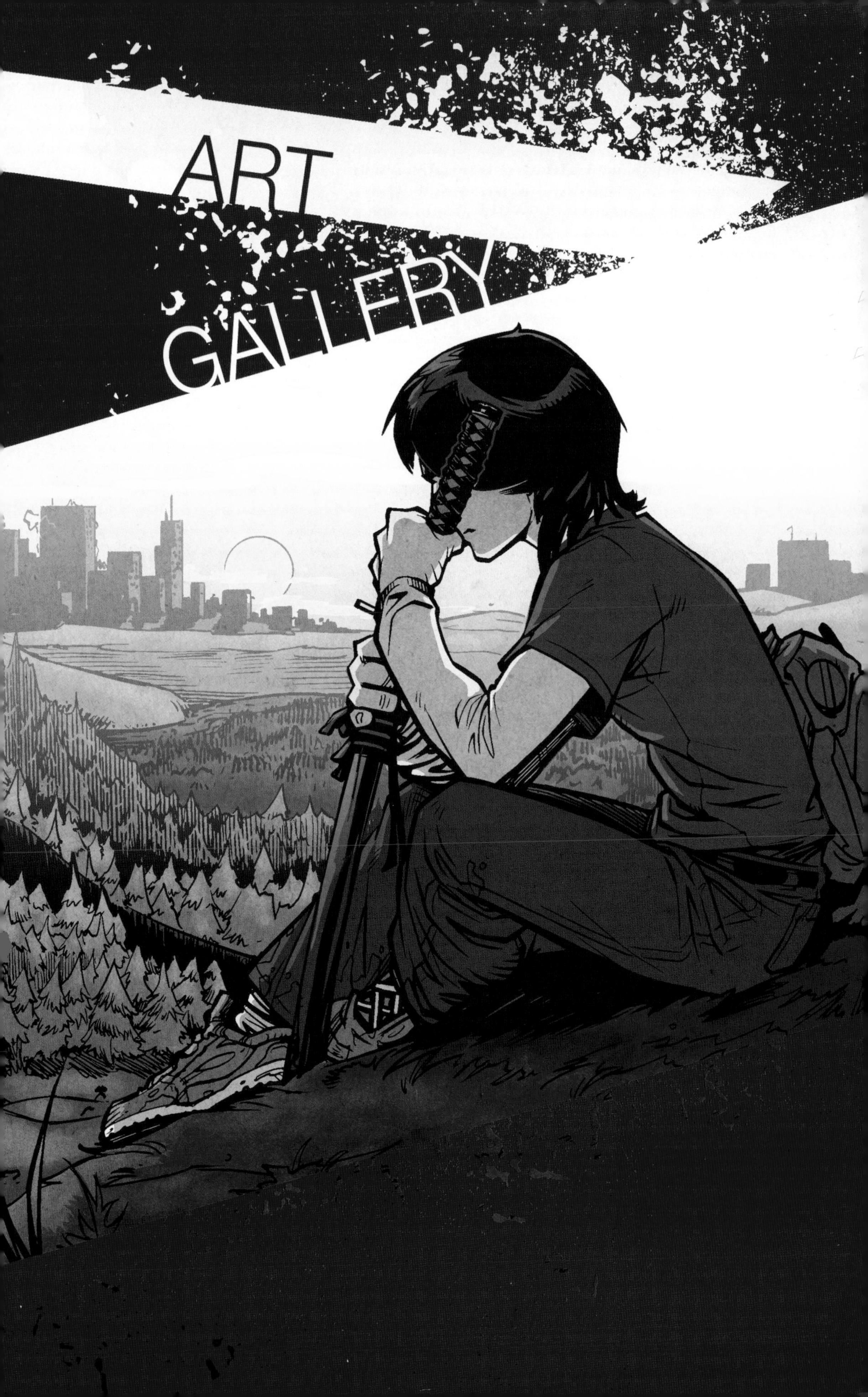
ART
GALLERY

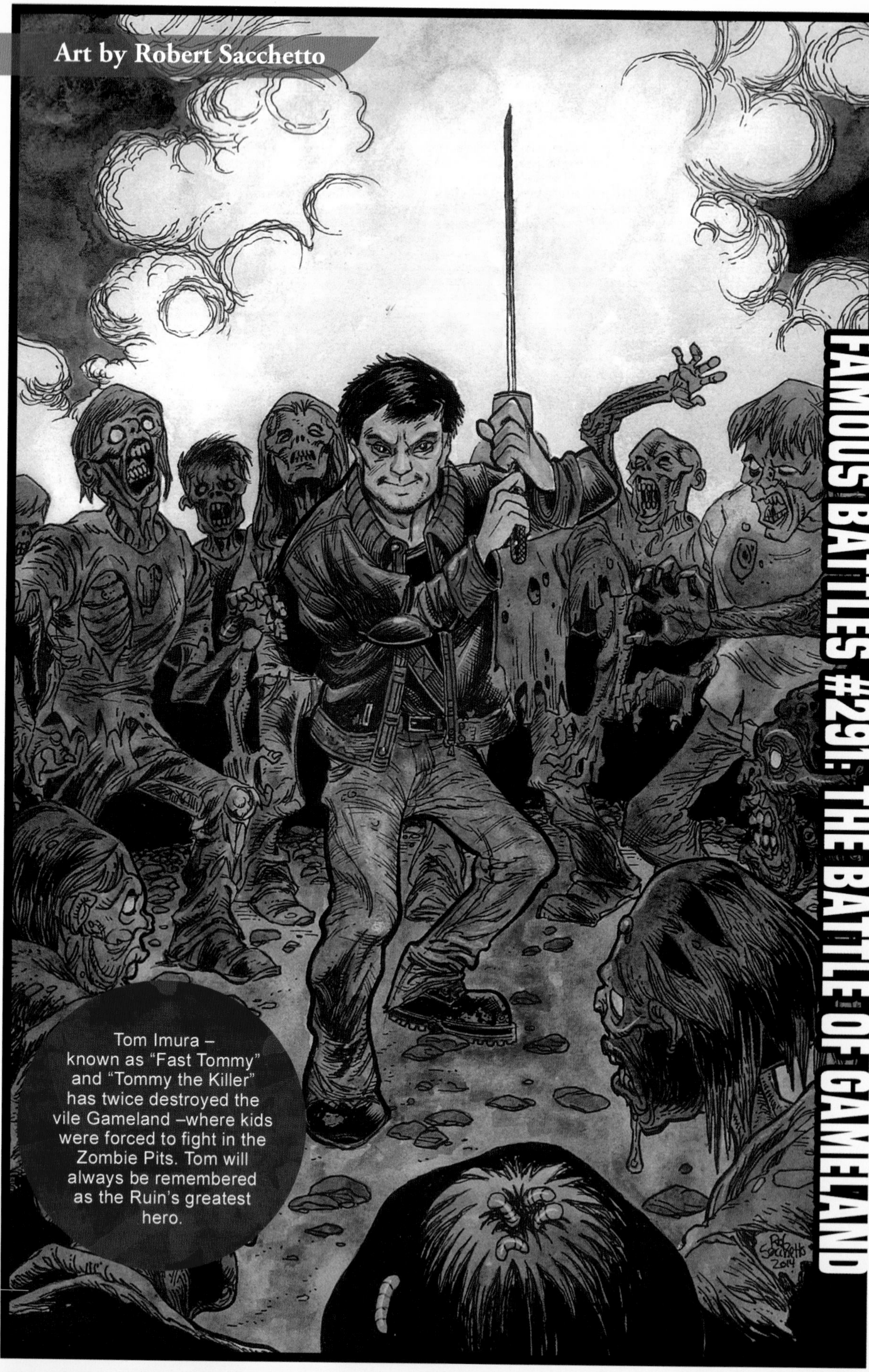
Art by Robert Sacchetto
FAMOUS BATTLES #291: THE BATTLE OF GAMELAND
Tom Imura – known as "Fast Tommy" and "Tommy the Killer" has twice destroyed the vile Gameland –where kids were forced to fight in the Zombie Pits. Tom will always be remembered as the Ruin's greatest hero.

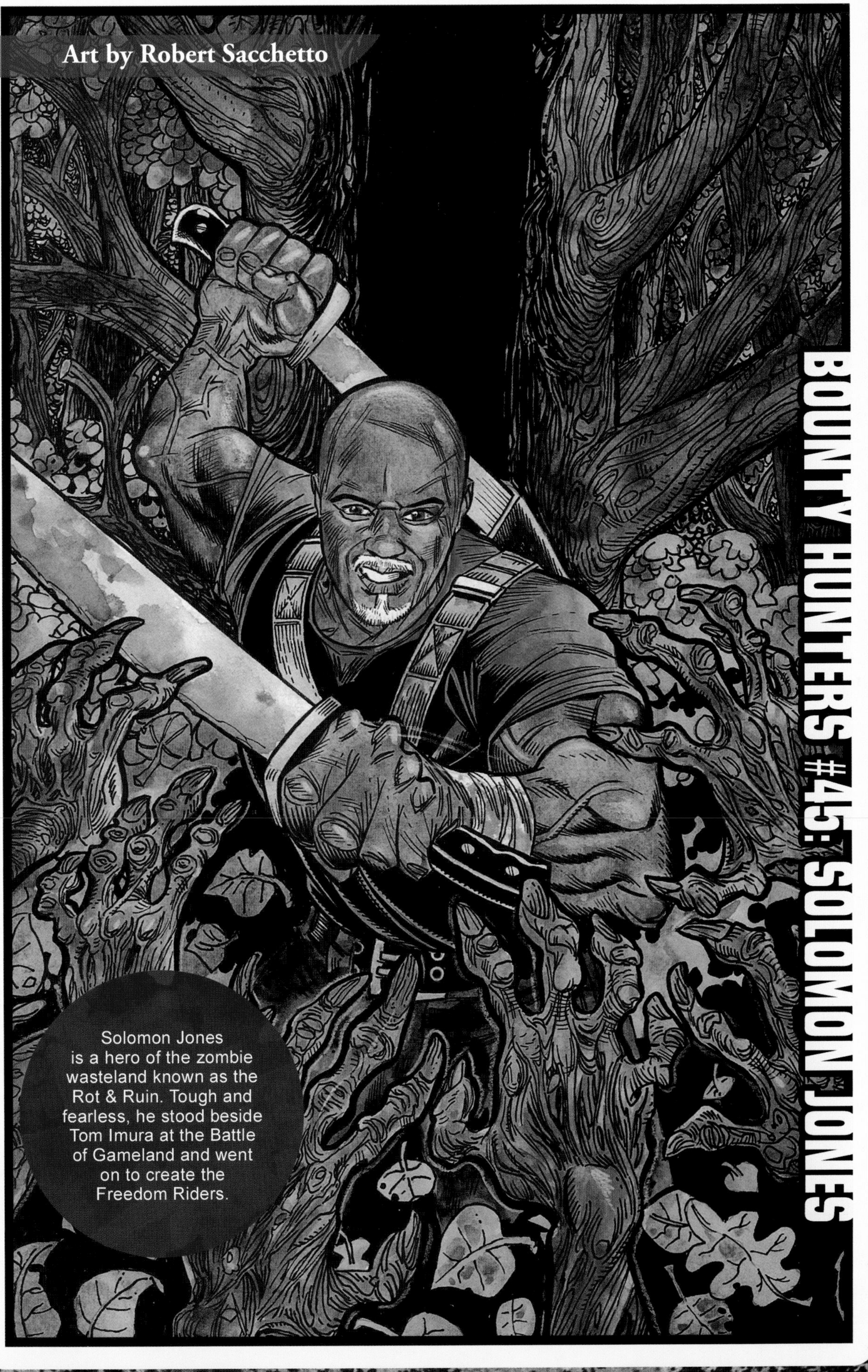
Art by Robert Sacchetto
BOUNTY HUNTERS #45: SOLOMON JONES
Solomon Jones is a hero of the zombie wasteland known as the Rot & Ruin. Tough and fearless, he stood beside Tom Imura at the Battle of Gameland and went on to create the Freedom Riders.

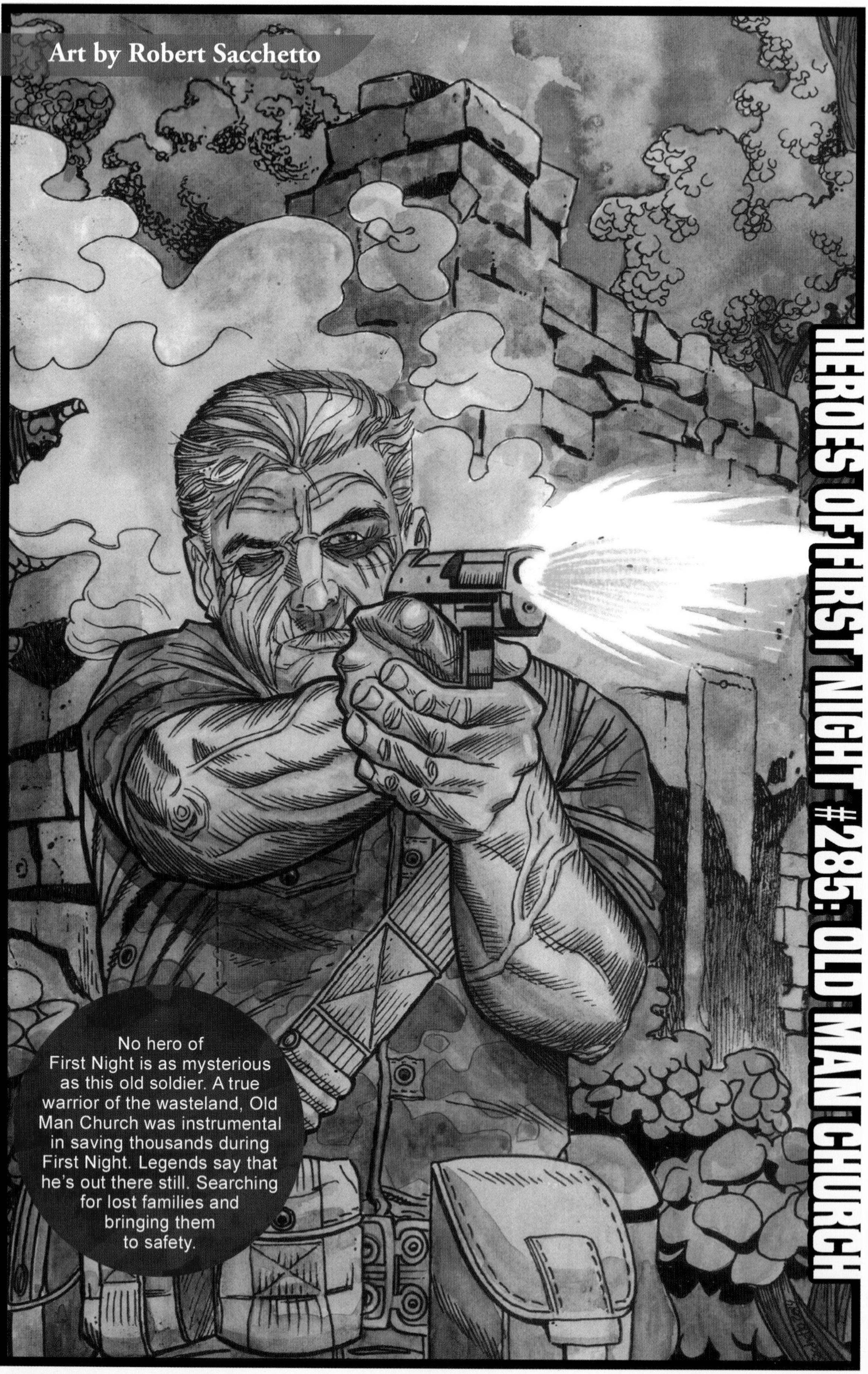
Art by Robert Sacchetto
HEROES OF FIRST NIGHT #285: OLD MAN CHURCH
No hero of First Night is as mysterious as this old soldier. A true warrior of the wasteland, Old Man Church was instrumental in saving thousands during First Night. Legends say that he's out there still. Searching for lost families and bringing them to safety.

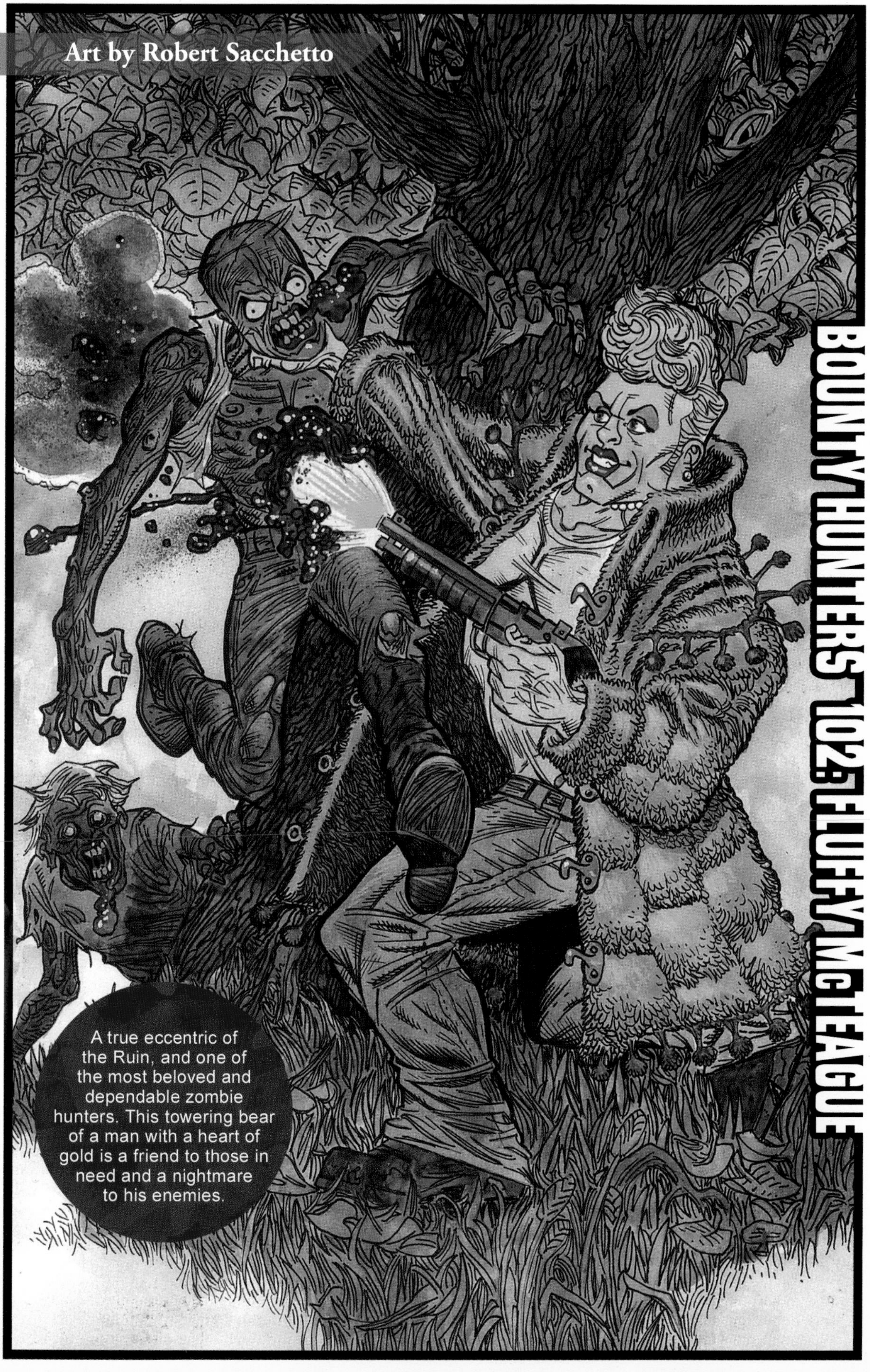
Art by Robert Sacchetto
BOUNTY HUNTERS 102: FLUFFY MCTEAGUE
A true eccentric of the Ruin, and one of the most beloved and dependable zombie hunters. This towering bear of a man with a heart of gold is a friend to those in need and a nightmare to his enemies.

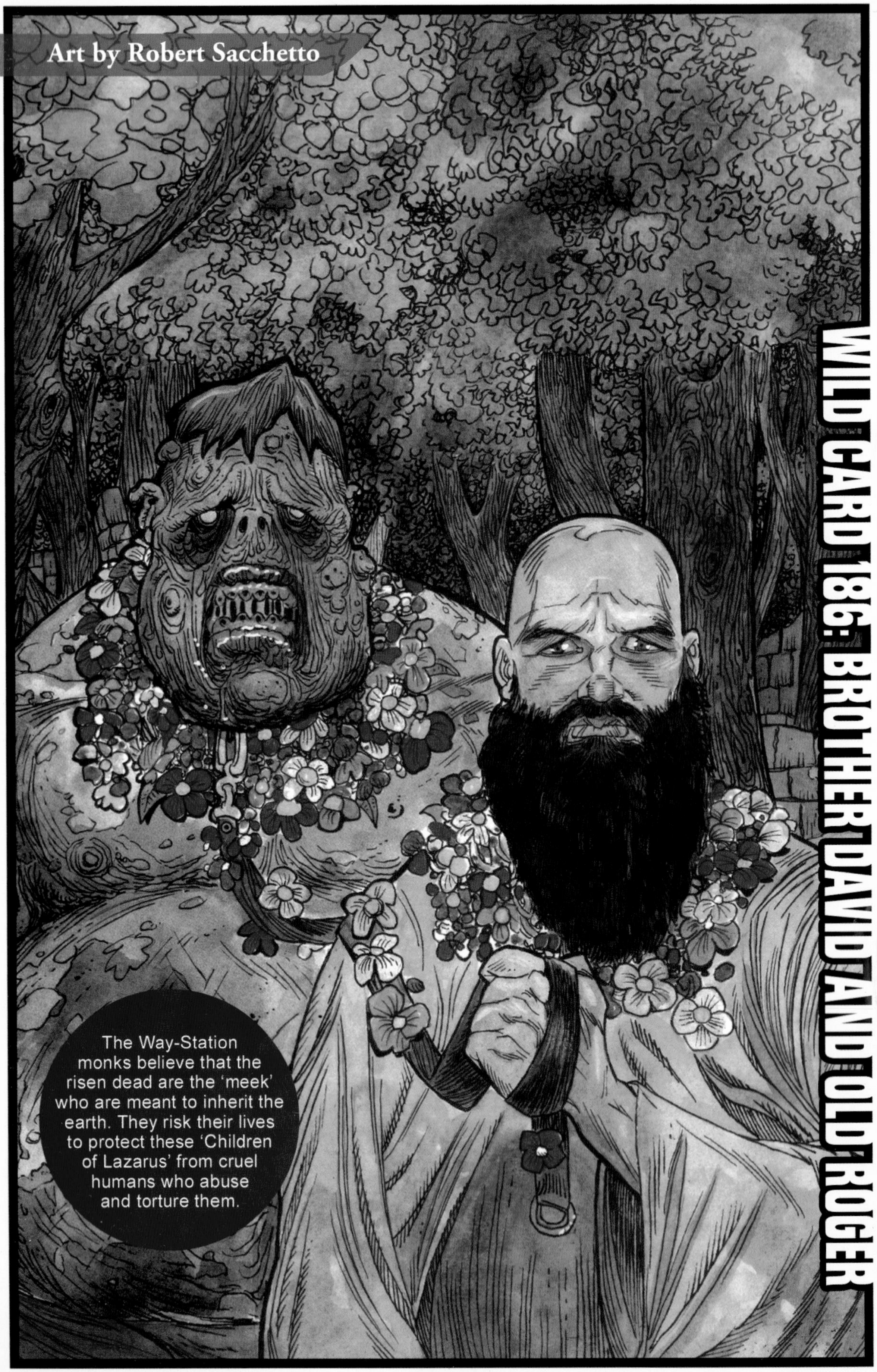
Art by Robert Sacchetto
WILD CARD 186: BROTHER DAVID AND OLD ROGER
The Way-Station monks believe that the risen dead are the 'meek' who are meant to inherit the earth. They risk their lives to protect these 'Children of Lazarus' from cruel humans who abuse and torture them.